The Mystery of the Crown of Thorns

by

A Passionist Father, C.P.

the author of
"The Christian Trumpet",
"Voice of Jesus Suffering",
and other works

Loreto Publications
Fitzwilliam, NH 03447
A. D. 2005

Published in 1879 by
D&J Saddlier & Co.

First Printing: 1999
Second Printing: 2001
Third Printing: 2005

Published by:
Loreto Publications
P. O. Box 603
Fitzwilliam, NH 03447
www.LoretoPubs.org

Published in collaboration with:
PCP Books
Boonville, NY, 13309

ISBN: 1-930278-38-1

Printed & bound at
Anaswara Offset Pvt. Ltd., Cochin
for Tansmith Publishers & Exporters, Cochin, India.

PREFACE

The special obligation contracted by the Religious of the Most Holy Cross and Passion, known under the name of Passionists, of promoting, in the minds and hearts of the faithful, the pious memory of, and the salutary devotion to, the sacred mysteries of our Savior's Passion, has suggested the idea of this book the Crown of Thorns of our divine Lord and Redeemer. In preparing for publication another work, entitled, *"The Voice of Jesus Suffering in the Mind and Heart of Christians,"* the author was deeply impressed with the terrible and affecting sight of the Incarnate Son of God, crowned with sharp thorns, mocked, insulted, blasphemed, and tortured by cruel executioners.

This extraordinary and awful spectacle, never before witnessed in the history of human suffering and human barbarity, naturally makes on the mind of the Christian believer the impression that some important mystery is intended by the divine Victim in consenting to endure such unheard-of tortures and deep humiliations. So far as his limited capacity and the means at his disposal would allow, the author has endeavored to study this very interesting subject, and ventures to give in this little work the result of his labors.

In the Office and Mass of the Crown of Thorns, appointed by our Holy Mother the Church for the first Friday in Lent, the most striking figures of the Crown of Thorns are pointed out to us in various parts of the Old Testament. These have been explained in the first six chapters of this book.

Through these instructive figures we are, step by step, led to the threshold of Pilate's palace in Jerusalem, and are introduced into the inner courts where we behold their realization in the person of our divine Lord, crowned with sharp thorns, as the King of ignominy and sorrow. Here his sufferings and humiliations are described, and their causes and effects examined at some length. The First Part of this book closes with a brief history of the real Crown of Thorns of our dear Savior.

The profound and sublime mystery of the Crown of Thorns will be found more fully developed in the Second Part of this work, wherein we shall see this glorious crown shining in the miraculous sun of Venerable Anna Maria Taigi in Rome, and impressed on the Sacred Heart of our Savior as manifested to his favorite servant, Blessed Margaret Mary Alacoque, at Paray Le Monial in France. We will admire and venerate it on the heads of more than fifty illustrious saints and eminent servants of God, who have glorified it with their devotion and sufferings, and adorned it with their tears and blood, during the last seven centuries.

The mystic Crown of Thorns is actually pointed out to us on the brows of several living servants of God, especially on the bleeding head of Louise Lateau in Belgium, and of Palma Maria of Oria in Italy, the two wonders of the present age.

In writing this new work on the Crown of Thorns of our divine Lord, we had no model for our guidance. Various events of different kinds suggested at first and gradually, developed the idea of this book. We have gathered together the fittest materials that we could find scattered in different works, and have endeavored to arrange them in the best order our judgment could suggest. The large work of the learned Dominican Father Angelo Pacciuchello, on the Passion of our Lord, has given us some valuable assistance. We are indebted to the celebrated Father Joachim Ventura, who also seems to have used Pacciuchello, for some sublime and useful ideas about the Crown of Thorns of our blessed Lord. The principal historical events relative to the mystical Crown of Thorns, enumerated in the last chapters of the Second Part of this book, and the sketch of Palma Maria's life, we have compiled from the second volume of the French work, *"Les Stigmatisées,"* by the illustrious and pious French author, A. Imbert Gourbeyre, an eminent professor in the medical college of Clermont Ferrard, France.

Our aim has been to instruct and edify, whilst endeavoring to please. In this age of superficiality the taste of modern readers has been vitiated by light literature. Grave, dogmatic, and didactic works, how learnedsoever they may be, will scarcely be noticed by the majority of Christians. We are convinced that an explanation of the symbolical portions of the Holy Scripture, relating to the sacred mysteries of our holy religion, and more especially to the Passion of our Lord Jesus Christ, has the charm of novelty and the power of attracting the attention of the ordinary Christian reader. A favorable opportunity is thus afforded of conveying directly and almost insensibly much useful information and practical instruction, which would be rejected if offered in a more direct and positive way. In explaining the figures of the Crown of Thorns, we have followed this plan, and have kept in view the proposed end. Comparatively few persons are either able or willing to make serious meditations on the Passion of our divine Lord: but many pious Christians are disposed to peruse a plain and affecting description of his bitter sufferings.

The candid reader will be able to judge how far we have succeeded in this portion of our work. Experience shows that a variety of judicious selections of edifying extracts from the lives of the saints and of eminent servants of God proves interesting to the generality of Catholic readers. This is in a special manner the case when supernatural facts are intermixed in the selection. The human mind aspires to the supernatural which is its final end, and prefers to be taught rather by example than by precept. A very considerable portion of this book will be found to contain historical events of this description, which will prove, we trust, both interesting and edifying to all piously disposed minds. Because our idea of a practical devotion to the Crown of Thorns of our divine Savior is more fully developed in the first chapter of the Third Part of this book, to avoid repetition, we refer the reader to its contents.

In submitting this work to the careful revision of competent ecclesiastic and lay persons, we have been highly encouraged by their kind approval, and, we may be allowed to say, by their flattering encomiums, in great part very likely dictated by their friendly dispositions and charitable condescension towards the humble author. From less favorably disposed critics we claim the right of being judged in conformity with the golden maxim of St. Augustine: "*In necessariis unitas: in dubiis libertas; in omnibus charitas.*" After long and mature consideration, and urged by the repeated advice and exhortations of several persons whom we esteem and respect, we have at last consented to lay before the public this little work on devotion to the Crown of Thorns. We can only claim one qualification for this undertaking, which is that of having experienced a small share of the physical and moral sufferings of the Crown of Thorns. Thus we can more easily enter into the spirit of this devotion, and feel some little compassion for the sufferings and humiliations of our thorn-crowned Savior. From what we have stated, this book will be found divided into three parts. In the First Part we assign the motives which should induce every Christian to have a special devotion to our suffering Lord crowned with thorns as the King of sorrows. In the Second Part we give a brief history of the mystic Crown of Thorns in the Church. In the Third Part we venture to propose some special practices of devotion, which we trust will be found conducive to the honor and glory of our thorn-crowned King, and to the spiritual welfare of pious Christians. We submit in anticipation this book and everything else we have written to the infallible judgment of the Holy Roman Catholic Church, the mother and mistress of all the Churches, whose obedient, respectful and affectionate son we wish to live and to die.

In sincere compliance with the decree of Pope Urban VIII and of any other supreme Pontiff, the author declares that, in giving any title of respect and veneration to any servant of God mentioned in this book, and not yet canonized or beatified, he intends to express his own personal sentiments only, without wishing in the least to anticipate the judgment of the Holy and Apostolic See.

G. R., C. P.
FEAST OF OUR MOST HOLY REDEEMER,
October 23, 1876.

CONTENTS

THIRD PART

THE MYSTERY OF
THE CROWN OF THORNS

FIRST PART

DEVOTION TO THE CROWN OF THORNS

INTRODUCTION

The Supreme Pontiff, Innocent VI, in his decree establishing the Feast and Office of the Lance and Nails, which pierced the body of our crucified Lord Jesus Christ, exhorts all the faithful to have a special veneration for, and devotion to, all the sacred instruments of our Savior's Passion. The following are his words: *"We should honor the most holy Passion of our Lord and Redeemer, Jesus Christ, in such manner that, meditating on all the mysteries and merits of the same Passion, we venerate also each sacred instrument thereof."*

Then this holy and zealous Pontiff, coming more directly to the honor due to the lance and nails, says: *"Although the lance and nails, and the other sacred instruments of the Passion, should be everywhere venerated by the faithful of Christ, and though every year the Church celebrates the solemn offices of the same Passion, yet we deem it proper and fitting that a special solemn feast should be instituted and celebrated in honor of those particular instruments of the Passion, more especially in those places wherein these salutary instruments are preserved. Hence we wish to encourage this devotion by special office and pivileges."* (Innocent VI in Decret. de Fest. Lanc. et Clav. Domini.) All that this holy Pope says about the lance and nails of our Lord's Passion is equally to be understood of his Crown of Thorns.

Moreover, if the lance with which the side of our crucified Lord was pierced after his death, and which just for an instant touched his dead body, and was hallowed by his Sacred Blood, should, according to the papal decree, be honored and venerated by all the faithful with a special office and with a solemn feast, surely we should, with greater reason, honor, with some special devotion, his Crown of Thorns that tortured his adorable head during the longest and most painful portion of his bitter Passion, and was for our divine King and Lord the sad occasion of endless insults, and of the most profound humiliations and cruel mockeries.

Our Holy Mother the Church has, in her grateful devotion, instituted a special office to be recited, and mass to be celebrated, by the clergy at the commencement of the holy season of Lent, namely, on the Friday after Ash Wednesday. But as the Crown of Thorns was endured by our most loving Savior both for the clergy and for the people, so both should unite in a special devotion to this sacred and august mystery of the Passion. St. Bernard, after having with fervid eloquence described the manifold advantages which he derived from this devotion, warmly exhorts all classes of men to contemplate our suffering Lord crowned with thorns. *"Go forth, ye daughters of Sion, and see King Solomon in the diadem wherewith his mother crowned him."* (Cant. 3:11) Come just souls, and contemplate with pious affection your sovereign King Jesus, in his crown of mercy, and learn to imitate his meekness and patience. If during your life you meditate often on the painful and ignominious mystery of the Crown of Thorns of your Savior, you will be invited to behold him on the day of universal judgment, crowned with glory, and will be made supremely happy in his blessed company, for all eternity, in heaven. *"Go forth, then, ye daughters of Sion, and see King Solomon in the diadem wherewith his mother crowned him."*

Come, ye sinners, also, and look at your Savior, crowned with sharp thorns on account of your sins, that, at the sight of his sufferings and humiliations, you may be moved to compunction and sorrow. If, obstinate in your crimes and ungrateful to your Redeemer, you refuse during life to meditate on his sufferings, and to contemplate your Lord and God crowned with the thorns of your sins, you shall be forced to see him crowned with justice, as your Judge, when he will condemn you as reprobates to the eternal punishment of hell. (St. Bernard. Serm. 50, de divers) A member that sympathizes not with its head, wounded or in pain, is either paralytic or in some way diseased. As all good Christians desire to receive, on the day of universal judgment, from the blessed and ever loving hands of our Savior, the crown of glory promised by St. Bernard to those devout souls that often meditate on the sufferings and ignominies caused him by his Crown of Thorns, so we wish to contribute, to the best of our power, to the realization of this happy and glorious end, by the publication of this book.

CHAPTER I

FIGURES OF THE CROWN OF THORNS

"Go forth, ye daughters of Sion, and see King Solomon in the diadem with which his mother crowned him." (Cant. 3:11)

St. Bernard contemplates and describes our divine Lord and King, Jesus Christ, wearing at different times four crowns. The first crown, this holy doctor says, was placed upon the head of our Infant Savior in the crib of Bethlehem by the loving hands of his Immaculate Virgin Mother. This was the crown of poverty and misery. *"Coronavit eum Mater sua in corona paupertatis, in corona miseriae."*

The second crown was more painful to him, because it was a Crown of Thorns, thrust and pressed upon his adorable head by the cruel hands of his heartless stepmother, the synagogue. *"Coronavit eum noverca sua corona spinea."*

The third is a crown of justice which his elect will place upon his glorious brow on the day of universal judgment. *"Coronandus a familia sua corona justitia, quando veniet ad judicium."*

The fourth and most illustrious crown is that which our blessed Lord has received from the hands of his Eternal Father. This is a crown of immense and eternal glory; according to the words of the psalmist: *"Thou, O Lord, hast crowned him with glory and honor."* (Ps. 8:6) *"Coronat eum Pater corona gloriae."* (S. Bernard, Serm. 2, in Epiph. Domini) ·

We will, like Saint Bernard, contemplate, with the help of God, these four crowns at the proper time. At the holy season of Christmas we will, in company with Our Blessed Lady, consider the crown of poverty and misery of our new-born Savior in the stable of Bethlehem. But at present we intend to meditate on the painful and ignominious Crown of Thorns which his stepmother, the synagogue, has barbarously pressed upon his sacred head. By so doing, we desire and hope to form for him that crown of justice with which his elect will honor our blessed Lord on the day of universal judgment, and thus deserve to contemplate him, in his crown of glory, which his Eternal Father has already placed upon his glorified human head. *"Go forth, then, ye daughters of Sion, and see King Solomon in the diadem wherewith his mother crowned him."*

We should reflect here that this invitation is more immediately addressed to the daughters of Sion, that is to say, to the Jewish nation. They are invited to see King Solomon, the wisest, richest and most glorious of their kings. But King Solomon was a figure of the Messias. The Messias could never be seen by the Jewish people crowned with a diadem of gold and precious stones, like Solomon; but they could contemplate him with a Crown of Thorns, which their calumnies and persecutions had prepared for his adorable head. Had they attentively perused the Old Testament, they could have discovered many striking figures of this mysterious Crown of Thorns. For, as every circumstance of the incarnation, birth, life, passion, death and resurrection of the Messias was clearly foretold, or prefigured in the Old Testament, so they could have found some special revelation about this mysterious crowning of thorns. But the carnal Jews could never be induced to think, much less to believe, that the expected Messias, or Great Deliverer, was to be a King, crowned with thorns, and covered with ignominy and contempt. We Christians, however, enlightened by faith, will very easily discover what the Jews have neglected to seek. We will soon have an opportunity of considering and admiring many striking figures of the Crown of Thorns of our dear Lord. Before examining them, we will make about the Word of God some general remarks.

The Word of God, contained in the Holy Scripture, says the angelic doctor, St. Thomas, has the special prerogative, which is exclusively its own incommunicable property, to signify things, and to impart to things signified the power of indicating other objects. (1 P. quest. I, art. 10) In books conceived by human minds, and written by human hands, words express only some idea, or state a special fact. Hence human words can have only one immediate and historic meaning, which results from the grammatical construction of a definite sentence. But the Word of God, besides this immediate historic signification, which is called the *literal sense*, has likewise another, very often more important, meaning, which emanates from the things signified, and which is called the *spiritual sense*.

17

We learn from this that the historic sense of the Word of God is immediate and proximate, confined to the expression of a certain truth, or to the statement of a particular fact. But the spiritual sense, which is also called the *prophetic meaning,* is more remote and mediate, relating to some future event. The first, or the literal sense is more easily understood by the generality of readers; but it is also more limited, and often incomplete without the second, or the spiritual and prophetic meaning. This is by far more elevated, and for this reason it is more ample in its capacity, more noble in its object, and more perfect in its end. Both meanings, however, are and must be true; both are real, because both are the intended signification of God's inspired Word, which is essential truth: and hence both are important, and should be studied with care and attention. The first meaning, or the literal sense, is expressed by God according to the circumstances of the occasion, and is used by His divine wisdom as a veil of the future; the second meaning, or the spiritual sense, contains the prophetic mystery, which it unfolds and explains. Hence in perusing the Holy Scripture, St. Augustine says we should constantly keep before our mind these two meanings of the Word of God. If in reading the Bible we confine ourselves to the proximate and immediate sense of the words, and are satisfied with its literal and grammatical signification, which is only the bark and the superficial covering of the stem, we shall never obtain a full and perfect intelligence of the divine oracles, and we shall receive very little or no instruction and edification from this superficial reading of the Bible. But, alas! this is almost exclusively the way in which the Holy Scripture is read by the generality of Christians, and by those especially who consider the Bible the only rule of their religious belief, and of their moral conduct. What edification can we draw, for instance, from the canticle of Solomon, without the knowledge of its sublime spiritual meaning? Let us illustrate this fact by one out of innumerable examples.

We read in Genesis that Abraham had two sons, Ismael and Isaac. Ismael, his first-born, he had by Agar. (Gen. 16) Isaac, the second, was born to him from Sara. (Gen. 21) Now this statement of the fact is literal, immediate, and historical, and most certainly true. It is a fact which we learn from divine revelation, and which every Christian is bound to believe. But, without the knowledge of its more comprehensive and sublime, spiritual and prophetical meaning, very little profit and edification can be obtained by its perusal. The magnificent grandeur of this historic fact appears only when the great doctor of the Gentiles, St. Paul, with his inspired genius, removes the veil from the mystery, and, as the herald of God's truth, proclaims that Agar and Sara are only figures of the Old and New Testaments, of the Jewish synagogue and of the Christian Church. *"It is written* (the great Apostle says), *that Abraham had two sons, one by the bondwoman, and the other by the free woman. ...which things are said by allegory. For these are the two testaments: ... therefore, brethren, we are not the children of the bond-woman, which is the synagogue: but of the free* (which is the Church), *by the freedom wherewith Christ has made us free"*. (Gal. 4:22)

Our present object allows us merely to remark that this most illustrious doctor among the Apostles, and the most enlightened interpreter of the spiritual meaning of the Old Testament, saw figures, not only in the *written Word of God*, but also in the *made Word of God*, which is this created universe. In connection with this allegory of Agar and Sara, Ismael and Isaac, the penetrating eye of St. Paul discovers and points out to us, a prophetic meaning intended by the wisdom of the divine Creator in the very geographical configuration of Mount Sinai and Mount Sion, on the latter of which the city of Jerusalem was built. *"For Sinai* (he says), *is a mountain in Arabia, which has affinity with that which now is Jerusalem, and is in bondage with her children; but that Jerusalem which, is above, is free, which is our mother* (the Church of the living God)". (Gal. 4:25)

We have more than one motive in dwelling as we have done upon the literal and spiritual meaning of the Word of God. Let us now conclude that the Holy Ghost, in inspiring the sacred writers of the Scripture to state certain facts and give details of the circumstances by which they are surrounded, has, very often, some further and more important object in view than that expressed in the immediate and grammatical sense of the words. Holy Moses, in relating, under the guidance of divine inspiration, the simple and material historical fact of the two sons of Abraham, was moved to give to us a figure and a prophecy of the Jewish synagogue and of the Christian Church.

The principles being now sufficiently explained, let us proceed to the examination of the figures of the Crown of Thorns. In the Old Testament, these prophetic figures are so numerous that we can only mention the principal ones, and make some suitable comments on the more important and more striking among them. We will treat of these in separate chapters.

CHAPTER II

FIGURE OF THE THORNS AND THISTLES
ADAM AND EVE

"Cursed is the earth in thy work ... thorns and thistles shall it bring forth to thee." (Gen. 3:18)

The history of Adam and Eve is well known. If deeply studied, it would afford an immense amount of useful knowledge. Bat we must not depart from our proposed brevity.

After the fall of our first parents God appeared to them in human form in the terrestrial Paradise. This we learn from the fact that *"The Lord God made* (on this occasion for) *Adam and his wife garments of skin, and clothed them."* (Gen. 2) In their state of original innocence the visible presence of God formed the purest joy and most perfect happiness of Adam and Eve; but now in their guilt the sight of Him is their keenest torment. Covered with shame and trembling with fear, they attempt to hide themselves behind the thickets of the desecrated Garden of Eden. But who can hide himself from the all-seeing eye of God? He appears to them and demands from them an account of their conduct. This was the first judicial trial of criminals upon earth. From its simple process it appears that Eve allowed herself to be first seduced by Satan under the form of a serpent. Adam was evidently absent from Eve, and was, in conformity with God's directions, engaged in some light employment in another part of the terrestrial Paradise; Eve was alone and idle. Idleness is the mother of curiosity and idle curiosity is the bait of temptation. The fallen angel perceived his opportunity, and promptly availed himself of it. Assuming the low condition of a serpent, he slyly glided to the feet of Eve, spoke to her of the admirable tree of the knowledge of good and evil, and excited in her youthful imagination an ardent desire of seeing it. She went at once to the spot, she looked with admiration at its beautiful fruit, she was delighted with its fragrance, she felt a longing for it. But she was deterred by God's prohibition. Satan, perceiving her hesitation, urged her to pluck one of the sweet smelling and ripe fruit and to eat it, promising an acquisition of extraordinary knowledge, and an elevation in power and dignity similar to that of God. *"You shall be as gods, knowing good and evil."* (Gen. 3:5) Ambition prevailed; and Eve fell into the snare.

Woman will never remain alone, either in virtue or in vice. If truly virtuous, she will promote piety; if vicious, she will corrupt society. Eve, after her fall, went in search of Adam, and became his stumbling block. Adam fell through Eve. But she was the first to hear from God the sentence of her condemnation in the following words: *"I will multiply thy sorrows and thy conceptions; in sorrow shalt thou bring forth thy children, and thou shalt be under thy husband's power, and he shall have dominion over thee."* (Gen. 3:6)

Consider the wisdom and justice of this divine sentence. Eve sought to enjoy happiness in idleness, which is the concentration of selfishness; she is punished by God with a multiplicity of sorrows. Sorrows mean cares, trials, crosses, sufferings, contradictions, anxieties. Woman has a large share of them, in whatever state, condition, or position of life she may be. As a wife and mother she is condemned to a multiplicity of conceptions. These conceptions are of two different kinds, namely, in her mind and in her body. As a wife she will have much to think of and to do to please her husband, and to secure his constant esteem and lasting affection. As a mother she will have more to think of and suffer than any man will be able to describe. This is the punishment of Eve's curiosity: because curiosity is a multiplicity of idle conceptions of the mind and of the imagination, which should be punished and cured by a multiplicity of sorrows, sufferings and cares. *"I will multiply thy sorrows and thy conceptions."*

The principal crime of Eve, however, was her extravagant ambition. As pride is the natural temptation of man, so ambition is that of woman. Eve was aware of her husband's superior knowledge; she wished to know at least as much as he did; moreover, she aspired to the knowledge and to the dignity of a goddess. *"You shall be as gods, knowing good and evil,"* the serpent said to her. It was this impious presumption that prompted her disobedience. Eve wished to be like God, possessing His attribute of universal wisdom, and consequently all His divine perfections, because to aspire to one perfection of God is to aspire to all. *"You shall be as gods."* Now, as pride is punished by the abasement of humiliations, so ambition is punished by forced subjection to power and authority. *"Thou shalt be under thy husband's power, and he shall have dominion over thee."*

If this power and dominion of man over woman were regulated by sound reason and just laws, her subjection would be rendered comparatively easy and light; but because her ambition was contrary to reason and to law, so woman is condemned to feel the tyranny of man's whims and passions. Who will attempt to describe the sad consequences of this terrible tyranny? Who will be able or willing to write the history of woman's slavery and degradation, misery and multiplied sorrows during the four thousand years of her bondage before Christianity came to her ransom? ...

But what we learn from history, compared with woman's secret and manifold sorrows; is a drop of water in comparison to an ocean of bitterness; How terrible woman's condition should have been if Mary the blessed had not come to raise her from the slough of her degradation, and brought to her the blessings of the divine Redeemer with the charity and liberty of the gospel!

This glorious lady is the privileged woman intended and promised by God, when He cursed the infernal Serpent, and said: *"I will put enmities between thee and the woman and thy seed and her seed; she shall crush thy head."* Whilst the Immaculate Mother of the Redeemer crushes with her virginal foot the serpent's head, she mercifully extends her maternal hands to Eve's oppressed daughters; she frees them from their bondage, and restores them to their forfeited dignity and honor in the Catholic Church. St. Bernard says: *"Eve was a thorn that pricked her husband unto death, and left her sting of sin to her posterity. Mary is a rose of heavenly love. Eve is the thorn of death. Mary is the rose of life."* (St. Bernard, serm; de Beata Maria)

We are now in the presence of Adam. His fallen condition is worse than that of Eve. He possessed more knowledge, and a heavier responsibility rested upon his head. Adam was the father and the representative of mankind; the consequence of his fall extended to all men, without exception. His punishment will be severe. God said to him: *"Because thou hast hearkened to the voice of thy wife, and hast eaten of the tree whereof I commanded thee that thou shouldst not eat, cursed is the earth in thy work; thorns and thistles shall it bring forth to thee .... In the sweat of thy face shalt thou eat bread, till thou return to the earth, out of which thou wast taken. For dust thou art and unto dust thou shalt return.*" (Gen. 3:7)

In these terrible words of divine justice we hear the sentence of God's punishment against Adam, and learn their historic, spiritual and prophetic meaning. Let us carefully and calmly consider them.

1. We will first consider the material and historic meaning of these divine words. On account of Adam's sin God cursed this earth, and rendered it sterile and barren. Hence man is forced to labor and toil in order to draw from it his scanty food to support life. Thus, in punishment of his prevarication, man is condemned by his offended Lord and God *to a life of hard labor,* and to manifold privations and sufferings. In aggravation of his labor and toil, this cursed earth, tilled by his hands and moistened by the sweat of his brow, shall bring forth to him thistles and thorns. "*Cursed is the earth in thy work; with labor and toil thou shalt eat thereof all the days of thy life. Thorns and thistles shall it bring forth to thee.*" This malediction is a true historical fact, the painful effects of which we have to experience every day of our lives in this land of exile.

2. The worse effects of this curse, however, are not confined to the earth. They afflict the body of man, and penetrate deeply into his very soul. Let us remember that the body of man was taken from the earth outside the terrestrial Paradise. "*The Lord God formed man of the slime of the earth.*" (Gen. 2:7) This earth being cursed by God, the body of man was also cursed with it. The thorns and thistles, produced by the earth in consequence of the malediction of God, are a figure of the manifold physical sufferings with which our body is afflicted. The countless maladies that worry and torment our body are the mystical thorns and thistles which spring forth from it, and which continually prick and irritate our physical constitution. St. Augustin says: "*Spinae quid significant nisi peccatores, qui, quasi ericiis spinis peccatorum cooperti sunt.*" (In Ps. 10)

Moreover, as Adam is the head of the human family, and man is the head of the material creation, so these mystical thorns and thistles seem in a special manner to be applied to our head. Hence come the headaches and neuralgias which afflict and sadden such a large portion of mankind. Bushes of these thorns evidently grow within our brain, from which spring so many troublesome, painful, and distracting imaginations. These bodily sufferings, that are the punishment of original sin, are frightfully multiplied by the indulgence of sensual passions, and by the commission of actual sin. The more sins we commit, the thicker grow the bushes of thorns and thistles that prick our senses, disturb our imagination, and sadden our heart.

Sin, however, being principally committed by the soul through an abuse of our free will, so these mystical thorns more cruelly torment our conscience. For as the earth, on account of Adam's sin, has been condemned by God to produce thorns and thistles, which render the soil barren, increase the work of man, and prick the hand of the laborer, so sin renders the soul sterile, encumbers it with the spiritual thorns that torture his conscience, and with the thistles of evil passions, stifle the production and growth of virtuous deeds. Hence St. John Chrysostom, commenting upon the words, *"Cursed is the earth in thy work,....thorns and thistles it shall bring forth to thee,"* says: *"The conscience of the sinner shall never cease producing thorns and thistles that will continually afflict his guilty soul. Conscentia tua punctiones tibi et aculeos procreare non desinet."* (Comment. in Mk. 14:17) Here we may deplore the fearful blindness of those sinners who, to stifle the remorse of their guilty conscience, plunge more deeply into the giddy vortex of vice. They are like the tired laborer who, to take rest, would throw his naked limbs upon a bed of prickly thorns. Better by far for them, had they imitated the example of the youthful and fervent Benedict, who, being strongly tempted to sins of lust, rolled his naked body upon a large heap of thorns and with his innocent blood extinguished the fire of concupiscence. Other saints and faithful servants of God have used with equal result the same remedy. Thus the thorns and thistles of sin were by Christian virtue changed into its antidote.

3. It is high time for us to pass to the consideration of the third and most important signification of the divine words: *"Cursed is the earth in thy work... thorns and thistles shall it bring forth to thee."* This is a remarkable prophecy of the Crown of Thorns of our Savior, Jesus Christ. Reflect that thorns are not only the effect and punishment of sin; but, as we have seen above, they are likewise its most striking and fittest emblem. Now, the incarnate Son of God, being eternal and essential holiness, being the primary source of all grace, virtue and blessing, could not assume *the guilt* of our sins. He could, however, take upon himself the exterior emblem of sin, as Jacob assumed the garments of his brother, Esau. He could, moreover, undertake to atone for our sins by consenting to undergo the punishment due to them, and demanded by divine justice. For this end our

24

blessed Lord, in his love and mercy, consented to wear on his adorable head the crown of real thorns which the earth produced for our chastisement in consequence of the malediction pronounced by the offended majesty of God. Thus the Crown of Thorns of our Lord is intended by him to signify that he has undertaken to ransom us from our sin, and to bear on his sacred body, and especially upon his adorable head, the effect of God's awful malediction.

"*Christ* (St. Paul says) *hath redeemed us from the curse of the law, being made a curse for us.*" (Gal. 3:13) We learn from these words that the malediction pronounced by God when he said, "*Cursed is the earth in thy work:.... thorns and thistles shall it bring forth to thee,*" was directed, through our fault, and for our sake, against the innocent head of His most beloved Son. But it had to be done. No other remedy remained for our evils. The nature of Adam's sin, and the necessity of our redemption and salvation, demanded the painful and humiliating sacrifice of the divine Victim. "*For as by the disobedience of one man, many were made sinners* (St. Paul says) *so also by the obedience of one, many shall be made just:... that as sin hath reigned unto death, so also grace might reign by justice unto everlasting life, through Jesus Christ our Lord.*" (Rom. 5:9)

25

CHAPTER III

FIGURE OF THE BURNING BUSH

"The Lord appeared to him (Moses) *in a flame of fire out of the midst of a bush."* (Exod. 3:2)

The Church of the living God, enlightened by the wisdom of the Holy Ghost in the unerring interpretation of the written Word of God, discovers and points out to us in the Holy Scripture various figures of the Crown of Thorns. In the Office of our Savior's Crown of Thorns this loving spouse of the Lamb directs our attention to the mysterious apparition on Mount Horeb, which in the Bible is called the *Mountain of God. "Whilst Moses was feeding the sheep of Jethro, the priest of Madian, his father-in-law, he drove the flock to the inner part of the desert, and came to the Mountain of God, Horeb; and the Lord appeared to him in a flame of fire out of the midst of a bush, and he saw that the bush was on fire, and was not burnt: and Moses said, I will go and see the great sight, why the bush is not burnt."* (Exod. 3:1) Let us follow the example of holy Moses, and contemplate with devout attention this great vision.

The learned Ventura says: *"That the fathers of the Church and the interpreters of the Sacred Scripture unanimously agree in asserting that this thorny bush enveloped by the flames of that mysterious fire, without being burnt or destroyed, is a figure of the incarnation of the eternal Son of God."* (La Madre di Dio. 2 part, ch. 5) Here is the explanation. The miraculous flames that surround the thorny bush are a figure of the divine Word, who assumed our human nature. The thorny bush represents our fallen humanity overgrown with the sharp and crooked thorns of malice and innumerable sins, creeping on the ground like a blackberry bush, puny, poor, and despicable among plants. Like our fallen humanity, it bears in its prickly thorns the marks of God's curse. God appeared to Moses in the thorny bush

26

in the form of fire to signify that the eternal Word of God would assume our poor, fallen, degraded humanity, with all the thorns or painful consequences of sin, without the guilt of it. Hence the flames enveloped the thorny branches of the whole bush, without burning or consuming them; because, by consuming the fuel, fire transforms the nature thereof into its own substance.

But it was impossible for the Son of God, who is essential holiness, to assume, in the least degree, any guilt whatever of our sins. Our merciful Lord could, however, and did in fact, assume their temporal effects, namely, the misery, sufferings, and degradation of the sinner, so strikingly represented in the thorns and in the puny, weak and useless branches of the bush. Hence, Moses saw with wonder that the mysterious bush was enveloped with fire, yet it was not burnt. *"Ignis in rubo est Deus in carne, seu Verbum Caro Factum."* (A Lapide comment. in Exod. 3:2) Lastly, the fire that leaps, is agitated and blazes up among the thorny branches of that mystical bush, represents in a sensible way the intense sufferings and agonizing spasms endured by our dear Lord under the horrible torture of the Crown of Thorns. May this magnificent vision excite in the mind and heart of every Christian the same ardent desire that it evoked in the breast of holy Moses, and induce him to draw respectfully near it, to contemplate the profound mystery which it represents in such an admirable manner.

The burning bush is a striking figure of the Incarnation of the divine Word; but, on account of its thorns, it calls more especially to our mind our Savior crowned with thorns during his Passion. Such in fact is the interpretation and sentiment of the Church expressed in the Office and Mass of the Crown of Thorns. In confirmation of this, our Holy Mother represents to us the Sacred Heart of our Lord crowned with thorns, and emitting flames of fire, like the burning bush of Moses. The figure could not be more expressive of the reality. Devout reader, if you are harassed by scruples of conscience, by the thorns of misrepresentations and the calumnies of men, by crushing humiliations and insults, you will find much comfort in meditating on the mystery of the Crown of Thorns. When you are afflicted with irksome headaches, and a feverish fire burns, as it were, in your brain, remember the burning bush of Moses, and reflect that it was only a weak figure of the excruciating torture endured by the King of sorrows crowned with thorns and insulted by a brutal soldiery. In these painful circumstances offer to the Eternal Father your sufferings and humiliations in union with those of His divine Son. This pious practice will bring comfort to your soul and body, and enrich you with merit for heaven.

In the life of the angelic youth, St. Aloysius Gonzaga, we read that he was often afflicted with painful headaches, and when exhorted by his compassionate fellow-religious to pray God to deliver him from his trouble, he mildly answered that he perferred to suffer and have a share in the Crown of Thorns of his divine Master. He who is crowned with thorns with Jesus upon earth will, with him, be crowned with glory in heaven.

St. Lydwina had during more than thirty years been afflicted with intense sufferings all over her body, but more especially in her head, when an angel appeared to her, announcing that her mystic Crown of Thorns was nearly completed, and she should be soon called to receive a brilliant crown of heavenly glory.

CHAPTER IV

FIGURE OF THE ARK OF THE COVENANT

"Frame an ark of setim wood:... and over it thou shalt make a golden crown round about." (Exod. 25:10)

In the Office of the Crown of Thorns the Church brings before our eyes the famous Ark of the Covenant, which among the Jews was the most precious and sacred object used in their religious worship. *"God said to Moses: Frame an ark of setim wood, the length whereof shall be of two cubits and a half, the breadth a cubit and a half, the height likewise a cubit and a half. And thou shalt overlay it with the purest gold within and without; and over it thou shalt make a golden crown round about."* (Exod. 25:10-11) In due time *the two tables of the Decalogue, the golden urn that had manna, and the rod of Aaron that had blossomed, were enclosed in this venerated ark.* This we learn from St. Paul's Epistle to the Hebrews. (Heb. 9:4) The angelic doctor, St. Thomas, says that the three sacred objects enclosed within the ark, or at least placed close to it, mystically signified the three divine attributes of Wisdom, Power, and Goodness. In fact, the law is the work of God's wisdom, the miraculous rod is both the emblem and the proof of His divine power, and the manna was the figure and the effect of His goodness. (St. Thomas, I. 2. Quaest. 102, art. 4)

1. This celebrated ark was also a beautiful figure of our Savior's Incarnation. The setim wood, by its natural soundness and incorruptibility, represents the sinless nature of our Lord's assumed humanity, and the incorruptibility of his sacred and glorified body. For the royal Prophet, David, quoted by St. Peter, says *"that God will not suffer His most holy One to see corruption."* (Acts 2:27) Again, this ark, formed of incorruptible wood, was overlayed within and without with the purest gold. This gold represents the Person of the Eternal Word inseparably united at His Incar-

29

nation with the soul and body of our Lord Jesus Christ. The two tables of the Decalogue were by the command of God enclosed in this ark, to signify that the law of God was deeply impressed in the most holy and most loving heart of our Blessed Lord. From the first moment of his Incarnation our unborn Savior could say: *"Sacrifice and oblation Thou (O Father) didst not desire; but a body Thou hast fitted to me. In the head of the book it is written of me, that I should do Thy will. O my God, I have desired it, and Thy law is in the midst of my heart."* (Ps. 39:7; Heb. 10:7)

2. The manna was in the ark as a proof of God's goodness, and of His providential care of His people. The Incarnation, however, is the most astonishing manifestation of God's goodness and mercy towards mankind. Moreover, the manna was a very expressive figure of the Eucharistic Bread, through which we are fed with the Sacred Body and Precious Blood of the divine Lamb of God. Hence our Lord said to the Jews: *"Your fathers did eat manna in the desert, and they died...If any man eat of this Bread, he shall live forever: and the Bread which I will give is my flesh, for the life of the world."* (Jn. 6:49-52)

3. The miraculous rod of the high Pontiff Aaron was also with this ark. The history of this famous rod will be found interesting and pregnant with meaning in this age of infidelity, when the sacred character of the Christian priesthood is despised by the infidel and degraded by the heretic.

Two hundred and fifty leading men of the synagogue, enticed by Core, a Levite, and by Dathon, Abiron, and Hor, caused a schism among the Jews, because in their pride and ambition they aspired to the dignity of the priesthood. Their sacrilegious presumption was punished by God in a terrible manner. By command of Moses, the whole Jewish nation was summoned to witness the most awful chastisement recorded in sacred history. In the sight of all Israel, Core, Dathon and Abiron, with their entire families, were swallowed up alive in the earth, *"and fire coming out from the Lord destroyed the two hundred and fifty men that offered the incense."* (Num. 16)

Then, by the command of God, twelve rods were selected, and upon each of them was written the name of one of the twelve tribes of Israel, and lastly another rod had the name of Aaron. These thirteen rods were placed by Moses side by side upon a table in the Tabernacle of the Lord, and shut up for the entire night, with the express understanding that the dignity of the priesthood should be considered awarded by God to the tribe or person whose rod should be found miraculously blossomed on the following morning. Early in the morning, an immense multitude gathered in front of the tabernacle, anxiously awaiting the miraculous manifestation of the divine will. Moses entered the tabernacle fully impressed with the importance of the occasion, and brought out before the people the thirteen rods, when, to the general amazement, it was found that, whilst the twelve rods were perfectly dry, that of Aaron alone had not only blossomed, but had also produced almonds. Thus, by divine interposition Aaron and his sons were publicly confirmed in the priestly dignity, for the priesthood is essentially a divine institution. Hence St. Paul teaches *that no man should presume to take this honor and dignity upon himself, except he be called by God, as Aaron was."* (Heb. 5:4) For the future remembrance of this prodigy, Moses commanded that the miraculous rod of Aaron should be preserved in the tabernacle with the Ark of the Covenant.

4. A crown of the purest gold surrounded the lid of this holy ark, as a figure of the Crown of Thorns that was to be placed by his enemies on the head of our dear Savior. Gold being among metals what charity is among virtues, the golden crown of the ark signified the ardent love of our blessed Lord in permitting himself, for our sake, to be subjected to the cruel torture of the Crown of Thorns.

The lid, being the uppermost extremity of the ark, indicates another mystery. It shows that our Savior had to endure the Crown of Thorns on his head in order that the Divinity may extract the thorns of sin from our guilty humanity: for his human nature could suffer, but his Divinity only could cure us of our sins. According to St. Paul, the head of Jesus is the figure of his Divinity. *"I would have you know that the head of every man is Christ; and the head of the woman is the man; and the head of Christ is God."* (1 Cor. 2:3) Hence, Theophilatus says, the head of Jesus indicates his Divinity. *"Per caput enim Deitas presignatur."* It therefore follows that our Lord Jesus Christ, by consenting to have his head transfixed by the thorns of our sins, and by undergoing the pain and ignominy of this cruel and humiliating torture, consumed and destroyed our guilt by the power of his Divinity. The Crown of Thorns, says Theophilatus, is our sins, which Christ consumed by his Divinity. *"Corana ex spinis peccata sunt, quae Christus sua Deitate cousumit."* (Theophil. comment. in St. Matt. 27:29.)

Here we discover another meaning in the golden crown round the lid of the ark. As gold is precious in the estimation of worldly men, so

31

devotion to the Crown of Thorns should possess for us a high value. If all the members of our Savior's body, on account of their union with the Person of the Eternal Word, are sacred and deserve our profound adoration, how much more profound should be our worship of his most holy head — the throne of his divine intelligence, the noble figure of the Divinity, and the august representative of the Godhead? Oh, how sublime and instructive is the mystery of the Crown of Thorns!

5. The more deeply we dig into this golden mine, the richer treasures we draw out of it. Gold brought out of the mine must pass through the crucible and be purified by intense fire. Had this precious metal sensitive faculties, it would, under the action of fire, feel an excruciating pain. The pain, however, is intended not for its destruction, but for its purification and refinement, and for the increase of its worth and value. Our Lord had the most refined and sensitive feelings. Though he had no need to suffer for himself, because he was essential holiness, yet, having assumed our human nature, he had to suffer for our purification, in order to remove from our fallen humanity the dross of sin, and to impart to our moral actions and sufferings the value of supernatural merit, which is infinitely more precious than gold. Our merciful Savior procured for us these two advantages in a high degree through the sufferings and humiliations of the Crown of Thorns. Because as life and action are communicated to the members of the body from the head, so the supernatural life of grace and the power of meriting is communicated to the faithful from the divine Head of the Church, Jesus Christ. *"For God hath made him Head over all the Church, which is his body, and the fullness of him, who is filled all in all."* (Ephes. 1:22)

All virtuous actions performed for God's sake, and all the sufferings and humiliations endured for the promotion of His honor and glory, are richly rewarded by God. Great must be the reward given by the Eternal Father to His divine Son for having endured the sufferings and humiliations of the Crown of Thorns to promote His glory and the eternal salvation of mankind. In fact, the Church sings with the royal Prophet: *"Thou, O Lord, hast prevented him with blessings of sweetness: Thou hast set on his head a crown of precious stones."* (Ps. 20:14)

Every soul saved will form a brilliant jewel in the diadem of glory of our blessed Lord, and increase the joy of his loving heart. Moreover, according to St. Bernard, God turned the very malice of His Son's executioners to His actual honor and glory. *"Though those cruel men* (says the Saint) *press a Crown of Thorns on the head of Jesus, in derision and mockery, yet contrary to their intention, and in spite of their malice, they proclaim him their crowned Sovereign. For upon bended knees they salute him, King of the Jews. Hence, in their harsh and cruel treatment of our Lord, their words and actions proclaim him to be their King."* (St. Bern. de Pass. Dom. cap. 19) Head of Jesus, pierced with thorns, open the intelligence of our minds, and make these sublime truths penetrate deeply into our soul. May all Christians be moved to meditate upon them and induced to offer to their suffering King their sincere homage and profound adorations.

CHAPTER V

FIGURE OF THE AZAZEL, OR
THE EMISSARY GOAT

"Let Aaron offer the living goat; and, putting both hands upon its head, let him confess all the iniquities of the children of Israel, and all their offenses and sins: and, praying that they may light on its head, he shall turn it out into the desert by a man ready for it." (Levit. 16:21)

The Old Testament is full of mysteries. It is, in fact, the shadow of Christianity, and the veil which indicates, whilst it conceals, Jesus Christ. Since the fall of Adam man feels two wants: the first is the necessity of acknowledging his fallen state; the second is the need of a Mediator and Redeemer, between him and God. The mysterious ceremony of the *Azazel,* or *emissary goat*, represents and expresses these two wants. We find in it the confession of sin, and the removal of it by a Mediator. Let us say something first about confession of sin and of human misery.

Even pagans, with the dim and flickering light of reason, could perceive that some terrible calamity had fallen upon our human nature. On one side they discovered in man something very noble, with high aspirations: on the other side they found him groveling upon the earth, degraded by low passions, and defiled by the filth of sin and vice. Hence St. Paul says: *"We know that every creature groaneth and is in labor even till now."* (Rom. 8: 22) Every one of us can cry with holy David, *"Have mercy on me, 0 Lord, for I am afflicted; my eye, my soul, my heart is troubled. . . . My life is wasted with grief, and my years in sighs."* (Ps. 30:10)

Sin being the cause of human misery, *because sin maketh people miserable* (Prov. 16: 34), hence arises in the sinner the want and the desire of removing sin from his troubled and afflicted soul. Sin is to the soul what poison is to the body. Both must be ejected if we wish to enjoy health, peace and rest. The commission of sin generates in man the necessity of confession: because sin, to be cured, must be acknowledged. Hence, in many parts of Sacred Scripture we find the obligation of confession imposed by God upon the sinner. As soon as Adam and Eve had fallen, God interrogated them, asking them what they had done, to oblige them to acknowledge their transgression. Cain murdered his innocent brother Abel; the body of the latter was still warm when God, in a visible form, appeared to Cain and asked: *"Where is thy brother Abel?"* (Gen. 4: 9.) Let Cain answer this question and he will confess the murder.

The more sin is multiplied on earth the more explicit the obligation of confession is made by the command of God. For the sake of brevity we must pass over the various ordinances of God contained in the fourth, fifth and sixth chapters of Leviticus, which are practical confessions of sin, as the angelic doctor, St. Thomas, observes. We will, however, make some few quotations from other parts of Scripture. *"The Lord spoke to Moses, saying: Say to the children of Israel, When a man or woman shall have committed any of all the sins that men are wont to commit, and by negligence shall have transgressed the commandment of the Lord and offended, they shall confess their sin."* (Num. 5:6) Again: *"He that hideth his sins shall not prosper; but he that confesseth and forsakes them shall obtain mercy."* (Prov. 28:13) From the Gospel we learn that the Jews at the time of St. John the Baptist observed the practice of confession: *"John was in the desert baptizing, and preaching the baptism of penance for the remission of sins. And there went out to him all the country of Judea, and all they of Jerusalem, and were baptized by him in the river Jordan, confessing their sins."* (Mk. 1:4-5; 4, 5; see also Mt. 3:6) This is more than sufficient to show that confession of sin was a duty among the Jews. This duty is too well known in the Christian Church to require proof from us in this place.

2. As we Catholics are commanded by the Church to confess our grievous sins at least once every year, so the Israelites were commanded by God to celebrate every year the feast of expiation, when the High Priest, by a mysterious rite, had to transfer publicly all the sins of the people upon the head of a living goat, in Hebrew called *Azazel,* or the *emissary goat.* On this solemn occasion the High Pontiff, in the presence of the assembled multitude, laid both hands on the head of the mysterious animal, confessing aloud all the iniquities of the children of Israel, and all their offenses and sins, and praying that they might light on its head; he gave the emissary goat in charge of a man appointed for this office,

who led it into a desert, and abandoned it to the universal execration of heaven and earth. (Lev.16:21.)

In this ceremony we have seen accomplished one of the two duties mentioned above, namely, confession of sin, and the acknowledgment, before heaven and earth that we are a fallen race of men. In consequence, however, of our fall, we feel a second want.

3. We feel the need of a mediator to relieve us from the crushing burden of our sins and miseries. In short, human nature feels the want of a Redeemer, who, in his goodness and merciful compassion, may vouchsafe to deliver us from the manifold evils that oppress our common humanity. Hence, the holy Patriarch Jacob, on his death-bed, foretold that the Redeemer who was to be sent *"shall be the expectation of nations."* (Gen. 49:10) It is evident that this Redeemer, to cure and save the sinner, must be innocent and free from sin, in order that his mediation and atonement may be acceptable to God. Among the Jews this office of mediator was on this occasion well prefigured in the *Azazel,* or emissary goat. This animal could not be guilty of any sin. Hence, being guiltless, the High Pontiff laid publicly and solemnly the iniquities, offenses and sins of the children of Israel upon its head, and drove it away from them, praying and hoping that, with the victim, all the sins were taken away from the people.

This rite or ceremony, however, without the profound mystery of the Crown of Thorns, would remain very obscure and unsatisfactory: because a senseless beast could not atone for the sins of man. But this animal was a striking figure of the divine Lamb of God, on whose adorable head all the iniquities, offenses and sins of mankind were laid by the Eternal God, represented in the person of the Jewish High Priest. *"All we, like sheep, have gone astray, every one hath turned aside into his own way, and the Lord hath laid upon him the iniquities of us all.... He shall be led like a sheep to the slaughter."* (Is. 53:6) This terrible mystery was fully revealed and accomplished when the divine Lamb of God, our Lord Jesus Christ, was crowned with thorns. It was then that the Eternal Father laid upon the innocent head of His Son the iniquities of us all. He was then made our true Mediator and our most merciful Redeemer: for, as holy Bede remarks, "by voluntarily assuming the Crown of Thorns, our merciful Lord undertook to atone for our sins, which, like thorns, germinate from the accursed earth of our corrupted hearts." (St. Bede comment in Joan. ch. 19) St. Augustine says, *"Corona spinea capiti ejus imponitur quia punctio peccatorum nostrorum.... aridis tribulis comparatur."*(Serm. 41, de Pass. Domini)

Contemplate, then, Christian soul, this divine Son of God in the hall of the Roman governor's palace, sitting upon a cold stone, crowned with thorns. Reflect that, whilst his cruel enemies torture his adorable head with a horrible crown of long and sharp thorns, the Eternal Father presses it deeply down by laying upon it the enormous load of all the sins of mankind. Whilst these sharp thorns torture our Savior's head, our sins transfix his divine heart and make him endure a double agony — one of pain in his body, and another of grief and shame in his most holy soul. Are you, devout reader, willing to promote, by your example and opportune words, the devotion of the Crown of Thorns, with the pious intention of making some suitable reparation to our dear Lord for the insults and sufferings endured by him on this occasion? You will surely be moved to show your gratitude to our common Redeemer if you reflect that, at his crowning with thorns, he fulfilled for our sake and welfare the two duties of confession and atonement. You remember that, as we observed above, thorns are both the punishment and the emblem of sin. Now, it is evident that our Lord, by allowing a Crown of Thorns to be placed upon his adorable head, acknowledged by this act of profound humility the existence of our sins, which in reality is a confession of them made by him publicly to God and man. Moreover, by voluntarily taking them upon his head, he, like the Jewish Azazel, undertook to atone for them, not in figure, but in truth, as our actual Mediator and real Savior, thus fulfilling the twofold duties of confession and atonement. In conclusion, we should learn that the sacrament of penance, instituted by him for the remission of sin, should be devoutly frequented by us if we wish to obtain from his mercy forgiveness for our transgressions.

4. When King Clovis, in the presence of an immense multitude of his people, presented himself to receive baptism from the holy Bishop Remigius, this latter placed his pontifical hand on the head of the kneeling monarch, and, with great solemnity and dignity, said to him: "Bow down your neck with meekness, great Sicambrian prince, and promise to burn what you have hitherto adored, and to adore him whom you have attempted to burn. As a pagan you adored idols: promise now to burn and destroy them, throughout the kingdom of France. In your pagan zeal you attempted to abolish the religion of Jesus crucified: promise now to adore and to worship him." The fervent royal neophyte promptly made to the bishop

these two promises, and received the forgiveness of all his sins through the holy sacrament of baptism. (Life of St. Remigius) Confession is a second baptism for the sinner. When we go to confession we should be resolved to destroy in our hearts all the secret idols of our sins and evil passions, and to love and worship Jesus Christ alone, who, by his humiliations, sufferings and death, atoned for them, and obtained for us the grace of pardon and reconciliation.

CHAPTER VI

FIGURE OF THE RAM AMONGST THE BRIARS : ABRAHAM AND ISAAC

"Abraham lifted up his eyes, and saw behind his back a ram amongst the briars sticking fast by the horns, which he took and offered for a holocaust instead of his son." (Gen. 22:13)

1. The most difficult and painful command ever given to any man was that received from God by the holy Patriarch Abraham. God said to him: *"Take thy only begotten son, Isaac, whom thou lovest and go into the land of vision; and there thou shalt offer him for a holocaust upon one of the mountains which I will show thee."* Isaac was the only son that Abraham had from his wife Sara. She had conceived him through a miracle, because she was old and naturally barren, and without a great prodigy Sara could not have given birth to any child. Abraham loved Isaac in common with all parents. Nature has implanted in the heart of parents a strong affection for their children. The helpless condition and manifold wants of childhood render this affection necessary. But parental affection is highly intensified when it is concentrated in an only child, and this a son. Such was Isaac. *"Take thy only begotten son, Isaac, whom thou lovest."*

But the love of Abraham for Isaac was enhanced and increased by other motives. Abraham was a most pious and virtuous father. If nature generates in the heart of parents a strong affection for their children, virtue purifies, enobles and strengthens it a hundredfold. Virtuous parental affection is an emanation of the love of the God-head, from whom all paternity in heaven and upon earth is derived, as St. Paul. says. (Eph. 3:15) Hence, the affection of a pious and virtuous father for his child has the tenacity and vigor of a manly and noble heart, purified, elevated, and fortified by divine love. The more this supernatural love increases towards God, the more parental affection is intensified towards the child. Happy child of such a father!

2. Now, Abraham was a most eminently devout servant of God. He is the father of the faithful, and a model of divine love. From this we may conclude how ardently he loved his son Isaac. Again, Isaac deserved his father's love. He was his only begotten son. He was in the flower of his age, and in the full blood of manhood. He was handsome, noble-looking, full of health and manly vigor. Isaac was the son of promise: he was to be the father of nations as numerous as the stars in the firmament. (Gen. 15:5) Promises of very numerous progeny were repeatedly made to Abraham by God, who said to him, *"I will make thee increase exceedingly .... I will bless Sara, and of her I will give thee a son, whom I will bless, and he shall become nations, and kings of people shall spring from him."* (Gen. 17) But what endeared Isaac to the heart of his saintly father was his respectful behavior towards his parents, his docility, and eminent piety. Young in age, Isaac was already ripe in the virtues that adorn and ennoble a youthful son. It is this precious child that Abraham is called upon to sacrifice with his own hands, and then to burn his body with fire, until it be totally consumed, as the victim of an holocaust. But this command has been given by God in order to render manfest to all future generations the eminent sanctity of father and son.

3. The sacrifice should have been painful, but the agony of the father's heart would have been shorter had the victim been immolated on the spot without delay; such, however, was not to be the case. Abraham had to undertake a long journey of three days' duration, having continually under his paternal eyes his innocent and beloved child. With his cheerful and affectionate attentions, Isaac, unconscious of his destination, rendered himself every moment more pleasing to his thoughtful father. With sentiments of deep devotion, Isaac spoke to his father of the inward joy of his heart in anticipation of the great sacrifice they were going to offer to Almighty God. Abraham looked at his son with more than usual tenderness, shed some tears, and was silent.

On the third day Abraham saw the mountain selected by God for the sacrifice of Isaac. He began at once to make his preparation. He left his two servants and provisions at the foot of the hill. He took the wood that he had brought with him for the holocaust, put it on the shoulders of his son; and he himself carried in his hands fire and a sword, and they went together, side by side. Isaac, with all the simplicity and confidence of childhood, said to Abraham: *"My father! behold we have with us the fire and the wood, but where is the victim for the holocaust?"* Oh! what emotions must at that moment have been excited in the heart of Abraham! But with an heroic self-possession he calmly answered: *"God will provide Himself a victim for an holocaust, my son."* Having at last arrived at the appointed place, Abraham laid the sword and the fire upon the ground, and took the dry wood from the shoulders of his son. With loose stones they immediately began to prepare a temporary altar about seven feet long, and three or four feet wide and high. Upon the stones they arranged some smaller kindling wood, and over this the larger pieces which they had split and brought along with them. Could we penetrate into the sanctuary of Abraham's heart and see what his feelings are at this awful moment! He is looking at the bright sharp weapon with which he has been commanded to slay his own most beloved child. He sees before him the altar, the wood, and fire with which he shall have to burn his lifeless body. Whilst we are reflecting, Abraham acts. Behold he affectionately embraces his son, kisses and with tears in his eyes declares to him the command of God. Isaac feels a shudder creeping through his frame, but, doing violence to his natural feelings, bravely consents, in obedience to God, to be immolated for His honor and glory. He steps on the altar, lays himself down on the wood, like an innocent child on his bed, allows himself to be bound with cords by his father, lifts up his eyes to heaven, and recommends his soul to God. His father seizes the sword, raises it up in the air, gives a glance at his son, and aims the mortal blow at his heart. But God is satisfied with the dispositions of father and son. An angel says to Abraham: *"Lay not thy hand upon the boy, neither do thou anything to him. Now I know that thou fearest God, and hast not spared thy only begotten son for my sake."*

4. Here is an example for parents and for children. When children receive a legitimate command from their parents which is painful to their feelings, they should reflect on the obedience of Isaac. The command of God manifested to him by the mouth of his father was extremely painful to nature. But this dutiful son was ready to sacrifice his very life in obedience to God's command. No such command will ever be given again to any child. But let children remember that they are obliged to obey their parents, when their orders are conformable to the law of God. If the command is painful to nature, let children reflect on the obedience of Isaac, and humbly obey.

41

Parents also have a bright example in the holy Patriarch Abraham. He loved his only begotten son as much, at least, and very likely more, than any modern parent can love his child. But when called by God to sacrifice him, he was ready to obey. Parents! Christian parents! God may require the sacrifice of a beloved child, not by your own hand, but by ordinary death. Learn from this holy father to be submissive to the will of God. God may call your child to a higher and holier state of life: as you desire your eternal salvation, and that of your child, beware of opposing his or her holy vocation. This vocation may demand a sacrifice from your human, perhaps too human, affection; but how great soever your sacrifice may be in your estimation, it cannot be compared to that of Abraham.

"This holy Patriarch was so determined upon executing the command of God (St. John Chrysostom wisely observes), that he carefully concealed it from his wife, lest she should, in her maternal affection and grief, attempt to dissuade and prevent the painful sacrifice of their beloved child. This wise precaution was suggested to Abraham by the sincerity and eagerness of his obedience to the command of God. For the same motive he began his journey very early in the morning, before he could be observed by any of his relations or neighbors. He was at some considerable distance from them before they could be aware of his departure: Moreover, they were kept in ignorance, not only of the object, but also of the place of his destination. Consider now how painful it must have been for the affectionate heart of this holy man to be conversing alone with his son, apart from all other persons, when the affections are more warmly excited, and attachment becomes stronger, and this not for a few hours, not for one or two, but for several days and nights. It would have been an heroic act of human fortitude to sacrifice his son immediately after receiving the divine command; but who can sufficiently admire the astonishing strength of character in Abraham, when we behold him free from any symptom of human weakness, or from any sign of parental tenderness towards his son when alone with him on the summit of Moriah? What language can describe his strength of virtue when we contemplate him, in obedience to God, calmly binding Isaac to the wooden altar, seize the sacrificing knife, and raise up the hand to inflict the mortal stroke on the heart of his only son? ... It is impossible to understand how it happened that his paternal hand was not paralyzed by horror, how the strength of his nerves was not relaxed by anguish, and the affecting sight of his prostrate son did not overpower his spirit. Behold, then, in Abraham the father and the sacrificing priest, with his own son as the divinely selected victim. God, however, did not wish to see the flowing blood of Isaac, but He desired to give us an example of perfect obedience. He wished to make known to the whole world the virtue of this admirable man, and to teach all mankind that it is necessary to prefer the command of God before children and nature; before all things, and life itself. The command given by God to Abraham, naturally speaking, was enough to stagger his reason, to throw him into the deepest perplexity, and to undermine his faith in the past. For who would not have thought that the promise which had been made to him of a numerous posterity was all a deception? But Abraham hoped against hope, and his faith in God triumphed. He descended from the mount, enriched with merits, replenished with the most precious blessings of God, and with his paternal heart overflowing with heavenly joy he returned to his home, in company with his son, full of life and happiness, and adorned with the crown of martyrdom. Thus in Isaac we behold a type of the death and resurrection of Jesus Christ. How can we be pardoned then, or what apology can we have, if we see that noble man obeying God with so much promptness, and submitting to Him in all things, and yet we murmur at His dispensations? With faith and hope in God, like Abraham, let us in all our trials and sorrows be perfectly submissive to God's adorable will." (St. John Chrysostom, serm. 5, de Lazaro)

5. To those who may be surprised at the command given by God to this holy Patriarch, we have only to say that God is the Master of life and death. God has absolute dominion over all His creatures. He could at any time demand the entire immolation of any person. God demands this sacrifice at the point of our death, and He sends death to us whenever He pleases. But in His paternal goodness, and in the exercise of His justice, God is satisfied with our resignation to His divine will, when the time of our death arrives. He has been pleased to substitute other victims when sacrifice is required for religious worship. In the Old Testament different animals were immolated among the Jews. In the Christian religion we have a more worthy Victim in the sacrifice of the Mass. No religion can exist without sacrifice. Pagan worship is a proof of this truth. The motive and the object of pagan sacrifices may be wrong, but the principle is sound: Since the fall of Adam sacrifice became an essential duty of man; and it has always been offered in every nation with any pretension to religion.

43

The only exception is found in Protestantism, and this fact alone is sufficient to demonstrate that Protestantism is no religion, because it has rejected Sacrifice, which is essential to religious worship.

After this digression, which is not without its object, we will return to Abraham, and from history we will pass to mystery.

6. In obedience to the command of the angel, Abraham unbound his son Isaac, bade him rise, and come down from the altar. Then, turning round, *"he saw behind his back a ram among the briars sticking fast by the horns to the thorny branches."* By a secret inspiration he understood the prophetic meaning of his own words, when a short time before Abraham said to his son: *"God will provide Himself a victim for the holocaust."* He took, therefore, this ram so providentially sent to him by God, *"and offered it for an holocaust instead of his son."*

In this wonderful history of Isaac we have a remarkable figure of our divine Savior, from his birth to his passion, death, and resurrection. The miraculous conception and birth of Isaac is a striking figure of that of our Lord. Both were beyond and above the laws of nature. Abraham and Sara were worthy figures of St. Joseph and our Blessed Lady. Isaac was about the age of our Lord when commanded to be sacrificed. The place of the sacrifice was the same for both. Mount Moriah and Mount Calvary are the same mountain. When we saw Isaac carrying upon his shoulders the wood intended for the sacrifice; when we saw him voluntarily laying himself down upon it to be immolated as a victim, we could not but see in his person a most striking figure of our Lord carrying his cross to Mount Calvary to be crucified and immolated upon it. Abraham, with fire in one hand and a sword in the other, is a figure of the Eternal Father. The fire signified the charity of the Eternal Father in giving us His divine Son, as an holocaust for our redemption. The sword showed that the death of His divine Son could only take place in obedience to his will. As no one but Abraham could immolate his son Isaac, so no created power could deprive of life the incarnate Son of God; He could die only when and how God decreed. God's omnipotent will was the sword that really inflicted the stroke of death on the Victim of Calvary. It was the same omnipotent will that restored life to him at his glorious resurrection. In this respect Isaac was also a figure of the Redeemer. Morally and in the sight of God, Isaac died when he consented to be immolated in obedience to His command, manifested to him through the mouth of his father. It was through the miraculous interposition of God that his life was spared. When Isaac sprang up from the sacrificial altar, full of life, vigor and joy, he represented the resurrection of our Savior. So far the figure seems to be perfect. *"Mortis et resurrectionis figuram in altari positam,"* St. John Chrysostom says.

7. But we have now to consider the Crown of Thorns. Look then, dear reader, at *the ram among the briars sticking fast by the horns to their thorny branches;* and what can we see in it, but the Lamb of God crowned with thorns? The ram has its head surrounded with thorns immediately before being sacrificed; Jesus is crowned with thorns before his crucifixion. The ram is bound with cords and placed by Abraham on the wood of the altar; Jesus is bound likewise, then laid on the wood of the cross. The altar upon which the mysterious animal is immolated was erected on Mount Moriah; this hill is a portion of Mount Calvary, whereon the cross of our Redeemer is planted. It was God who sent the ram to Abraham; and God only could send to us His divine Son. God sent to Abraham the victim as a substitute for his son Isaac; God sent Jesus to be sacrificed for our redemption and eternal salvation. Behold how the mysteries of the Old Testament are fulfilled in the Person of the Incarnate Word.

We have seen that among these mysteries the Crown of Thorns has a very prominent part. We might have mentioned more figures of the Crown of Thorns. But for the sake of brevity we will merely indicate them. The altar within the tabernacle whereon incense was burned was surrounded with a golden crown. (Exod. 30:3) The table for the service of the altar had also a crown of gold. (Exod. 25:25) Crowns formed of chains adorned the heads of the pillars in Solomon's Temple, and were graven in the ceiling. (2 Paralip. 3) Wreaths of network were carved on the chapiters of all the pillars (Paralip 4:13). The miter on the head of the high Pontiff, and the crown of golden chains on the top of the *Rational,* and the *Ephod* which he carried on his breast, were all figures of our Savior's Crown of Thorns. (Exod. 28) Other figures could be gathered from the Old Testament; but what we have brought forward should be more than sufficient to show that God has always been anxious to keep before the eyes of faith the great mystery of the crown of our Savior. We are therefore deeply convinced that the devotion which we advocate in this little book will be pleasing to Him, and will prove both agreeable and profitable to Christian souls. From the figures we will now pass to the reality.

CHAPTER VII

JESUS CROWNED WITH THORNS :
PRELIMINARY REMARKS

In order to form some faint idea of the excessive sufferings endured by our Lord at his crown of thorns, we should reflect that his bodily constitution was extremely refined, and most sensitive to every kind of physical suffering. This is what we shall have to do before proceeding to the contemplation of the Crown of Thorns.

1. Let us consider then, in the first place, the difference between a person seriously in earnest, and firmly determined to obtain an important end, and another very lukewarm about it. This latter will be slow and careless in the choice and application of the means. But the former will, as soon as possible, select the fittest instruments, and apply them in practice, at the earliest opportunity, with the utmost vigor.

Now it is a fundamental dogma of Christianity that the eternal Son of God became man to satisfy divine justice offended by the sins of man, and thus redeem and save mankind. This merciful object of Our Savior's Incarnation was promised by God in the Old Testament, foretold by His holy prophets, and lastly announced by His holy angels. The Angel Gabriel said to St. Joseph, the virginal spouse of the holy and immaculate Virgin Mother of our Lord; *"Thou shalt call his name Jesus: for he shall save his people from their sins."* (Mt. 1:21) This was the end of Jesus' mission upon earth, *"For God sent his Son a propitiation for our sins,"* St. John says. (1 Jn. 4:10) *"Our Lord Jesus Christ* (St. Paul teaches) *gave himself for our sins that he might deliver us from this present wicked world."* (Gal.1:4) Behold here, then, the object of our merciful Redeemer's Incarnation. Jesus became man to satisfy the justice of God, offended by the sins of man, and thus to redeem and save mankind.

46

Now this propitiation with God, this deliverance from sin, this salvation from eternal misery, had to be effected through the bodily sufferings of Jesus, by the shedding of his sacred blood, and through his actual death upon the cross. This is another article of the Christian faith; hence St. Paul says: *"Whereas you were some time alienated, and enemies in mind in evil work, yet now he, Jesus, hath reconciled in the body of his flesh through death to present you holy and unspotted and blameless before him."* (Col. 1:21-22) *"Jesus loved us* (St. John says) *and washed us from our sins, in his blood."* (Apoc. 1:5) *"He himself bore our sins in his body,... by whose stripes you were healed."* (1 Peter 2:24) Devout reader, fix well your attention upon these words of divine inspiration. Consider the end of our Savior's Incarnation. This was fully to atone for all the sins of mankind. Now the means and instrument which our Lord adopted and used for the perfect attainment of this sublime end, was the assumption of a real human body and true created human soul, in order that he might suffer and die, and through his sufferings and death satisfy divine justice for our sin, and thus redeem and save mankind. *"He himself bore our sins in his body,... by whose stripes you were healed."*

It is evident to any ordinary intelligence, and besides daily experience shows, that the more refined the human body, or any member or organ of it is, the more keenly sensitive it becomes to every kind of physical pain. Therefore, out of respect for the wisdom and earnest sincerity of our divine Lord and Savior, we must conclude that the body assumed by him in his Incarnation must have been exceedingly refined and consequently most keenly sensitive to all kinds of suffering..

2. From these premises we learn another mystery. It is this: Jesus Christ, who styles himself the Son of Man, was the only child ever born upon earth for suffering. Suffering is the effect of sin; hence, as man was not and could not be created for sin, so he could not be created for suffering. Man, on the contrary, was created and intended by God for happiness both in time and eternity. It was the curse of sin that brought upon guilty man both suffering and death. Now, because the eternal Son of God became man to atone for the sins of mankind, therefore the immediate object of his Incarnation was to suffer and die a victim of charity for our redemption and salvation. Hence the admirable adaptation of his bodily constitution to the most exquisite sensibility in every kind of physical pain. And, in fact, if we who were not originally created nor intended by God for

sufferings, feel them so keenly, we should from our own experince judge how incomparably more acute every kind of pain must have been to our divine Lord, who, by the wisdom and justice of God, was in his human nature created and destined as a victim of immolation upon the altar of suffering and death. This will appear more evident if we proceed to make two additional reflections: one in relation to his sacred body, the other about his most holy soul.

3. It is certain that the more refined the subject of pain is, the more intense suffering becomes. A tender and delicate child feels the same kind and amount of suffering — as cold weather, a severe blow — more keenly than a grown-up, robust person. A delicately-reared lady suffers more, under the same circumstances, than a tough, hard laboring man. The same must be said of different parts of the body. The prick of a pin or of a thorn in a callous hand or foot will scarcely be felt; but the same puncture in the eye, or in some internal vital organ as the brain or the heart, will cause intense agony: because the subject of pain is more refined, and consequently more sensitive to suffering.

Now, the whole body of our divine Savior was most exquisitely refined in its constitution. It was, in fact, so wonderfully refined in every lineament, as to be compared by learned and pious authors to the delicacy of the human eye, or to the keen sensibility of the internal vital organs of an ordinary human body. Devout reader, you may be surprised at this assertion; but be not incredulous, I pray. Please do consider attentively the origin of our Lord's body, and the singular elements of its miraculous formation. Then you will be able to draw your conclusion, and form a definite judgment.

4. Nobility of blood, in the general opinion of mankind, greatly contributes to the delicate refinement of the child's body. For the sake of truth, let us, at least on this serious occasion, lay aside the vulgar prejudices of human pride. Jesus will be pleased with the docility of our Christian humility, and reward it with his heavenly light. Now, then, Christian reader, piously reflect and consider who the Mother of Jesus was in her human pedigree, blessed Mary was the noblest lady in the Jewish nation and in the whole world. She was a descendant from the princely tribe of Juda, and more particularly of the royal family of David.

From her saintly father's side, our Blessed Lady had concentrated in her virginal veins the royal blood of no less than eighteen kings, her direct ancestry. On her holy mother's side, she was a descendant of the supreme Pontiff Aaron. We learn this fact from the holy evangelist St. Luke, who says that *"St. Elizabeth, the wife of St. Zachary, a Jewish high priest, was of the daughters* (namely a descendant) *of Aaron."* (Lk. 1:5) And the Blessed Virgin Mary is by the Archangel Gabriel called: *"the cousin* (or near relation) *of Elizabeth."* (v. 36) In the person, then, of our most holy Lady we see the union of the highest and noblest pedigree that can be desired by any person on earth. Her virginal body is hallowed by the sacredness of the Jewish priesthood, and ennobled by kingly dignity. Now, if the children of noble and royal parents are remarkable for the refinement of their bodily constitution, we may, if we can, imagine how great must have been the beauty and delicacy of Jesus, the blessed fruit of her virginal womb. Most holy Mary is the beautiful Lily of Israel, and the fragrant Rose of Juda, from whom Jesus, the Flower of humanity, sprang. *"And there shall come forth a rod out of the root of Jesse, and a flower shall rise up out of this root, and the spirit of the Lord shall rest upon him."* (Is. 11:1)

Moreover, Blessed Mary, our Savior's Mother, was the most chaste and the purest of virgins. Virgins in comparison with the Queen of Virgins are like thorns by the side of a lily. *"Sicut lilium inter spinas, sic amica mea inter filias."* (Cant. 2:2) Good God! who can conceive how refined and delicate ought to be the child of such a Virgin Mother? .... But let us proceed.

5. Grace and holiness are the perfection of human nature. As sin, crime, vice, blunt and harden man, so grace, virtue, habitual holiness, soften, embellish and refine him. Now the thrice-blessed Mother of Jesus had never been touched in body or soul by the foul breath of original or actual sin. Mary was an immaculate Virgin Mother. She was young in age at the time of her maternity, but far advanced in virtue. Mary was eminent in sanctity and full of divine grace: Her heart loved God more ardently than did all the saints and angels. By an archangel she was saluted as *"blessed among women, and filled with divine grace and love. Hail Mary, full of grace."* (Lk. 1:28)

Mary heard this angelic salutation before a word was uttered to her about the intended Incarnation of the Son of God. This evidently shows that Blessed Mary was replenished with grace, burning with God's love, eminent in sanctity, even before receiving in her immaculate virginal bosom the Author of all grace, the God of holiness. But to what degree of eminence will this fullness of Mary's grace and sanctity be raised during the nine happy months of her most intimate maternal union with the incarnate Son of God; Good God! who but Thy divine wisdom can fathom this profound ocean of love and grace, and grace and love? Love every instant expanded the heart of Mary, grace entered immediately to fill up this new capacity. Love every moment drew more closely the immaculate heart of Mary to the divine heart of Jesus; grace linked them together like twins in charity and holiness! O immaculate heart of Mary! O Sacred Heart Of Jesus! you were so similar, you were so very near each other, you were so closely united; most holy hearts! See how the heart of the Son, the fountain of all grace, pours down in the heart of the Mother a constant stream of the water of grace. See how every new flow of grace enlarges the capacity of Mary's soul, and excites her maternal heart to more intense love for her unborn child, Jesus. See how the heart of Jesus, the furnace of divine charity, redoubles every instant the flames of their reciprocal love. *"My beloved unto me, and I unto him."* (Cant. 1:12) Thus kept on constantly advancing this wonderful process of grace, love and refinement, in the heavenly forge of Mary's virginal womb, until the hour arrived when the angelic choirs, in an ecstasy of admiration sang at the cave of Bethlehem, *"Glory to God on high."* The angels saw the Infant Son of Mary, and, whilst adoring him in her arms, they admired the beauty, the perfect symmetry, the exquisite refinement, and most delicate complexion of his little human body. Considering, then, our Redeemer's conception and birth from an immaculate, most holy Virgin Mother of the royal house of David, we should conclude that his body ought to have been exceedingly delicate in constitution, and consequently extremely sensitive to every kind of physical pain.

6. We have, however, to consider more important and more conclusive arguments. Even an immaculate virgin mother must have a spouse in order to conceive a divine Son. We must now pass to examine the qualifications of this spouse of Mary and true Father of Jesus. We read, in the first chapter of St. Luke's gospel, that *"the Angel Gabriel was sent from God into a city of Galilee, called Nazareth, to a virgin espoused to a man, whose name was Joseph, of the house of David, and the name of the virgin was Mary."* (Lk. 1:27)

Observe, devout reader, how carefully the inspired evangelist, twice in a single verse, calls our attention to the fact that, though our Blessed Lady was married to St. Joseph, nevertheless she was a most pure virgin.

Mary and Joseph, on the first day of their holy wedding, made by common consent a solemn vow to God of perpetual virginity. A short time after their marriage, God sent to this most holy Virgin the Angel Gabriel. The angelic messenger, after saluting her with words never before heard by mortal ears, announced to Mary that she had been chosen by God to be the Mother of the promised Messias. At these words of the angel, Mary's profound humility and her high esteem for virginal purity were alarmed. She immediately said to the angel: *"How shall this be done, for I know not man?"* The answer of the heavenly messenger will now teach us who the Father of Jesus is. *"The Holy Ghost,"* the angel said to Mary, *"the Holy Ghost shall come upon thee, and the power of the Most Holy shall overshadow thee. And therefore the Holy One, who shall be born of thee, shall be called the Son of God."* (Lk. 1:35) Jesus, then, is the Son of God, not only in his eternal and divine, but also in his temporal and human generation. Hence in his humanity our blessed Lord has a most holy and immaculate virgin for his Mother, and the Holy Ghost as a substitute for his Father. Let now human reason, purified and enlightened by Christian faith and piety, conclude how supremely refined must have been the body of Jesus, our Lord, formed by the miraculous operation of the Most Holy Spirit, conceived and born of a most pure, most holy, immaculate Mother!... The angelic doctor, St. Thomas, teaches that what is done by God through a miracle is always more perfect than art or nature can make it. In the conception and birth of Jesus there is a chain of the most wonderful prodigies ever wrought by God in heaven and upon earth. How sublimely perfect, therefore, the humanity of Jesus must be, which has been the subject of all these astonishing miracles from the first moment of its existence! O most sacred body of Jesus! I admire, I adore thee. O God of justice! is it this body that has to be scourged, crowned with thorns, and fastened with nails to a cross? O most loving Mother of Jesus! you were so kind, so gentle, so tenderly careful of the body of your most beautiful and innocent Son! But he is now going to be crucified.

7. Whilst the executioners are preparing for this bloody deed, let us keep ourselves recollected, and make two more reflections about the share which the soul of Jesus had in the refinement of his body, and in increasing the intensity of his suffering at the crucifixion.

Christian philosophy has discovered in the economy of this universe the grand and sublime principle of assimilation. God is the beginning and last end of all being. He is the Model and the Author of all things. All creatures bear the impress of God's image. Created intelligences, or the angels nearer to God, partake more abundantly of His divine attributes, and through these they both enlighten and draw towards God, as to the common center, inferior angels and human souls. The angelic doctor says: *"The image of God is more perfect in the angels than in the human soul, and in the higher angels this divine image is brighter than in the inferior angels. It is likewise more perfect in man than in woman."* (Thom. q. dist. xvi. 9, i, a. 3.) Now, the human soul is united to a material body. The human body is a microcosm, or the compendium of material creation. Hence the soul, by informing the body, by infusing life into it, by acting upon it and through it, refines its carnal nature, assimilates it to itself, and, in a certain sense, it spiritualizes the body. This admirable process has been going on continually upon earth, among countless millions of men, during almost six thousand years. We may conclude from this what immense work of assimilation has silently, but effectively, been performed by human souls in this material world. The human soul, operating upon the body, refining it and, as it were, spiritualizing it, indirectly operates upon, refines, and spiritualizes all material creation. Finally, the bodies of the elect, being exalted and sublimated by spiritual grace during life, and by glory at the general resurrection; all material creation, in and through all these countless millions of glorified bodies, will be assimilated as much as possible to God, and united to Him in glory through Jesus Christ. Thus Jesus Christ is truly *"the Alpha and Omega, the beginning and end of all things."* (Apoc. 1:8)

We learn this beautiful, grand and sublime philosophy from St. Paul, who says: *"It is sown an animal body, it shall rise a spiritual body. If there be an animal body, there is also a spiritual body.... It is sown in corruption, it shall rise in incorruption; it is sown in dishonor, ti shall rise in glory; it is sown in weakness, it shall rise in power.... As we have borne the image of the earthly man, Adam, we will also bear the image of the heavenly man, Jesus."* (1 Cor 15:42)

8. The human soul proceeds in this divine-like work of assimilation and spiritualization of the body through its intelligence and affections. Hence, the higher and more active is its intellectual life and action, and the purer, holier, and more intense are its affections upon and through the vital and nobler organs of the body, the sooner the body will be refined and assimilated to the soul, and consequently rendered more keenly sensitive to every kind of physical pain during our mortal life upon earth.

52

These principles will enable us to give a reason for the faith that is in us about the Passion of our divine Lord, which is the grandest and most sublime work of God's wisdom and power. The ordinary way of superficially viewing the Passion of our Savior detracts from its dignity, and cannot produce much fruit of virtue in Christian souls. Consider, attentively, what has been stated above, and it will help you, dear reader, to understand more clearly, and appreciate more justly, the intensity and high value of our Redeemer's sufferings. We will now pass to consider the relation which the body of Jesus bears towards the soul.

9. We begin with an admirable figure which we find in the book of Exodus. God commanded Moses to prepare the Ark of the Covenant for the reception of the two tables of the Decalogue. He described every detail about its length, breadth, and height. He ordered that it should be framed with precious and incorruptible setim-wood, and overlaid within and without with the purest gold. (Exod. 25:10) Now, if God so strongly insisted upon having so rich and beautiful an ark prepared for the reception of the two material tables of the law, what body will He prepare for the reception of the spiritual and immortal soul of His divine Son, Jesus?... The soul of Jesus was the greatest, the noblest, the holiest, the most intelligent spirit ever created, or which will ever be created by God. Such a superior soul was strictly due to blessed Jesus' high dignity and mediatorial office. He was the beginning, the end, and the perfection of all creation. Jesus was the first and the fairest Flower of humanity. He was the first-born of the elect of God. He was constituted the Head of the Church, the Redeemer and Savior of men. Jesus was the supreme Monarch of heaven and earth, the first Lawgiver of the world, the universal Judge of mankind. Very extraordinary gifts and graces, virtues and wisdom were granted by God to the youthful King Solomon, to the end that he might be able to govern wisely, for some years, a few million men within his small kingdom. (3 Kings 3:5)

But what gifts and graces, what intelligence and wisdom, what virtue and power should have been communicated by God to the soul of Jesus, the King of kings, and sovereign Lord of men and angels? The mission of Jesus upon earth was not, like that of Solomon, confined to Palestine. Hence, on a certain occasion, our Lord said to the Jews: *"The Queen of the South came to hear the wisdom of Solomon, and behold a greater than Solomon is here."* (Mt. 12:42) *"In him* (St. Paul says) *are hidden all the treasures of wisdom and knowledge."* (Col. 11:3) The eternal Son of God came upon earth, became man to regenerate and elevate all nature, to establish a universal and everlasting empire over all souls and spirits, to teach the most sublime doctrines and profound dogmas to all men, to subdue to his faith and love all human intellects and wills, and, finally, to elicit the most sincere admiration, the most enthusiastic love, and the heartiest homage and profoundest adoration from the highest and holiest intelligences of men and angels during an endless eternity. He assumed a true human soul. Now, such soul must surely have been enriched and adorned with the best gifts and graces of God. This, thanks be to God, was the fact with the soul of Jesus. The holy prophet Isaias says: *"There shall come forth a rod out of the root of Jesse."* This root of Jesse is the most holy Virgin Mary. *"And a flower shall rise up out of this root."* Behold here the beauty and refined delicacy of our Savior's body. The prophet continues: *"And the spirit of the Lord shall rest upon him: the spirit of wisdom and understanding, the spirit of counsel and of fortitude, the spirit of knowledge and of godliness: and he shall be filled with the spirit of the fear of the Lord."* (Is. 11:2) Behold the blessed soul of Jesus filled with the seven gifts of the Holy Ghost.

Now, if God commanded Moses to prepare the ark of the old covenant for the reception of the material tables of the law, and this ark had to be framed with setim-wood, overlaid within and without with the purest gold, what kind of body will be prepared by the power of the Most High, through the operation of the Holy Ghost, for the reception of the great and most holy soul of Jesus? For a soul endowed with so many extraordinary gifts of nature and of grace, for a soul raised to the most sublime dignity, authority and power, the most perfectly organized and refined body will certainly be prepared by God. Such was indeed, the sacred body of our divine Lord. *"Therefore, coming into the world, he saith: Sacrifice and oblation, Thou, O Father, wouldst not, but a body thou hast fitted to me."* (Heb. 10:5)

10. But we should carefully observe the essential difference intended to exist between the tables of the Decalogue laid in the ark, and the soul of Jesus infused in his body. These two tables were two well-polished but material stones. The soul of Jesus was a most pure spirit. These two stones lay down heavily within the ark and could not naturally have the least physical influence upon it. They could neither communicate the life of vegetation to the wood, nor increase the intrinsic value of the gold. But

the soul of Jesus was the form of his body pervading every organ, every limb and member, infusing life through every vein and artery, communicating motion to every nerve and muscle; thinking in the brain, loving in the heart, hearing through the ears, seeing through the eyes, speaking with its tongue, living with its life, thoroughly identified with Jesus, God and man.

During thirty-three years and more, the blessed soul of Jesus acted, without the least difficulty or interruption, upon this most perfectly organized body. Ordinary children do not arrive at the use of reason until they are seven or eight years of age. The soul of Jesus had the most perfect use of reason from its first union with the body. Considering the vast amount of time we squander away in thoughtless evagations of the mind, in material pursuits, with the soul buried in the earth in sensual gratifications of the body, with the soul steeped in flesh, eating, drinking and sleeping, we must come to the humiliating conclusion that we pass the greater portion of our years without any wholesome exercise of our reasoning faculties. This is at least the general conduct of the vast majority of mankind.

But very different from this was the life of our divine Lord. Night and day, and day and night, his soul was constantly in the full exercise of its mental faculties. In the Gospel we find one instance only in which Jesus seemed to be sleeping. But even then his heart was watching: *"I sleep, but my heart watcheth"* — *"Ego dormio, et cor meum vigilat."* (Cant. 5:2) Whilst Jesus appears sleeping, he watches the conduct of his apostles during the storm, and promptly chides them for their want of confidence in him. (Mt. 8:24) *"Behold, he shall neither slumber nor sleep, that keepeth Israel."* (Ps. 70:4)

During the three years of his apostolic life he passed the days in traveling and preaching, in instructing and working miracles —going about doing good to every one. At night he retired to the mountain, and persevered watching and praying until the following morning, when he reassumed his apostolic labors. As the soul of our blessed Lord was, from the moment of his Incarnation, in perpetual active and affective union with the Divinity, so it was in constant action upon the noblest organs of his most sacred body. This action was two-fold: active and affective. The mind of our Lord was constantly exercising its intellectual faculties, his heart was burning with divine-human love. Jesus was perpetually thinking of God, and loving Him with all the fervor of his inflamed heart. In every instant of his human existence, the soul of our Savior was worshipping the Godhead for itself and for us; he was studying how to promote his Father's greatest glory, and continually doing His adorable will in every action and motion of his life, and in every breath and pulsation of his heart. Not a single action was performed by our blessed Redeemer, not a word was uttered by him, not a step was ever taken without actually referring it to the greater honor and glory of his heavenly Father. In every action of his life the soul of Jesus aimed at the highest degree of perfection. In short, the mind and heart of our Lord were constantly burning with the most ardent love of God. He truly loved God with his whole mind and heart, soul and strength, and for the same reason he loved men as a Man-God alone can love his most cherished creatures. This exercise of divine charity was in constant operation with Jesus, in his human nature, composed of a most exquisite body and and a most holy and most intelligent soul. We remarked above that intelligence and holiness refine the human body. We may now imagine, if we can, to what sublime degree of refinement the body of our divine Lord must have been raised during the thirty-three years of his most holy life upon earth.

11. Before we conclude, we have to make another most important reflection in relation to the body of our Lord, which is suggested to us by the two mysterious tables of the Decalogue in the ancient Ark of the Covenant. One of these tables contained the first three commandments that have immediate relation to God. The other had inscribed upon it the seven commandments relative to man. This was a most beautiful figure of our Savior's Incarnation. A few words of explanation will make it very clear. The living ark of the body of Jesus was prepared by God, and intended by him to receive a human soul enriched and adorned with the seven gifts of the Holy Ghost. This admirable soul of Jesus is represented and prefigured by the second table of the Decalogue enclosed within the Ark of the Covenant, upon which table the seven commandments were inscribed by the finger of God.

The first table, which relates immediately to God, represented and prefigured the divine Person of the Eternal Word made flesh, dwelling in that privileged body, the visible living ark of the new covenant of grace. Upon this table the first three of the divine commandments were inscribed, which are the foundation of the whole Decalogue; and of every law. Now, observe the admirable analogy between the figure and the reality. The sacred body of Jesus, the living ark of the new covenant of faith, grace and love, in receiving at the Incarnation the eternal Word of God, received at the same time, as Catholic theology teaches, all the three persons of the most adorable Trinity, Father, Son, and Holy Ghost. Because, where the Son is, so likewise the Father and the Holy Ghost must be. For the Trinity of persons is inseparably united in one divine nature. Hence, St. John says: *"There are three that give testimony in Heaven: the Father, the Word, and the Holy Ghost: and these three are one."* (1 Jn. 5:7) *"Believe you not* (our Savior says), *believe you not that I am in the Father, and the Father in me?"* (Jn. 14:10) *"I and the Father are one."* (Jn 10:10) Behold now what is contained in the sacred body of Jesus! First, a most holy, most noble and most intelligent soul: a soul that informs it, as philosophers say, pervades it through every pore, gives life to it, animates it, acts in it and through it. In the second place, the soul of Jesus is the immediate link of the hypostatic union of the eternal Word of God with this particular body of our assumed humanity. St. Bernard says: "The eternal Word, the created soul of Jesus, and his most holy body, are united indissolubly in one person." (St. Ber. serm. 2, in Nativ. Domini.) Finally, to the second person of the eternal Word, as faith teaches, the Father and the Holy Ghost are linked by the eternal, everlasting union of the divine nature. Hence, *"in Jesus Christ,"* as St. Paul says, *"dwelleth all the fullness of the Godhead corporally."* (Col. 2:9) The body of Jesus Christ is the true living temple of God, the living tabernacle of the most holy Trinity, the animated ark of the new covenant of grace, the seat of divine wisdom, the throne of holiness, majesty, authority and power. In this most sacred body of Jesus *"are hidden all the treasures of grace, wisdom, and knowledge."* (Col. 2:3)

If God required that the Ark of the Covenant should be framed with incorruptible setim wood, and overlaid within and without with the purest gold, what body will God have prepared for the soul of His divine Son? This body was to be the immediate instrument of our redemption, sanctification and salvation. Through his body Jesus was to glorify God more than by the creation of the whole universe. Through this glorified body Jesus will, during a blessed eternity, give more honor and glory to the most holy Trinity than all the angels and saints of heaven united. After having attentively considered all these solemn truths, every intelligent Christian must wonder how the body of Jesus could have remained during thirty-three years a natural body of flesh, without being transformed into a glorified state, as it was for a short time on Mount Thabor. But our divine Lord and Master solved this mystery when he said, *"Ought not Christ to have suffered all these things,"* the scourge, the Crown of Thorns, the crucifixion, *"and so enter into his glory?"* (Lk. 24:26)

What horror would the Jewish people have felt had they seen a number of their Pagan enemies break in pieces the sacred Ark of the Covenant, and trample them under their impious feet …. Christian reader! we are now going to witness the most holy, most beautiful, most delicate body of Jesus cruelly tortured by a horrible Crown of Thorns. This most holy temple of God will be disfigured by cruel hands. This living tabernacle of the most holy Trinity will be sacrilegiously profaned by impious men. The sacred feet, the most holy hands of Jesus will be barbarously gashed by rough nails, and his most loving heart will be transfixed with a lance. Let us devoutly draw near Jesus, and witness the most horrible crime committed by man's wickedness.

CHAPTER VIII

THE CROWN OF THORNS – A CROWN OF PAIN

"Platting a Crown of Thorns, they put it upon his head." (Mt. 27:29)

1. The bad example of superiors is contagious, and strongly affects the life and conduct of their subjects. The soldiers of the Roman Governor Pilate had during the morning repeatedly heard him giving to Jesus of Nazareth the title of *King of the Jews.* They presumed that such a high title had by the President been used in irony and mockery. This was the reason, says St. John Chrysostom, why those barbarous men, after having, during the scourging at the pillar, covered our Lord from head to foot with wounds and blood, resolved to make sport of him, by treating him in every possible way as a mock king, and by forcing upon him all the ridiculous theatrical insignia and the affected homages of a sham royalty. *"Quia Pilatus dixit eum Regem, Schema ei contumeliae apponunt."* (Chrysostom Homil. 88). Our Lord had been scourged in the court of the palace. From this place the soldiers of the Governor took him into the hall, and gathered together around him the whole band of the garrison, which served as a body guard to Pilate. Now, for his greater shame and confusion, they rudely strip our Savior once more. They make him sit down upon a cold stone, as his royal throne; and affect to offer him the flattering homages of obsequious courtiers. *"The soldiers of the Governor,* (St. Matthew says), *taking Jesus into the hall, gathered together unto him the whole band."* (Mt. 27:27) Whilst the majority of these heartless men heap outrages and insults upon the incarnate Son of God, another small party, more malignant and cruel, is eagerly engaged in weaving together, in the form of a helmet or cap, a horrible and ignominious crown of Red-Sea bulrushes, the thorns of which are very long, hard and sharp. St. Vincent Ferrer says, that the Crown of Thorns intended for our Lord was made in the shape of a hat covering his whole

59

head. *"Domini Corona erat ad modum pilei, ita ut totum togebat caput."* (Serm. in Parasc.) Such an instrument of torture could only be formed with long and pliable thorns like Red-Sea rushes. This is also the opinion of St. Augustine and St. Anselm, who mention a revelation of the Blessed Virgin Mary, and of others. (See above, ch. 15) The famous St. Vincent of Lerins, on the authority of eyewitnesses, states that these Red-Sea thorns are so strong and sharp as to perforate the soles of the shoes of travelers. In fact, some of the thorns of our Savior's crown are to the present day religiously preserved in various Catholic sanctuaries, and the sight of them always produces a shudder of pious horror.

2. The pagan soldiers then, having prepared this horrible crown, proceed to place it on the adorable head of our Lord. Two of the stoutest executioners plant themselves at opposite sides, close to him. They put the thorny cap over his head, and, taking hold of the two extremities of a strong knotted stick, they cross it over the Crown of Thorns, and press this thorny bush down in different directions, right and left, back and in front, with such force and violence as to cause the internal long and sharp thorns to pierce the skin, penetrate the skull, and prick the very brain of our dear Lord. *"Spinarum punctiones cerebrum perforantes."* (St. Lawrence Justin. de Triumph. Christ. Agon. cap. 14) Some of the longest thorns tear and torture the most delicate and sensitive tissues of that adorable head, forcing their way out of the occiput, whilst others take an opposite direction, and appear projecting with their bloody points outside the forehead and temples. Some of these terrible thorns penetrate as far as the ears, the eyes, the nose and cheeks of our agonizing Savior.

Blessed Tauler says: "The most handsome countenance of Jesus was disfigured by these thorns and by the streams of blood that flowed upon it." (B. Taulerus, con. 10 de Passione) See how the blood is running from every part of the perforated head and face! The long Nazarean hair of our Lord's head, his sacred countenance and his beard are covered and saturated with his divine blood, which trickles down in large red drops upon his wounded shoulders, and bruised chest. *"Divinum illud caput multiplici spinarum densitate perforatum usque ad cerebri teneritudinem confixum est."* (St. Peter Damian, serm. de Exalt Crucis.)

We learn from the revelations of St. Bridget that the most holy Mother of our Lord was present at his scourging and crowning with thorns. Our Blessed Lady gave the Saint the following description: *"The soldiers of the Roman Governor, after having scourged my Son at the pillar, adapted a Crown of Thorns to his adorable head, and, pressed it with such violence that blood was made to gush so copiously from it as to cover his eyes, fill his ears and imbrue all his beard."* (Lib. 2 cap. 10)

This torture of the Crown of Thorns made such an impression on the imagination, mind and heart of the afflicted Mother of our Lord, that she revealed it twice to her favorite servant. Here is the second revelation: *"A Crown of Thorns, reaching to the middle of his forehead, was most violently pressed upon the adorable head of my Son. Through the numerous wounds caused by those perforating thorns so many streams of blood were flowing in every direction, and in such a quantity, as to soak the hair of his head, fill his ears, cover his face, and saturate his beard. His whole countenance was covered with blood. His eyes were so filled with it that, when he wished to look at any object, my Son was obliged, by compressing the eye-lid, to squeeze the blood out of them."* (Lib. 4 chap.7)

4. Reflect now, devout reader, that the head, on account of the brain, is the most sensitive portion of the human body. Who will then be able to imagine, and much less to express, how intensely painful must have been the agony caused to our dear Lord by that horrible Crown of Thorns piercing all at once, like a thorny bush, every part of his adorable head! *"Ipsa corona .... Mille puncturis speciosum caput ejus devulnerat."* (St. Bernard, de Passione Domini) Consider, moreover, that the brain is most intimately connected with every portion of the human body, and especially with the heart. The head is the seat and center whence radiate all the muscles, nerves, veins and arteries that branch out and pervade every member, limb and organ of our body, diffusing a thrill of joy or pain everywhere, according to the actual condition of the head and affection of the brain. Hence it naturally follows that even a slight pricking of the brain, or wounding of the head, produces intense suffering, causes convulsions, swoons and apoplectic strokes. A severe headache, an intense neuralgic pain, prostrates the strongest man. See whether you can now conceive what agonizing martyrdom that frightful crown of long and sharp thorns must have produced in every part of the most refined and sensitive body of our divine Savior .... "When the pricking of one single thorn is sufficient to produce in our foot intolerable pain, who can form an idea of the intense agony caused to our Lord by so many thorns perforating all at once his adorable head?" exclaimed St. Vincent Ferrer. *"Spinarum punctiones cerebrum perforantes,*

Christus debuisset mori tanto dolore transfixus." (S. Laurent. Justin. de Triumphali Christi Agone.)

Reflect, finally, that all these terrible sufferings were directed as to a common center and compressed within his palpitating heart, submerging it into a rushing flood of overwhelming anguish .... Ah! our suffering Lord could indeed cry out, *"Save me, O God, for the waters of affliction and sorrow are come in even into my soul."* (Ps. 68:2)

The thorns that perforated his head were a figure of those more piercing that penetrated into his heart. For this motive our Lord showed his heart to blessed Margaret Marie Alacoque, surrounded by a Crown of Thorns, and the Church represents it to us in this painful condition. The thorns and the lance have left their impression upon it. The lance, however, is not there; but the thorns remain, to attract our attention, excite our compassion and stimulate our devotion.

Meditate often and deeply, Christian reader, upon this painful mystery. It will give you some faint idea of the harrowing agony endured by your Redeemer on account of that terrible Crown of Thorns. This, however, represents only his physical sufferings.

Catharine de Sandoval, a young Spanish lady of high aspirations, experienced in a very extraordinary manner the powerful attractions of the King of Sorrows crowned with thorns. She was very wealthy, beautiful and highly acomplished. All these qualifications obtained for her the attentions and homages of many of the Spanish nobility anxious to solicit her hand. But she rejected them, with haughty disdain as far beneath her ambition. Catherine had often been heard to protest that she should never consent to marry any person except a king with a royal crown over his head, or at least a prince of royal blood. One of the Spanish grandees, who was very persevering in his suit to the young lady, succeeded to engage in his favor the chamber-maid of Catharine, to whom he promised a handsome reward if she helped him in obtaining his intended object. The servant agreed to use all her influence in his favor with her young mistress. From that day she seized every favorable opportunity for speaking in his praise, and extolling his personal qualities and merits but without any visible effect upon Catharine.

One morning, after having with great care accomplished the toilet of her young mistress, the wily chamber-maid burst into expressions of high admiration of her charming beauty, and began to relate a most agreeable dream of the previous night, wherein she delighted to witness her splendid wedding with that noble and handsome cavalier. At the mention of his name Catharine, with great indignation, strictly forbade her servant ever to speak of him in her presence, and raising up from the chair with an air of great dignity, she said: "How often have I told you that I will never consent to marry any person except a king? Now remember this well, and begone immediately out of my room." After this ebullition of pride and ambition, Catharine began to pace up and down in the room, stopping once or twice before a large mirror in admiration of her handsome and majestic form, saying to herself: "I am made to be a queen. I should marry only a king."

With these thoughts in her head, she turned from the mirror, and her look fell upon a silver crucifix standing on the table. The Crown of Thorns first attracted her attention; then she read the inscription over the head of the sacred image, *"Jesus of Nazareth, King of the Jews."* A strong interior inspiration was moving her to choose this great King for her only spouse, when she heard in a sensible manner a miraculous voice, saying: "Behold the King who loves thee more than anybody else, and desires to be thy sponse. Take me as I am." At these words Catharine fell in terror prostrate to the floor of the room, when she saw our Savior coming near her, who said: *"Fear not, I am He."* Consoled by the heavenly sweetness of these words, she rose upon her knees and, shedding abundant tears, she addressed to our Lord the following prayer: "My Lord and my God, Thou knowest how often and how far I have fled from Thee. But now I surrender myself entirely and forever to Thy most holy cross. I accept Thee as my Lord, my King and my Spouse, just because Thou art crowned with thorns. I renounce every thought and affection for the world, and offer my whole heart to Thee, beseeching Thee never to permit it to escape from Thy hands." Hereupon our Lord extended his right arm to embrace his new bride, saying: "I stretch forth my omnipotent arm to communicate to thee the strength necessary for the accomplishment of my divine will, and for keeping the promises thou hast made to me. *Be thou faithful unto death, and I will give thee the crown of life."*

From that moment Catharine was completely dead to the world, and lived only for her divine Spouse crowned with thorns, as the King of Sorrows. After having for some years edified her household and the whole city by her profound humility, self denial and detachment from creatures, she offered herself to St. Teresa as one of her first companions in the reformation

63

of the Carmelite nuns. She requested to be called in religion *"Catharine of Jesus,"* in order that, whenever she heard her name, she might remember the promises she had made to our Lord, and thus remain faithful to him. (Boscape cant. 3, and instruzioni in forma di catechismo di Padre Maria Ferreri, S. J., art. 4 Credo.) Having so far considered the physical sufferings caused to our Lord by the Crown of Thorns, we will now proceed to reflect on the deep humiliations and internal anguish endured by the great Son of God on that memorable occasion.

CHAPTER IX

THE CROWN OF THORNS A CROWN OF IGNOMINY

"And, bowing the knee before him, they mocked him, saying, Hail, King of the Jews." (Mt. 27:29.)

1. When we behold any person in great suffering, a common sentiment of humanity evokes feelings of compassion in our hearts. This sentiment is so deeply rooted in human nature that it extends its sympathies even to animals. Suffering has for the human heart something sacred and mysterious. It calms passions, it quells hatred, and subdues revenge. These effects are produced even by the public sufferings of a condemned criminal. His punishment is, in a certain sense, an atonement to justice. His resignation in suffering, and his willingness to shed his life's blood, is a sacrifice offered to the sanctity of law and order; and the restoration of order and law, thus effected, reacts on the victim, and sanctifies it in the estimation of mankind. Hence, in all civilized nations, some public respect is shown to a poor criminal who accepts the punishment decreed against him by legitimate authority, and bears it with virtuous resignation.

2. Our most holy Lord was not and could not be a criminal. But the more innocent and holy he was, the more patiently and meekly he endured the flagellation to which he was condemned by the Roman Governor Pilate. During the scourging at the pillar his delicate body had been covered with wounds. His sacred flesh had been harrowed and lacerated with horrible whips, armed with iron hooks. But Jesus bore this martyrdom without a word of complaint, without a murmur. We have seen him crowned with thorns and he was silent. Such heroic fortitude in suffering, such virtuous patience should gain for him the respectful compassion of all beholders, and the commiseration of his executioners. Soldiers, above all classes of

65

ordinary men, are disposed to admire manly courage and fortitude in suffering. But every feeling of humanity seems extinguished in the hearts of these cruel men towards our suffering Lord. Their malice exceeds the barbarity of savages. No savage cruelty ever crowned any human victim with thorns, as those pagan soldiers have done with the innocent Son of God. Instigated by the demons of hell, they proceed to heap insults and mockeries upon the Victim of their barbarity. We will stop to witness this new outrage of human malice against our blessed Lord, that, whilst impiety mocks him, our faith and devotion may honor and worship his adorable person.

3. We have to consider the deep humiliations endured by the incarnate Son of God, on the occasion of his crowning of thorns. It was then that the prophecy of Isaias was fully realized when our Lord was despised and made to appear the most abject of men. Every honest feeling of self-respect, every sentiment of manly honor was crushed in him and trampled to the ground by those heartless executioners. God has implanted in the human heart deep sentiments of honor. These are reminiscences of our former greatness, and the cherished badge of our original dignity. Man had been created by God great and glorious. *"We were made a little less than the angels. We were crowned with glory and honor. We were set by God over all the works of His hands."* (Ps. 8:6)

The sin of our first parents has not entirely degraded the dignity of our human nature. We are conscious of our superiority over all the material creation in the possession and use of our intellectual faculties. Man, standing erect on this earth, and calmly surveying this vast universe, hears an inward voice, proclaiming him *the lord of all visible creatures. "I have said you are God's, and all of you the sons of the Most High."* (Ps. 81:6) No wonder, then, that man conceives in his breast a high sentiment of his dignity, and deeply feels and resents every humiliating insult offered to him. Sentiments of honor are engendered in the human mind, not only by the remembrance of our former dignity, and by the consciousness of our present powers, but much more by faith in our future destiny. *"Behold what manner of charity the Father hath bestowed upon us, that we should be named and should be the sons of God.... Dearly beloved, we are now the sons of God; and it hath not yet appeared what we shall be. We know, that when he shall appear, we shall be like unto him; because we shall see him as he is."* (Jn. 3:1) Our origin, our present condition and future destiny are the three sources of all our honest sentiments of honor and self-respect. The better these are understood and appreciated, the more exalted and refined our idea of honor will grow in our mind. Hence, the wise man says: *"A good name is better than riches, and good favor is above silver and gold."* (Prov. 22:1) And in another place the Holy Ghost says: *"Take care of a good name; for this shall continue with thee more than a thousand treasures precious and great. A good life hath a number of days; but a good name shall continue forever."* (Eccli. 41:15) This sentiment of honor and self-respect, having been implanted in the human heart by our divine Creator and first Teacher, the more wise and virtuous any person grows, the more anxious he is to preserve his good name. Hence, we find by experience that all wise and prudent persons, and more especially all saints and servants of God, were and are extremely careful to avoid everything that may bring disgrace and infamy upon their character.

4. Now let us reflect that our Lord is the incarnate wisdom of God. He is eternal and essential holiness. It is he who has infused this noble sentiment of honor and self-respect in the human heart. It is the light of his wisdom and the heat of his divine charity that enhances it in our soul. It is he who, through his inspired word, commands us to take care of our good name. Can we, therefore, for a moment suppose that his good name was not very dear to him? . . . Surely not. We read in the Gospel that when the Jews contemptuously called him a Samaritan possessed by an evil spirit, our Lord mildly rebuked them for this insult, saying: *"I have not a devil, but honor my Father, and you have dishonored me."* (Jn. 8:48) Our blessed Redeemer deserves the most sincere honor and profound homage of angels and men on account of his divine perfections, being equal and co-eternal to the Father, *"who hath appointed him heir of all things, by whom also he made the world; who, being the splendor of His glory and the figure of His substance, and upholding all things by the word of His power, making purgation of sins, sitteth on the right hand of the Majesty on high, being made so much better than the angels, as he hath inherited a more excellent name above them."* (Heb. 1) The extraordinary sanctity of his life among the Jews, his constant practice of the most exalted virtue, his admirable wisdom and prudence, his stupendous miracles, his active charity, his universal beneficence, his humility, patience and meekness, should have gained for him the universal respect of mankind. Our divine Lord desired this esteem and respect in proportion as he desired the glory of his heavenly

Father and the true happiness and eternal salvation of men. He came upon earth to redeem and save mankind. For this object he preached the gospel of grace; he instituted Sacraments; he selected his Apostles, and appointed them heralds, ministers and representatives to all the nations of the earth. He commanded them to establish his spiritual kingdom for the happiness and salvation of mankind. But, to obtain this grand object and sublime end, it was absolutely necessary that the founder of this holy religion should enjoy among men a very high and unexceptional reputation for wisdom and sanctity. Fix well, Christian reader, this maxim in your mind, before you undertake your meditation on the humiliations, outrages and insults heaped on your divine Lord and Master at his crowning of thorns.

5. Before proceeding, however, we must make another reflection. The science of good and evil, of pain and joy, of honor and dishonor, is acquired more fully by contrast. We cannot form a correct idea of evil except we learn first what is good. Joy is better relished when we have suffered pain, and pain is never fully understood except by persons who have enjoyed the blessings of perfect health. Nobody feels more deeply the crushing burden and oppressive weight of disgrace and insult than he who has been high in dignity and in the esteem and favor of the great ones of this world. Our divine Savior had been esteemed and honored by the people of Palestine. They admired his wisdom, they were charmed by the power of his popular eloquence; they were attracted by his sweetness and kindness; they wondered at his miracles, they honored him for his extraordinary holiness, His very enemies were forced to acknowledge his superior gifts and qualities. The Pharisees envied his virtue; the scribes dreaded his doctrines; the Jewish priests were angry at his burning zeal for the glory of God and the salvation of souls, which they had no courage to imitate. The Roman Governor and King Herod gave evident proofs of the esteem they had for him.

6. All this, however, is but a thin shadow of the real honor and high esteem manifested towards our Lord by the angels of heaven. One of the highest archangels was sent to announce the profound mystery of his Incarnation, and to proclaim the titles of his sublime dignity. *"Behold,"* Gabriel said to his most holy Mother, *"Behold, thou shalt conceive in thy womb, and shall bring forth a son; and thou shalt call his name Jesus. He shall be great, and shall be called the Son of the Most High: and the Lord God shall give unto him the throne of David his father: and he shall reign in the house of Jacob forever, and of his kingdom there shall be no*

end." (Lk. 1:31) Nine months after this, our Savior's birth was by angelic messengers heralded to mankind in the following words: *"Behold I bring you good tidings of great joy, that shall be to all the people; for this day is born to you a Savior, who is Christ the Lord, in the City of David. . .. And suddenly there was with the angels a multitude of the heavenly host, praising God, and saying: "Glory to God in the highest; and on earth peace to men of good will."* (Lk. 2:10)

Whilst a portion of the angelic hierarchy announces the birth of our divine Lord, and proclaims his dignity to mankind upon earth, this glorious event is solemnized in heaven with greater magnificence and glory. God the Father addresses these words of loving welcome to our infant Savior: *"Thou art my Son: this day have I begotten thee."* . .. Then, turning to the countless millions of His angels, He says: *I will be to him a Father, and he shall be to me a Son,"* and immediately commands all the angelic spirits, in heaven and upon earth to do homage to His Incarnate Word; *"Let all the angels of God adore him."* . . . Hereupon St. Paul remarks: *"He that maketh His angels, spirits; and His ministers, a flame of fire, says to His Son: Thy throne, O God, is forever and ever; a scepter of justice is the scepter of thy kingdom. Thou hast loved justice and hated iniquity; therefore God, thy God hath anointed thee with the oil of gladness above them that are partakers with thee .... Thou in the beginning, O Lord, hast founded the earth; and the heavens are the works of thy hands."* (Heb. 1) At these magnificent words of the Godhead, all the angelic spirits fell down prostrate in profound adoration before the majesty of the incarnate Word and exclaimed: *"Thou art worthy O Lord our God, to receive glory and honor and power; because Thou hast created all things."* (Apoc. 4:11) This angelic homage and adoration, which began with the incarnation and birth of the Son of God, has never ceased for a moment; but it has been continued ever since and will last during all eternity. Legions of angels remained round the crib of Bethlehem to protect our infant Savior from the crafty and cruel designs of the impious King Herod. They escorted him in his exile into Egypt; they faithfully ministered unto him on the mount, and were ever ready to serve him at the least indication of his will. An angel comforted our agonizing Lord in the garden of Gethsemani, and legions of angelic spirits, armed with swords of fire, would in an instant have destroyed all his enemies, had he granted them permission. All these holy angels in an attitude of the most profound respect accompanied our Savior in every stage of his sorrowful passion, and witnessed his dreadful sufferings and deep humiliations during the mystery of the Crown of Thorns.

7. To the honor and adoration offered to our Lord by the angels of God, we should add the marks of respect, homage and love manifested to him by the highest and holiest person upon earth. We shall not attempt to describe, because we are unable to conceive the depth and intensity of adoring love which filled the mind and heart of his immaculate Virgin Mother, and of his adopted father, St. Joseph. Holy Elizabeth and her saintly husband Zachary, honored our Lord before his birth. We behold humble and simple shepherds in profound adoration before the crib of our new-born Savior; and the wise Kings of the East, kneeling before him, profess their belief in the mystery of the Incarnation, by their words and by their conduct. They offer to our Lord the emblematic gifts of gold, frankincense and myrrh, intending thereby to express their faith in the reality of his assumed human nature, honoring him as their King and worshipping him as their God. Holy Simeon and the venerable prophetess Anna adored our infant Savior in the temple of Jerusalem; *"praised the Lord, and spoke of him to all that looked for the redemption of Israel"* (Lk. 2:25, 36)

St. John the Baptist, the greatest among the prophets, and most holy among the children of men, speaking of our Lord, said to the Jewish people: *"I indeed baptize you with water: but there shall come one mightier than I, the lachet of whose shoe I am not worthy to loose. He shall baptize you with the Holy Ghost and fire."* (Lk. 3:16) The apostles, the evangelists and all the disciples of our Lord were filled with admiration at the sublimity of his doctrine, the power of miracles, and splendor of his sanctity. They worshipped him as the incarnate Son of the living God; and preached this dogma through Judea and Galilee to all the people.

We learn from our Lord that many ancient prophets and pious kings ardently desired to see and worship him. But this extraordinary and miraculous privilege was granted to two only. These were Moses, the most meek among men, and Elias, the most zealous of the prophets. We will learn this fact from St. Mathew, and close our remarks with it: *"Jesus taking with tim, Peter, James and John, his brother, bringeth them up into a high mountain apart. And he was transfigured before them. And his face did shine as the sun; and his garments became white as snow. And behold, there appeared to them Moses and Elias talking with him... And a bright cloud overshadowed them. And behold a voice out of the cloud saying: This is my beloved Son, in whom I am well pleased; hear ye him. And the disciples hearing, fell upon their faces."* (Mt. 17:1) We are now called upon to witness the most astounding spectacle ever beheld by angels or by men since the creation of the world. Our divine Lord in the hall of Pilate, is the object of the most complete and astonishing contrast. The prophecy of holy Simeon is now fully realized. He is made the sign and the center of the most opposite contradictions. Whilst God with His angels, and the holiest persons upon earth, unite in honoring him; the most wicked and vilest of men heap upon our Lord the most cruel outrages, and the most humiliating insults. Here, indeed, the contrast is most complete and striking. It is painfully humiliating to be disgraced and outraged, soon after having been highly praised and honored. But what is singular in the person of our Savior is, that whilst he is actually honored, praised and worshipped by countless millions of angelic spirits and by the greatest saints, he is at the same time publicly derided, mocked, outraged and insulted by the most wicked and impious men instigated by the devils. The knowledge our divine Lord has of the sacredness of his person, the holiness of his life, the sanctity of his mission, and of his sublime dignity, intensify his feeling of disgrace and humiliation beyond the comprehension of created intelligences. Hence, deeming it impossible to explain by words this profound and astonishing mystery of the crowning of thorns, let us contemplate it in its awful reality ....

8. Behold, then, the King of Kings sitting on a cold stone, crimsoned with his own blood, an old military cloak is contemptuously thrown on his wounded and gory shoulders. A reed is thrust between his hands tightly bound with cords.... Look and see the sovereign Lord of heaven and earth with a reed of derision in his divine hands for a scepter, a filthy scarlet rag on his bleeding shoulders for his kingly mantle, a crown of sharp thorns on his adorable head as his royal diadem. A cold stone forms his imperial throne. Only a stony heart can behold him without emotion. These pretended courtiers, having placed upon our Lord all the insignia of mock royalty, proceed now to offer him their affected homage... They assume the most insulting attitudes of profound contempt for his person. They fill his ears with vulgar expressions of coarse ribaldry, and vent upon him the most opprobrious and blasphemous epithets. These cruel men snatch the reed from the hands of our dear Lord and repeatedly strike with it the Crown of Thorns over his head, causing it to shake all over and driving the thorns more deeply into his head, sending a thrill of pain through every limb and

71

a pang of agony to his sorrowful heart. These heartless monsters brutally slap the face of the eternal Son of God, and disgorge their disgusting phlegm upon his divine countenance. In conclusion, bending their knee in mockery to the ground stained with his life's blood, these impious men salute our Lord, and jeeringly say to him: *"Hail, thou King of the Jews."* (Mt. 27:29) Thus the prophetic vision of Isaias is more fully realized. The appearance of the most beautiful of the sons of men is so horribly deformed that his nearest relations and most intimate friends can no longer recognize him; here are the sad words of the Prophet: *"There is no beauty in him.... Despised and the most abject of men: a man of sorrows, and acquainted with infirmity, his look was, as it were, hidden and despised .... Surely he has borne our infirmity and carried our sorrows, and we have thought him, as it were, a leper, and as one struck by God and afflicted....But he was wounded for our iniquities, and bruised for our sins...The Lord hath laid upon him the iniquities of us all."* (Is. 53:2)

9. We cannot find in history any man so covered and overwhelmed with opprobrium and contempt, as the divine Son of God. *"Truly he is the most abject of men."* Derision is hard to bear. No man with any sense of honor can submit to it, without at least doing great violence to his feelings. Derision can proceed only from the low mind and corrupt heart of vulgar persons. But to be mocked and derided in public, to be derided when we are enduring agonies of pain; to be derided and mocked for virtues and for our meek behavior in suffering, to be mocked and derided by our own executioners, to bear all this with meekness surely requires a virtue superior to that of human nature. Derision, however, has a sharper and more pungent sting when directed against an innocent victim of oppression, against a noble and high personage, and especially, against a man of superior wisdom, held in high estimation by the largest and best portion of mankind. Derision in words is painful enough, but when to derisive expressions are added acts of mockery and insult, each of which increases the pain and confusion of the noble and innocent victim, then indeed the martyrdom of suffering and debasement is complete. *He is the most abject of men.* Dionysius the Carthusian says: *"The Jews, not satisfied with inflicting cruel blows upon his body, heaped insults, derisions and blasphemies upon the head of our Lord Jesus Christ."* Could we believe that if God became man for man's salvation, he should receive this horrible treatment from the objects of his divine charity? Yet to the eternal confusion of human nature, such has been

the fact, and this awful fact is described in the Gospel. *"Then the soldiers of the Governor, taking Jesus into the hall, gathered together unto him the whole band: and stripping him, they put a scarlet cloak about him. And platting a Crown of Thorns, they put it upon his head, and a reed in his right hand. And bowing the knee before him, they mocked him, saying; Hail King of the Jews."* (Mt. 27:27) St. Mark adds that these cruel and brutal men: *"struck his head with a reed and spat on his face."* (Mk. 15:19) Lastly we learn from St. John, who most likely was present at this horrible scene, that the executioners struck with hard blows our suffering Lord in various parts of his wounded and bleeding body. *"They came to him and said: Hail King of the Jews, and they gave him blows."* (Jn 19:3) This conduct of our Savior's enemies is so extraordinary that the wisdom of God must have concealed under it deep and useful mysteries which we are now going to consider in the following chapter...

CHAPTER X

JESUS CROWNED WITH THORNS, IS SHOWN BY PILATE TO THE JEWISH PEOPLE

"Behold, I bring him forth to you, that you may know that I find no cause in him... So Jesus came forth, bearing the Crown of Thorns and the purple garment, and Pilate said to the Jews: Behold the man." (Jn. 19:4) Every circumstance in the passion of our Lord is a ray of divine wisdom and a token of his mercy. The eternal Son of God became man to save mankind from everlasting misery. Among all the nations of the earth the Jewish people were the object of his predilection. In his human generation Jesus belonged to the tribe of Juda. He was born in Judea, and lived among the Jews, doing good to every one. They have returned to their best benefactor evil for good. Their malice and hatred have reduced him to the most piteous condition, for which they deserve the severest punishment. Before going to die, however, our merciful Lord desires to make a touching appeal to the hearts of his enemies that, being moved by his sufferings and converted to God by his grace, they may avert the terrible chastisements that are already impending upon their guilty and stubborn heads. In his divine wisdom and mercy, our loving Savior allowed himself to be severely scourged and crowned with thorns that the sight of his excessive sufferings may move the heart of the Jews to commiseration, more towards themselves than for him. On this remarkable occasion our divine Lord employed three powerful motives to obtain his end, namely, the example of the Roman Governor, his own innocence, and the severity of his sufferings. All this we learn from the words which Pilate addressed to the Jewish people. Let us examine them.

1. *"Pilate went forth again and saith to them: Behold, I bring him forth to you, that you may know that I find no cause in him."* Light and darkness, truth and error, good and evil, vice and virtue are better known by contrast. The Jews had the true religion of the living God. They were taught by His heavenly doctrines which had been revealed to them by Him.

They should therefore be guided in their conduct by truth, justice and charity. The noblest sentiments and the best feelings of human nature should appear developed in their character. The Jews should be models of all virtues to the pagan world, by which they are surrounded. *"Be ye holy, because I am holy,"* God said to them. Pilate is an idolater in religion; he was born and brought up in paganism; he could have but very little knowledge of Jewish moral laws, and of their religious practices. As a Roman Governor and the representative of the Roman Empire he was sent to Judea to administer justice and law according to Roman jurisprudence. Nevertheless, Pilate, deprived of the light of revelation, but guided by principles of sound reason, and of natural law, fully perceives the innocence of our Lord, and boldly proclaims it to the chief priests, Jewish magistrates and people. *"Behold, I bring him forth to you, that you may know that I find no fault in him."* Pilate is so thoroughly convinced of the innocence of our Savior, that he insists upon this fact on three different occasions, though he perceives that his appeal to justice was highly disagreeable and irritating to the Jewish people. *"He said to them the third time: What evil hath this man done? I find no cause of death in him."* (Lk. 23:22) Pilate, a pagan—Pilate, a high officer of a powerful emperor and the authorized representative of the vast Roman Empire, officially recognizes and proclaims the innocence of Jesus of Nazareth, whilst the Jewish people, his compatriots and co-religionists, are obstinately determined upon condemning him to the most infamous and cruel death of the worst of malefactors. Neither the example of the Roman Governor, nor the well known fact of the innocence and extraordinary holiness of Jesus, have any effect upon the stubborn minds of the Jews. They deserve to be abandoned to their malice and reprobate sense. Their reason being willfully obscured by prejudice, our merciful Lord makes the last and strongest appeal to their innate feelings of humanity, and to their natural sentiments of commiseration for his extreme sufferings.

He has for himself no fear of torments, no dread of death. He ardently desires to be immolated for the salvation of man. But our merciful Savior is most anxious for the conversion of the Jewish people. He knows that this cannot be effected, if he succeed to excite in their heart feelings of natural compassion which, through the power of his divine grace, he intends to raise to sentiments of supernatural charity that will convert their hearts and sanctify their souls. Can we hope that his merciful intentions will be understood and appreciated by the Jewish people? Let us see.

2. Among the Romans there was a truly wise and humane custom of placing the culprit in the presence of his judge before this magistrate officially pronounced the final sentence. It was reasonably supposed that the presence of the unhappy prisoner, haggard, confused, trembling at his impending doom, suffering from internal anguish, pale and emaciated from long imprisonment in some horrible dungeon, and then wounded and bleeding from bodily tortures inflicted upon him during his trial, would naturally move to compassion the heart of his judge and thus be pardoned and acquitted by him altogether, or at least be induced to grant a more mild and lighter sentence. The sight of human misery naturally affects the heart of our fellowmen. A wounded and bleeding human being strongly excites to compassion every well-disposed person. Quintilian relates, that the Roman Emperor Julius Caesar, having been treacherously assassinated by Brutus and his fellow conspirators, Mark Antony took in his hand the bloody tunic of the murdered emperor, and from the steps of the Capitol he showed it to the Roman people, urging them to detest and punish the authors of that horrible crime. The sight of the imperial dress riddled with numerous stabs and crimsoned with the fresh blood of their great emperor, excited the deepest feelings of horror in the breasts of the vast multitude of people, assembled for the occasion. They immediately, by a common impulse, started in search of Brutus and of his colleagues to wreak vengeance upon them, but not being able to find them, because they had hastily escaped from the city, the people burned their houses down to the ground. (Quintil. Lib. 6. inst. 1) The Roman Governor Pilate, being well informed in the history of his country, was fully aware of this fact ... He perceived, however, his advantage over Mark Antony, who could exhibit to the Roman people the bloody garment only of the murdered emperor; but Pilate could show to the chief priests, Jewish magistrates and people, the wounded and bleeding body of our suffering Lord, wearing upon his adorable head the horrible Crown of Thorns. *"Behold, I bring him forth to you, that you may know that I find no cause in him.... So Jesus came forth bearing the Crown of Thorns and the purple garment."*

3. From the first moment that the Roman Governor saw our Redeemer, he was deeply struck with his noble, dignified and saintly appearance. During his examination Pilate discovered in our Lord great wisdom, prudence and virtue. He conceived for him great esteem and respect; and was anxious to save him from the hands of his enemies. But when our Lord

was brought before him after his horrible scourging and crowning with thorns, his heart was deeply moved.... Supposing the same feelings of humanity to exist in the breasts of the Jews, the Governor led our suffering Savior to the rails of the balcony of his palace, facing a large square whereon a vast multitude of people were assembled. As soon as he appeared, the eyes of all were turned upon our Lord, who stood before them with his eyes modestly cast down. The people beheld his head crowned with sharp thorns which made the blood flow in streams upon his face, wan with suffering sorrow. He wore a scarlet cloak upon his shoulders, which partially covered and concealed his wounded body. Pilate remained standing in a dignified attitude at the right side of our Lord, surveying for some moments the excited multitude of human beings before him. Then with his left hand he lifted up the limb of the red mantle of our Savior and, with an expression of profound emotion, pointing with his right hand to the wounded and bleeding body of our meek and suffering Lord, Pilate, with a deep and tremulous voice, said to the Jews: *Ecce Homo* –"Behold the Man." Pilate evidently intended to say more, for this short sentence is incomplete. Reflect that he went to the balcony determined to appeal in his behalf to the Jewish people, and more especially to the chief priests and civil magistrates to obtain our Savior's acquittal.

Why, then, did he utter only two short words? The reason evidently is that the Roman Governor was horrified at the barbarity with which our dear Lord had been treated by the heartless executioners at the scourging and crowning with thorns. He was deeply afflicted at their savage cruelty, and keenly felt the injustice and excessive severity of the punishment inflicted, contrary to his expectation, upon the holy and innocent Victim bleeding and agonizing before his eyes. As he attempted to speak, Pilate was overcome by his feelings. Stretching out his hand, trembling with emotion towards our suffering Lord, he uttered with a faltering voice these affecting words: *Ecce Homo.* "Behold the man."... Children of Israel—Pilate intended to say—Children of Israel, this suffering person before your eyes is a man like you. Look at him .... See the pitiable condition to which he is now reduced. Look at his head crowned with thorns .... Behold his face livid and swollen, disfigured by hard blows, and besmeared with gore .... Look at his whole body, covered from head to foot with gaping wounds, streaming with blood. He has scarcely the appearance of a man. In this horrible condition he cannot naturally live long. He must soon die. Even barbarians are moved to compassion towards a wounded and dying enemy. The very beasts of the forest cease tearing an unresisting and helpless victim. Children of Israel, have pity on Jesus of Nazareth, who has done so much good to you and has caused no harm to any person. Let him now die in peace. Were he to recover from his present desperate condition, and live for some years longer, his body shall remain so disfigured with scars, and the shame of his present degradation will ever be so overwhelming upon his mind, that he could never dare to appear before you, or before any civilized society. Have, therefore, mercy upon him. *Ecce Homo.* "Behold the man."

4. These moving words of Pilate were chiefly intended for the leading men among the Jews. As Governor of the province he was well aware of the power and influence of the Jewish magistrates and priests over the people. It was the chief priests and magistrates who had delivered our Lord into his hands and manifested great eagerness for his condemnation to death. Pilate justly thought that if he could succeed to gain them to his views, our Lord could be saved. He naturally felt that the sight of our Savior, most horribly scourged and crowned with thorns, should touch and move their hearts, as it had affected his own. St. Lawrence Justinian, the holy Patriarch of Venice, in his admirable book on the Passion of our Lord, treating on this very subject, the *Ecce Homo,* says: "I believe that the most efficacious means to calm the anger of irritated men and to excite in their breasts feelings of compassion towards any suffering person threatened by them with more serious injuries is to place before the eyes of his enemies and persecutors his actual sufferings and anguish of mind. The misery of a fellow man in pain, with the anguish of his soul depicted by the hand of death on his pale and sad countenance, easily moves the heart of men and draws out of their breasts those feelings of commiseration that the God of nature has mercifully implanted in them. This is the result that the Roman Governor Pilate intended and expected to obtain when he showed to the infuriated Jewish people our Lord Jesus Christ crowned with thorns, and covered all over his sacred body with gaping and bleeding wounds .... "*Hoc egit Pilatus in judaeorum turba furenti.*" (De Triumphali Christi Agone. Cap. 15)

5. St. Paul says *"As the body is one and has many members, yet all these members constitute one body only. Hence, if one member suffer anything, all the members suffer with it."* (1 Cor. 12) Human nature is the same in each individual man. Individuals are to the human race, what the

different organs, limbs and members are to the human body. Hence, every human heart should, at the sight of any man in suffering and sorrow, be moved to feelings of commiseration.... We should observe, however, that in the human body there are superior and inferior members. The head is above, the feet are beneath. Some of our limbs are more refined and useful, some others are less so. Some organs of our body, as the heart and the brain, are more essential to our physical health and life than some other external or internal organs.

Now, daily experience shows that the noblest, most refined and most essential organs of our body, as the head and the heart, when in pain and anguish, more promptly and more forcibly communicate their sufferings to the other organs and members of the same body. Again, when other members suffer, the head and the heart more promptly and more keenly sympathize with them. Let these principles of nature, daily illustrated by personal experience, guide us in our present consideration of our suffering Savior exhibited by Pilate to the Jewish magistrates and chief priests. All superiors in a moral body occupy the position of the head. They are raised in rank, that from their more elevated position they may more easily survey and discern all the wants of their inferiors.

Their dignity and responsibility oblige them to possess the knowledge necessary for the direction, government and protection of their subjects. The head has been furnished by God with two eyes, to the end that it should watch and see the wants and sufferings of all inferior members of the body. Ears have been fixed in the head, in order that they may listen at every time, and in every place to the cry of distress and to the groans caused by oppression and pain. The tongue is with the head that they may promptly rebuke injustice and condemn the oppressor. But if the voice of command and the precept of authority be not heeded, the feet of solicitude and the arm of executive power should be employed with vigor for the defence and protection of innocence calumniated, of oppressed weakness, and of persecuted virtue. The weak are the special and immediate wards of the guardians of human society. Innocent and virtuous persons are the most beautiful ornaments and the most valuable treasures of mankind. All superiors should cherish them more dearly than the other subjects under their jurisdiction and power. The criminal neglect of this sacred duty deprives society of the true living models of obedience to law, of respect for authority, order and justice. Disregard for virtuous and upright persons in superiors is an encouragement to vice and an official fostering of injustice, oppression and impiety, which must inevitably draw severe punishments upon the whole commonwealth. *"Hear this,* (says the prophet Micheas) *hear this, ye princes of the house of Jacob, and ye judges of the house of Israel, you that abhor judgment, and pervert all that is right; you that build Sion with blood, and Jerusalem with iniquity,.....therefore because of you, Sion shall be ploughed as a field, and Jerusalem shall be as a field of stones, and the mountain of the temple as the high places of the forest."* (Mich. 3:12) If these threats and warnings of the holy and zealous prophet were originally addressed to their predecessors, they are, however, well adapted to the Jewish magistrates to whom Pilate showed our Savior, scourged and crowned with thorns, appealing to their sentiments of justice and compassion in his behalf. In his case they had abhorred judgment and had perverted every principle of right and equity. They were actually shedding his innocent blood in Sion, and filling Jerusalem with iniquity. Shall the official proclamation of our Lord's innocence by Roman Governor make them suspend their iniquitous proceedings? . .. Will not the sight of his wounds and blood excite any feeling of commiseration in their heart? But . . . *Oh! ye heavens be astonished at this, and ye gates thereof be vehemently desolated.,* . . These unjust and cruel magistrates are the first to raise their voices and cry aloud to Pilate, *"Away with him; away with him....Crucify, crucify him.*

6. When the civil magistrates and the judges of any nation openly trample under foot law and equity, and have lost every sentiment of humanity, we cannot expect to see justice done to calumniated innocence and to persecuted virtue. At the unexpected clamor of the Jewish magistrates and civil officers, the Roman Governor was deeply disappointed and grieved. A ray of hope, howevor, still remained to him. From the high balcony he recognized in the square close to his palace large number of Jewish priests headed by their ecclesiastical superiors. Pilate was well aware that these sacred ministers of religion had great power and influence over the Jewish people. The Jews looked upon them with awe and respect, as they were commanded by God in these words: *"With all thy soul fear the Lord and reverence his priests .... Honor God wih all thy soul, and give honor to his priests."* (Eccli. 7:31) The Jewish priests had been selected by God to be the intrepid heralds of his holy law, and the faithful champions of justice and charity. They were clad with the *Ephod* of holiness, and had to wear on their breast the *Rational of judgment* upon which were clearly engraved

the words *"Doctrine and Truth."* (Exod. 28:30) Hence, they were reminded that doctrine should continually illumine their mind, truth should ever shine on their lips, and charity should always reign in their hearts. Their mind should be well stored with the knowledge of the law of God, whose ministers they were. Their heart should be inflamed with love for mankind, and their voice should ever be raised in defense of innocence and virtue. Priests are the divinely appointed champions of justice and charity, because they are the living representatives, and the sacred ministers of God to mankind upon earth. *"The lips of the priest,* the Prophet Malachy says, *shall keep knowledge, and they shall seek the law at his mouth, because he is the Angel of the Lord of hosts."* (Malach. 2:7)

It was to the chief priests that the Roman Governor Pilate addressed his words in behalf of our persecuted and suffering Savior, as to the last court of appeal. Though a pagan in religion, yet he had in his heart some fear of God, and respected His ministers. He had a natural love for justice, and was moved to compassion at the sight of human misery. The sufferings and heroic meekness of our dear Lord had deeply moved his heart. Pilate naturally expected that the Jewish priests, who professed to be the ministers of the God of Israel, and the zealous defenders of His holy law, should be animated by a spirit of charity, by sentiments of justice, and by feelings of compassion for human suffering and oppression. Holding up the limb of the scarlet cloak on our Savior's shoulders, Pilate called the attention of the chief priests to his bleeding wounds; he pointed out to them the horrible Crown of Thorns that was torturing his adorable head and appealed to their innate feelings of commiseration by those moving words: *"Ecce Homo."* "Behold the Man."

St. John the beloved disciple, who was present at this awful scene, describes it in the following words: *"When the chief priests and the officers had seen him, they cried out, saying: Crucify him, crucify him; Pilate says to them, take him you and crucify him: for I find no cause in him....They answered: We have a law; and according to the law he ought to die: because he made himself the Son God. When Pilate therefore had heard this saying, he feared the more."* Alas! that Pilate, a pagan, fears at these words, but the chief priests fear not.... *"Now, when Pilate had heard these words he brought Jesus forth and sat down in the judgment seat....and he saith to the Jews: Behold your King. But they cried out: Away with him, away with him: Crucify him. Pilate saith to them: Shall I crucify your King?...."* The

Roman Governor with these words intended to call the attention of the Jewish magistrates and chief priests to the fact that no noble personage and much less a king, is ever condemned to the infamous and cruel death of the cross. This wise and kind remark drew out again the chief priests who answered: *"We have no king but Caesar."* (Jn. 19) *"Pilate* St. Matthew says, *seeing that he prevaileth nothing, but rather a tumult was made, having taken water, washed his hands before the people saying: I am innocent of the blood of this just man; Look you to it. And all the people answering said: His blood be upon us and upon our children."* (Mt. 20:24) Having heard these words Pilate delivered them Jesus our Lord to be crucified. *"And they took Jesus and led him forth. And bearing his own cross he went forth to that place which is called Calvary, but in Hebrew Golgotha, where they crucified him."* (Jn.19)

7. The awful tragedy is thus brought to a close. The principal actors therein have been the chief priests and the Jewish magistrates. The people have followed the example of their civil and ecclesiastical superiors. This is very natural, because, *"As the judge of the people is himself, so also are his ministers, and what manner of man the ruler of a City is, such also are they that dwell therein."* (Eccli. 10:8) Woe to the nation where judgment and justice is perverted by the rulers and magistrates, and the true or pretended ministers of religion become their associates in iniquity. *"A kingdom is translated from one people to another, because of injustices and wrongs, and injuries and diverse deceits."* (Eccli. 10:8) The Jewish magistrates, senators, officers and chief priests have conspired to commit injustices, wrongs, injuries and all manner of deceits against the essential holiness, truth and honesty of the incarnate Son of God, the Messias and the Savior of the world. More cruel than savages, worse than the beasts of the forests, they are not moved by his extreme sufferings, but with a diabolical frenzy they clamor for more terrible tortures, for the horrible death of the cross. *"Crucify him, Crucify him."* Our divine Lord on the balcony deeply feels this cruel outrage. He knows that the chief priests and Jewish magistrates demand his crucifixion that he may die in extreme pain and deepest ignominy, and thus his memory may forever be branded with infamy. Our Lord knows that these bad and malicious men not only desire to deprive him of life, but by the nature and circumstances of his death, they are anxious to render his name infamous and detestable among all future generations. St. John Chrysostom asks: "Why do the chief priests and Jewish magistrates

demand the crucifixion of Jesus? And answers: because it was ignominious."
They were afraid lest his memory should be transmitted to posterity with
honor; hence, to prevent this, they select the death of the cross, not reflecting
that truth shines more powerfully when an attempt is made to conceal it.
"Cum impeditur magis apparet veritas." (A Lapide in Matt. 27:22)

The royal prophet, speaking in the person of our suffering Lord,
compares the Jewish magistrates and chief priests to savage beasts. *"Many
dogs have encompassed me. The council of the malignant hath besieged
me. They have opened their mouths against me as a lion ravening and
roaring."* (Ps. 21:14) *"My inheritance,* the Synagogue, *is become to me
as a lion in the wood: it hath cried out against me."* (Jer. 22:8) *And now,
O ye inhabitants of Jerusalem, and ye men of Juda, judge between me and
my vineyard. What is there that I ought to do more to my vineyard, that
I have not done?....For the vineyard of the Lord of hosts is the house of
Israel, and the men of Juda....And I looked that they should do judgment,
and behold iniquity: and do justice, and behold a cry .... Therefore is my
people led away captive,...their nobles have perished with famine, and their
multitudes were dried up with thirst. Therefore hath hell enlarged her soul,
and opened her mouth without bounds: and their strong ones and their
people, and their high and glorious ones shall go down into it. And man
shall be brought down, and man shall be humbled, and the eyes of the lofty
shall be brought low...And the Lord of hosts shall be exalted in judgment,
and the holy God shall be sanctified in justice."* (Is. 5)

In the following chapters we shall consider the realization of these
terrible threats announced by the prophet, in the name of the Lord to the
guilty children of Israel.

CHAPTER XI

JESUS CROWNED WITH THORNS IS REJECTED BY THE JEWS

"When the chief priests and the officers had seen him, they cried out saying: Away with him: Away with him. Crucify him." (Jn. 19:15)

St. Peter Chrysologus, the zealous and eloquent Archbishop of Ravenna, undertook to examine in one of his sermons, the principal cause of the reprobation of Dives mentioned by our divine Savior in the gospel. (Lk. 16:19) Dives, he says, would not be condemned to hell, on account of his material wealth: because riches in their nature are good, though in a moral sense they are indifferent, becoming good or bad, according to the intended or actual use made of them by the legitimate owner. When material wealth has been lawfully acquired, when it is justly possessed, and properly used, then it is both physically and morally good. Instead of censure and punishment the virtuous possessor deserves prise and reward. The holy Patriarch Abraham, holy Job, Judith and many other saintly personages in the old dispensation, were rich yet they are highly praised in the holy scripture, and are among the great saints of heaven. Dives was clad in fine linen and purple. But every person is allowed to dress in conformity with the legitimate customs of the country, and according to his rank and position in society. Holy King David, Queen Esther, and that illustrious model of chastity, prudence, honesty and fidelity to duty, Joseph the viceroy of Egypt, used in due season, rich and splendid robes. For so doing they are neither condemned nor blamed in any portion of the Bible. Dives *feasted sumptuously every day,* St. Luke says; but the sons of holy Job did the same, and are nowhere condemned for their conduct. Hence the eloquent Archbishop concludes, that the above enumerated actions of Dives were not the principal cause of his eternal condemnation.

He was condemned to hell on account of his hardness of heart, for his total want of commiseration for the famishing beggar Lazarus, who, exhausted by want and suffering, *lay at his gate full of sores.* (St. Peter Chrysologus serm. 22) Dives in sound bodily health and vigorous strength could roam at ease in a large and comfortable mansion, whence he in the hardness of his heart could bear to see laying down upon the bare ground near his princely gate a poor, sick and starving man, exposed in the open air day and night to all the various changes and rigors of the season and of the weather. This poor beggar was scarcely covered with a few rags, whilst he was clad in fine linen and purple robes. Dives witnessed the sufferings, beheld the sores of the virtuous but starving beggar; yet he had no feeling of pity for him. He obstinately refused to give to Lazarus a morsel of bread or a glass of water, but let him starve and perish in a public road in front of his princely mansion. His very dogs evinced more sympathy for the sufferer by whining caressingly at him and by gently licking his putrid sores. What wonder that God refused to show mercy to this human monster, worse than the very beasts, who had no bowels of pity for the starving beggar, Lazarus? *"For judgment without mercy to him who hath not done mercy."* (James 2:13)

Our divine Lord and Master related the above mentioned event to the Jewish scribes and pharisees as a real fact. It was certainly a striking figure foreshadowing their conduct, when after his flagellation and crowning with thorns, he was shown to them, by the Roman Governor Plate in his suffering condition. As no feeling of compassion was evinced by Dives towards Lazarus; so no pity, no mercy was manifested by the Jewish people to our divine Lord in his extreme suffering and deep humiliations. Lazarus died through pain and want, so did our blessed Savior. But both are now more glorious and happpy in heaven. As Dives was swiftly punished by a premature death and by eternal reprobation; so we shall have to consider in this chaper the manifold and severe punishments inflicted by the justice of an offended God on all those who had no mercy, no compassion for His divine Son, crowned with thorns.

1. The Jewish nation has been severely punished by divine justice for the awful crime of Deicide. But the severity and long duration of the punishment has by far fallen short of the astonishing malice of that perverse people. They could have no possible cause or occasion for the persecution of our divine Lord. They were fully aware of his unimpeachable innocence

long before they began his trial at the tribunal of the Roman Governor. Our Lord had publicly challenged the scrutiny of his character and daily conduct to convince him of any sin and of the least violation of the law of God. *"Which of you shall convict me of sin?"* (Jn. 8:46) *"Think not that I am come to destroy the law or the prophets: I am not come to destroy but to fulfill."* (Mt. 5:17) From his infancy, childhood, youth, manhood to the moment of his condemnation, not the least violation of God's holy law could be brought against Jesus of Nazareth. But on the contrary he was on every occasion found most zealous and careful in the perfect observance of the law and of the sacred ceremonies of religion. He assisted with exemplary piety and profound devotion, at the solemn festivals in the temple of Jerusalem, and at the public prayers in the synagogue. He promptly obeyed all legitimate superiors, and paid all due taxes and tributes, even when his extreme poverty compelled him to work a miracle to obtain the necessary money for himself and his Apostle Peter. (Mt. 17:26) The scribes, pharisees and Herodians remember well the wise answer given them a short time before, when our Lord said: *"Give to Caesar what belongs to Caesar and to God what is due to God."* (Lk. 20:25) He was the most perfect model of humility without the least ambition for public dignities or places of honor. He fled away and hid himself in a mountain, when on one occasion he discovered that an admiring crowd believed him to be a prophet, and wished to proclaim him their sovereign Lord and King. (Jn. 6:15) His persecutors knew all this. They knew our most holy Lord never by word or deed injured any public or private person. They knew that Judas, enticed by their impious bribes, betrayed him, but, repenting of his treason had a short time before publicly protested in their presence his firm conviction in the innocence of his persecuted Master. (Mt. 27:3) Why then in the name of justice, do the chief priests and Jewish magistrates persecute this innocent man? ... Why do they bring Jesus of Nazareth to trial for his life before the civil tribunal of the Roman Governor Pilate?...Alas! it is not their zeal for the law of Moses, nor is it their love for justice but on the contrary it is secret envy, it is a deadly hatred engendered in their malicious hearts by disappointed pride and ambition.

2. The Jewish priests, scribes and pharisees persecute our Savior on account of his superior virtue. They are corroded by envy because of his eminent sanctity, because of his admirable wisdom and heavenly knowledge, because of his ardent and active zeal for the glory of God, for

the conversion of sinners and for the salvation of souls. They are embittered against him by jealousy at his extraordinary success in preaching to the people, at his numerous conversions of neglected sinners, at his manifold and wonderful miracles, at the admiration in which he is universally held by the people that follow him in crowds everywhere through Palestine. In their secret conventicle the chief Jewish priests and the hypocritical pharisees have betrayed the motive of their malignant conspiracy against our Savior's life by the following words: *"What do we, for this man (Jesus) doeth many miracles?...If we let him alone so, all men will believe in him."* (Jn. 2:43) These words expose the plot and the object of these malignant persecutors of our blessed Lord. The sanctity of Jesus is a reproach to their hypocrisy. The admiration with which he is regarded by the people, disappoints their pride and ambition. Not to forfeit the esteem of men they have impiously conspired to put to death the author of life and the Savior of mankind. They are resolved to make of him an object of public contempt, by condemning him to the cruel and infamous death of the cross. Behold the real motive of their persecution. During the trial every law of equity and justice has been violated. The enemies of our Lord have suborned venal and perjured witnesses who by their contradictions prove his innocence. They have accused him as guilty of several grievous crimes, none of which can be supported by the least shadow of proof. Before the Roman Governor these wicked men manifest the most shameful disregard for consistency. With overbearing arrogance they demand that Pilate should sanction the sentence of death which they have pronounced against our innocent Lord without proffering against him any accusation. Pilate firmly refuses his official approbation to such arbitrary and tyrannical proceedings; but the chief priests and Jewish magistrates insist by saying: *"If he were not a malefactor we would not have delivered him to thee."* (Jn. 18:30) This impertinent answer offended rather than satisfied the Roman Judge. The Jews are compelled to specify their accusations against our dear Lord. They make three distinct charges against him. 1st, they accuse him of impiety by uttering blasphemies against God, and by making himself the Son of God. 2nd, they denounce him as the corrupter of the people. 3rd, they impeach him as an ambitious pretender to the kingdom of Judea, refusing to pay tribute to Caesar, and making himself a king.

3. Pilate having questioned our Lord found him entirely innocent. He perceived that personal envy and hatred on the part of the Jews was

the real cause of this bitter persecution. Hence, he publicly proclaimed his innocence. But the Jewish magistrates and chief priests clamored more violently than ever for his immediate condemnation: they excited the feelings of the people against the Roman Governor, they passed from one accusation to another to see which made most impression upon his mind. They tried him first about religion. *"We have a law,* they said, *and according to the law he ought to die, because he made himself the Son of God."*

Pilate promptly disappointed their expectation by answering: *"Take him you, and judge him according to your law."* (Jn. 18:31) Foiled, but not discouraged, these malicious men betake themselves now to political charges, the final refuge of disappointed persecutors. They boldly say to the Roman Governor, *"If thou release this man, thou art not the friend of Caesar."* Thus by threats of personal violence, by seditious tumults, by maliciously impeaching his loyalty to Caesar, the chief priests and Jewish magistrates forced Pilate to confirm the iniquitous sentence of death which they have already pronounced against our innocent Lord. But, if under the pressure of this violent proceeding, Pilate reluctantly consented to become the accomplice of that horrible Deicide, are the Jews less guilty who compelled him to it? ...Certainly not says St. Agustine. *"Sed si reus quia fecit vel invitus . . . illi innocentes qui cogerunt ut faceret? Nullo modo."* Moreover, when the Roman Governor manifested his disapprobation of their iniquitous conduct, washing his hands in their presence, publicly declaring his innocence of the blood of our guiltless Lord, the Jews in a most horrible and blasphemous manner unanimously assumed the terrible responsibility of the awful crime of Deicide. *"Let his blood,* they exclaimed. *Let his blood fall upon us, and upon our children."* Perfidious nation, wicked parents, wretched children! The essential holiness, the eminent virtue, the known innocence of our Lord, officially recognized and proclaimed by the Roman Governor cannot appease their hatred.

Pilate uses every legal means to baffle their malignant conspiracy against the life of our Savior, but the Jews counteract and frustrate his efforts by the open violation of every right and law. Their thirst for his life's blood becomes every hour more ardent. The moving spectacle of the incarnate Son of God, the true Messias, Supreme Pontiff and rightful King of the Jewish nation, the Savior of the world, meekly standing on the balcony of the palace of the Roman Governor with his divine and beneficent hands manacled, with his adorable head crowned with sharp thorns, and his sacred body covered with bleeding wounds, instead of eliciting their compassion, inflame the anger of the Jews, who in a tumultuous manner exclaim: *"Away with him, Away with him...Crucify, crucify him...Let his blood be upon us, and upon our children..."* Ah! That no innocent blood can be shed with impunity!...If the blood of Abel the just, cried from the earth for vengeance against the crime of fratricide; O God of eternal justice, what must be the punishment of Deicide committed in the most holy person of your divine Son?...We expect the most terrible calamities to fall upon the Jewish magistrates, chief priests, and upon the entire Jewish nation. When the sacred rights of justice are violated by public men, the sword of divine justice must vindicate them. When feelings of humanity and sentiments of mercy are extinguished in the breast of civil magistrates and of ecclesiastical persons, then the utter destruction of the guilty nation becomes inevitable. *"For judgment without mercy to those who have not done mercy. Learn ye that are the judges of the ends of the earth. Give ear you that rule the people and please yourselves in multitudes of nations; for power is given you by the Lord, and strength by the Most High, who will examine your works, and search out your thoughts, because being ministers of his kingdom, you have not judged rightly, nor kept the law of justice, nor walked according to the will of God. Horribly and speedily will he appear to you, for a most severe judgment shall be for them that bear rule."* (Wis. 6:2)

In the next chapter we will consider the justice of the divine judgment, and the terrible severity of God's punishment against the Jewish nation.

CHAPTER XII

PUNISHMENT OF THE JEWS

1. Strong and plain warnings had been given to the Jewish people, almost in every page of the Holy Scripture, of the most severe chastisements, if they violated the commandments of God. Their banishment from Palestine, their dispersion among the nations of the earth, the destruction of their cities, and especially of Jerusalem, their capital, are repeatedly foretold in many parts of the Old Testament, from Moses to the last of the Prophets. *"Hear this, ye princes of the house of Jacob, and ye judges of the house of Israel, you that abhor judgment, and pervert all that is right, you that build Sion with blood and Jerusalem with iniquity. Therefore, because of you, Sion shall be ploughed as a field, and Jerusalem as a field of stones, and the mountain of the temple as the high place of the forests."* (Mich. 3:9) St. John the Baptist announced to the Jews their impending punishments. *"Ye offspring of vipers,* he said to them, *who hath showed to you to flee from the wrath to come? Bring forth therefore fruits worthy of penance . . . For now the axe is laid to the root of the trees. Every tree therefore that bringeth not forth good fruit, shall be cut down, and cast into the fire."* (Lk. 3:7) The astonishing perversity and malicious obstinacy of the Jewish people drew upon their guilty heads the following severe rebuke and terrible threat of our meek and loving Redeemer, *"Woe to you scribes and pharisees, hypocrites; who build the sepulchers of the prophets and adorn the monuments of the just and say: If we had been in the days of our fathers, we would not have been partakers with them in the blood of the prophets. Wherefore you are the witnesses against yourselves, that you are the sons of them who killed the prophets. Fill up, then, the measure of your fathers. You serpents, generation of vipers, how will you escape the judgment of hell? Therefore behold l send to you prophets, and wise men, and scribes:*

And some of them you will put to death, and crucify; and some you will scaurge in your synagogues, and persecute them from city to city: that upon you may came all the just blood that hath been shed upon earth, from the blood of Abel the just, even unto the blood of Zacharias, the son of Barachias, whom you killed between the temple and the altar. Amen, I say to you, all these things shall come upon this generation. O, Jerusalem, Jerusalem, thou that killest the prophets, and stonest them that are sent unto thee! How often would I have gathered together thy children, as the hen gatherest her chickens under her wings and thou wouldst not? Behold, your house shall be left to you desolate...Amen I say to you, there shall not be left here a stone upon a stone that shall not be thrown down." (Mt. 23:29)

If these terrible punishments were threatened against the Jews for the killing of the prophets, of the apostles, and other holy servants of God, what chastisements are due to them for condemning to the death of the cross the Incarnate Son of God, their Messias and the Savior of mankind? The warning of prophecy was soon realized. The most frightful calamities befell that guilty nation. Political dissensions and civil wars tore it to pieces: famine and pestilence devoured that wretched people: parents saw their children dying of starvation. The destroying angel visibly appeared with a flaming sword in the air above Jerusalem, having its fiery point directed against the doomed city. Rebellion against the Roman empire swiftly brought the Roman legions around the walls of Jerusalem, inside of which the largest portion of the Jewish people, from every part of the country, had taken refuge. This memorable siege under the Roman General and Emperor Vespasian, continued by his brave son Titus, was one of the most terrible recorded in history. By a disposition of divine justice, it began a few days before the Jewish paschal solemnity, in which thirty seven years before, our Lord was condemned to death and crucified on Mount Calvary.

2. On that occasion, both on account of the great national solemnity, and because of the war with the Romans, an extraordinary number of the Jewish people were congregated in the city. At least one million and a half of those wretched Jews, some say more, were shut up within the walls of Jerusalem. No adequate provisions were made, or could be made, for the support of that vast multitude. The siege lasted several years. The defense on the side of the Jews was fierce and stubborn. The position of the city and the strength of its fortifications, prolonged the struggle beyond the expectation of the Roman general. The combatants on both sides performed

prodigies of military valor. Hecatombs of slain soldiers were putrefying round the walls and infecting the air with a pestilential atmosphere. Hence the plague was added to the scourge of war. The Roman general, to force the surrender of the city or to starve its doomed inhabitants, did not allow any person to come outside of the walls under penalty of being crucified in the sight of the beleagured people. In accordance with our Savior's prophecy, the Roman army dug a deep trench round about Jerusalem. Starvation or unconditional surrender was the order of the day. To famine and pestilence internal seditions among the Jews were added to their common war with the Roman Empire. In the despair and frenzy of starvation grownup men snatched like ravenous wolves the least morsel of food from the trembling hands of starving and weeping children. A mother maddened with hunger killed her full grown baby, roasted the body at the fire, eating a portion of it, and reserved the rest for subsequent meals. The smell of roasted flesh attracted to her house a crowd of hungry persons, who insisted with threats of violence, in having a share of her prepared food. The woman, forced by the people, opened a pantry room, where they were horrified at the frightful spectacle of the roasted body of her own child, portion of which she had been eating. The famous Jewish historian Josephus states that several other mothers were on that occasion guilty of similar unnatural barbarities. (Lib 6 Belli Cap 14) The accumulating horrors of famine, pestilence, and civil factions in the doomed city forced daily hundreds of the despairing inhabitants, in spite of the prohibition of the Roman General Titus, to attempt a flight to the Roman camp. But they were immediately seized by the soldiers, nailed upon crosses, which were erected, between the breastworks of the Roman army and the wall of Jerusalem, in full sight of the terrified inhabitants. More than five hundred persons of every class, sex and condition were daily crucified. In his history Josephus relates that the number of these executions increased to such an extent that sufficient timber could not be obtained to form the crosses, and that all the space between the Roman trench and the wall of the besieged city was entirely covered with crosses and with putrefying corpses. *Ut tandem locus crucibus deesset, et corporibus cruces.* (Lib. 6 Belli, Cap. 12) The Holy Ghost says: *"By what things a man sinneth by the same also is he tormented."* (Wis. 11:17) Is not this a just retribution for their impious cry against our divine Lord, their holy Messias, when the Jews clamored before the Roman Governor, Pilate: *"Away with him, away with him, crucify, crucify him, Let his blood fall upon us and upon our children?...* After having suffered all the horrors and miseries of a close and protracted siege, devoured by famine, decimated by pestilence, distracted by internal anarchy, the sacrilegious city was taken by storm and was totally destroyed by the Roman army. Thus were literally verified the prophecies of the old testament confirmed by the infallible words of our divine Savior, when he said: *"Daughters of Jerusalem, weep not for me, but for yourselves and for your children... for if in the green wood they do these things, what shall be done in the dry?* If the justice of my heavenly Father demands the excessive sufferings which you bewail in me, His divine and innocent Son, because I have undertaken in mercy to atone for the sins of your nation and of mankind: what punishment, do you think, will the justice of an offended God inflict upon a people that to all their former black ingratitudes, and manifold transgressions, now add the awful crime of crucifying me, their divine Messias and the true Redeemer of the world?" . . . *"Oh! Jerusalem, Jerusalem, if thou also hadst known, and that in this day, the things that are for thy peace, but now they are hidden from thy eyes .... for the days shall come upon thee, and thy enemies shall cast a trench about thee and compass thee round, and straiten thee on every side, and beat thee down to the ground: and thy children who are in thee.. And they shall not leave in thee a stone upon a stone: because thou hast not known the time of thy visitation."* (Lk. 19:42)

All these threats were literally accomplished against the guilty city of Jerusalem, which by the order of Titus, the victorious Roman General, was razed to the ground in the month of September, thirty-seven years after our Savior's crucifixion and death. According to the above mentioned Jewish hisorian, Josephus, more than one million and one hundred thousand Jews perished on that ever memorable occasion. The surviving portion of that wretched people was dispersed all over the face of the earth, to testify to all nations, tribes and tongues, how heavily during nineteen centuries *"The blood of Jesus has fallen upon them and upon their children."* The most dreadful, however, of all the punishments is their impious rejection of the Messias, by their insane cry: *"Away with him, away with him,"* followed by their obduracy in their malicious impiety, and the inevitable damnation during a miserable eternity of the vast majority of that guilty nation. Thus another prophetical warning of our divine Lord is unhappily verified. *"Amen, I say to you, that many shall come from the east, and the west, and sit down with Abraham, and Isaac and Jacob in the kingdom of heaven. But the children of the kingdom shall be cast out into exterior darkness: There shall be weeping and gnashing of teeth."* (Mt. 8:11) Behold the crime and the punishment of the perfidious Jews! The punishment has been severe and long, because the crime was the most atrocious ever perpetrated by any nation upon earth ... It was committed with premeditated malice; it was consented to by the representatives of the people; it was consummated with the most barbarous cruelty. Hence the sacrilegious murderers of the incarnate Son of God must feel and bear the just indignation of heaven, and the scorn of horrified humanity. Modern nations guilty of similar persecutions against the Church of Jesus Christ will likewise soon have to feel the effects of the offended justice of God.

3. We have observed that the degenerate chief priests, and Jewish magistrates were the principal and most active persecutors of our divine Lord. Corroded by envy, and inflamed by hatred, they conspired against his life, and in secret conventicle they agreed to condemn him to death on the first opportunity. For this end they bribed Judas with money; and furnished him with a band of armed men, to capture his betrayed Master in the garden of Gethsemani. Twice in a public assembly they pronounced sentence of death against our innocent Lord, before delivering him to the civil tribunal of the Roman Governor. It was entirely due to the influence of their authority, example, and active energy that the Jewish people were induced to demand from Pilate, the condemnation of our dear Savior to the death of the cross. Now, then, if the Jewish nation in general has been so severely punished for having consented to the crime of deicide, what punishments must we expect to fall upon the chief priests and Jewish magistrates who have been the principal authors and the most malicious instigators of this awful crime? More severe must be the chastisement where greater is the guilt. *"To him that is little mercy is granted, but the mighty shall be mightly tormented"* (Wis. 6:7) The holy Prophet Osee had foretold that: *"The children of Israel shall sit many days without king and without prince and without sacrifice and without altar and without ephod and without Theraphim."* (Osee 3:4) This is an evident threat that the Jewish priesthood and magistracy were to be abolished. Symptoms of dissolution appeared soon after the death of our Savior. During the thirty-seven years preceeding the complete destruction of the city of Jerusalem and of the temple, and the utter dispersion of the Jews from Palestine, serious commotions were excited, and bloody riots occurred among the Jewish magistrates and

94

chief priests, caused by their ambition, and their thirst for filthy lucre. These scandalous contentions grew more frequent and fierce in proportion as the final catastrophe approached. Josephus relates, that during the long seige of Jerusalem by the Roman army, the people within the beleagured city were divided into several factions which provoked frequent bloody encounters, hating and persecuting one another more cruelly than they fought against their common external foe... Moreover, the people maddened by famine and despair often threatened the life of the civil magistrates and Jewish priests for neglecting or refusing to provide them with the necessary means of subsistence. Frequently the magistrates were forced to abdicate their office which was transferred to other ambitious men who made, before election, flattering promises to the mob. But being unable to satisfy the people they were in turn deposed and others substituted in their place to be expelled again in a short time. Thus to the crushing pressure of external war, the disintegrating progress of internal anarchy, being added, the city was stormed and captured by the soldiers who, provoked and maddened by the long and stubborn resistance of the Jews, rushed upon them with uncontrollable fury; but wreaked their vengeance in a more special manner on the Jewish magistrates and officers, whom they sought in every direction. Very few could escape the gory blade of the exterminating sword. No mercy was shown to them in punishment of their barbarous cruelty against our innocent Savior. Divine Justice had warned them that *"Judgment without mercy should be executed against those who have done no mercy" "Learn ye that are the judges of the ends of the earth. Give ear you that rule the people.., because being ministers of his kingdom, you have not judged rightly, nor kept the law of justice, nor walked according to the will of God. Horribly and speedily will he appear to you: For a most severe judgment shall be for them that bear rule."* (Wis. 6:2) May modern avowed and secret persecutors of the Church of Christ, heed in time this merciful warning of infallible truth. Let present rulers and magistrates hostile to the venerable head of our holy religion, learn a useful lesson from the terrible and speedy punishment inflicted by divine justice upon the guilty Jewish magistrates, who persecuted Jesus Christ.

4. No less severe was the chastisement of the Jewish priesthood. These unworthy ministers of religion had been the most malicious, bold and persistent persecutors of the Messias. It has been through their active exertions that our Lord was captured in the garden of Gethsemani, that he

was insulted and struck on the face in the house of the high priest Annas, and twice condemned to death by the high pontiff Caiphas. They were the principal and most influential instigators of the mockeries and outrages heaped upon our Savior in the palace of King Herod. They are now before the Roman Governor, Pilate, the most zealous actors in the awful tragedy. They sacrilegiously abuse their authority and influence with the people to stir up the multitude to hatred against our innocent Savior, and are the first to utter the impious city: *"Away with him, away with him. Crucify him."*

Horrible crime which bears with it its due punishment! By rejecting Jesus of Nazareth, the chief priests deprive themselves of the dignity and office of the priesthood. Our divine Lord, being the author, the head, the life and the only fit victim of religion, this is necessarily abolished whenever he is rejected. His death was the complete abrogation of Judaism, as his glorious resurrection was the real birth of Christianity. The figure passes away as soon as the reality appears. Hence in his magnificent letter to the Hebrews, St. Paul says: *"There is verily an abrogation of the former commandment, for the weakness and unprofitableness thereof. For the law brought nothing to perfection, but an introduction of a better hope, by which we approach to God... Jesus Christ being a priest forever according to the order of Melchisedech, having an everlasting priesthood, whereby he is able also to save forever them that come to God by himself; always living to make intercession for us."* (Heb. 7:18) These words announce the realization of the prophecy made to the Jewish priests by St. Malachy, speaking to them in the name of God, about four hundred years before. *"I have no pleasure in you, saith the Lord of hosts; and I will not receive any gift of your hands... you have departed out of the way and have caused many to stumble at the law: you have made void the covenant of Levi ... Therefore have I also made you contemptible and base before all people."* (Malac. 1:10, 2:8) Behold here the terrible sentence of divine abrogation of the Jewish priesthood. How base, ignoble, and contemptible they are before all nations is proved by their conduct towards our Savior, and subsequent history testifies to the fact.

The same holy prophet who foretold the abrogation of the Aaronic priesthood, clearly announced the institution of the perpetual and universal priesthood of Christianity in the following words. *"From the rising of the sun, even to the going down, my name is great among the gentiles; and in every place there is sacrifice, and there is offered to my name a clean oblation."* (Malac. 1:2) Behold the consequence of the impious rejection of the Messias by the Jewish priests, when they cried aloud to Pilate: *"Away with him, away with him."* Our divine Lord departed from them, and thus they were deprived of the true religion of God, and of the priestly dignity. The Christian church and religion was firmly established on the immovable rock of Peter against which the gates of hell shall never prevail. The dignity of the Christian priesthood, more holy in its nature, more sublime in its object, more efficacious in its effects, more universal in its scope, and everlasting in its duration, has been by our Lord conferred on the apostles, and through them perpetuated in his holy church. Hence St. Paul says: *"Others were indeed made priests without an oath; but this with an oath, by him who said to him: The Lord hath sworn, and he will not repent: Thou art a priest forever, by so much is Jesus made a surety of a better testament . . . For that he continueth forever, hath an everlasting priesthood."* (Hebr. 8:20) This everlasting priesthood is firmly secured to the Christian religion in the person of the apostles and of all their legitimate successors, in the unbroken chain of the sacred ministry, by the infallible promise of our divine Lord, when he said: *Behold I am with you all days, even to the consummation of the world."* (Mt. 28:20) At their ordination the apostles were commanded by our divine master to exercise the sacred office of the Christian priesthood to the end of time. *"Take ye and eat: this is my body which shall be delivered for you. Do this for the commemoration of me. This chalice is the new testament in my blood. This do ye, as often as you shall drink it, for the commemoration of me. For as often as you shall eat of this bread and drink of this chalice, you shall show the death of the Lord, until he come."* (1 Cor. 11:24) On this memorable occasion, on the very eve of his death on the cross, our blessed Lord repeats the command twice in order to impress it more deeply in the mind of his apostles, and to insure the fulfillment of his injunction. This command has relation to the future and is extended to the end of time, when he would come to judge mankind. By his order, this the most sacred and sublime exercise of the Christian priesthood, has frequently to be repeated by the apostles and by their legitimate successors. *"For*, the apostle says, *as often as you shall eat of this bread, and drink this chalice, you shall show the death of the Lord, until he come."* Hence the existence of this divine command evidently demonstrates the existence of the power in the apostolic priesthood to execute it. For God never commands what is impossible. St. Paul who was not one of the twelve apostles, when these were ordained priests by our Lord, but who was selected three years after, claims this power for himself and for his fellow apostles and priests in the following words. *"The chalice of benediction which we bless, is it not the communion of the blood of Christ?...And the bread which we break, is it not the partaking of the body of the Lord?..."* (1 Cor. 10:16) The Bible, the authority of the fathers, and the whole history of Christianity perfectly agree in affirming the abrogation of the Jewish priesthood, and the establishment of a more sublime sacerdotal dignity in the Christian religion, which will last to the end of ages.

We have dwelt at some length upon this important subject, to show to the world that our faith and confidence in the Christian priesthood is not in the least degree shaken by the present general and violent storm of persecution, directed against it by the impiety of wicked men, instigated by the malice of the infernal powers. "For the gates of hell shall never prevail against an authority established, guaranteed, and supported by the omnipotent hand of God." *"Portae inferi non prevalebunt."*

5. We must now turn to consider the punishment inflicted upon the guilty Jewish magistrates and rulers of the people. We have seen the chastisement which these perverse men received during the siege of Jerusalem, and after the capture of the doomed city by the Roman army under Titus. But that was only the beginning of their humiliation and sorrow. From that epoch their authority and magisterial power were completely abolished. St. Paul justly remarks that: *"The priesthood being translated, it is necessary that a translation also be made of the law."* (Hebr. 12:12) But when the law is translated and changed, the former rulers and magistrates are deposed. After the chief priests, the Jewish magistrates, senators, and civil officers had the largest share in the persecution of our innocent Lord. By them Pilate was morally compelled to pronounce the sentence of his condemnation to the most cruel and infamous death of the cross. These iniquitous men had promptly joined their voices to the cry of the Jewish priests, clamoring aloud against our Savior and saying: *"Away with him, away with him. Crucify, crucify him...Let his blood be upon us and upon our children."* Their impious voices unhappily for them prevailed. Behold our Lord, and their Messias fastened to the cross. Their condemnation is written above his adorable head crowned with thorns. These words written by command of Pilate, the Roman Governor, *"Jesus of Nazareth, King of the Jews,"* proclaim the abolition of the Jewish monarchy, and magistracy. For when the legitimate King is

condemned to death, and the monarchy is abolished, the magistracy is deposed. The terrible threat of the holy prophet Osee is fully realized: *"The children of Israel shall sit many days without king, and without sacrifice, and without altar."* (Osee 3:4) During nineteen long centuries the wretched children of Israel have, by the just judgment of God, been dispersed among the different nations of the earth, without ever being allowed to elect any king, prince, or magistrate for their exclusive race. Like men infected with a mysterious moral leprosy, the effect of the awful malediction which they invoked upon themselves, when they *assumed* the terrible responsibility of the blood of Jesus, they are condemned to a perpetual exile among their fellow-men. Similar to their true prototype Cain, they bear on their gloomy foreheads the brand of God's malediction. Naturally ambitious for dominion, the coveted scepter of power invariably eludes like a phantom their eager grasp. They succeed in amassing the mammon of iniquity, they can acquire wealth, but they cannot obtain any lasting civil power. In punishment for their impious rejection of the Messias, the source and center of all authority and jurisdiction, the offended Majesty of God has wisely and justly dried up against them the fountain of all legitimate civil and religious power in society. The voice of prophecy and the testimony of history confirm this fact.

The *Civilta Cattolica*, one of our ablest Catholic periodicals, published in Florence, Italy, by a select staff of learned Jesuit Fathers who are under the special protection of the Pope, in reviewing a work of a German writer on the struggle of the so-called modern civilization, says: "The author sustains with much reason that Judaism is one of the principal moving powers in this present anti-christian warfare. The following are his words."

"In the conflict for modern civilization, the central point of which is now in Germany, the Jews wield a very important part. Being the avowed enemies of Christianity and of true Christian progress, they have during more than fifteen centuries, in spite of their oppression and degradation, preserved their vital energy with a pertinacity unexampled in the history of mankind. Wherever freedom has been granted to the Jewish race, these men have with wonderful elasticity sprung up to high eminence, and have succeeded in obtaining a remarkable preponderance in society. The Jews have at the present moment rendered *tributaries* to their enormous *banking* systems in both the governments and the nations of Europe. They actually monopolize and dominate over the financial markets of the world. In these latter years they have secured the control of the public press, and of the telegraph. Many influential Jews are actual members of legislative assemblies, and can be found sitting at the council-boards of modern governments, among the ministers of states, of kingdoms and of empires that profess to believe in Christianity.

"We can, without fear of contradiction, assert that the downfall in later years of Austrian power and influence has been precipitated through the perfidious intrigues and vigorous agency of the Jews; and that in union with Bismarck they are at present the staunchest prop to the haughty position, and domineering attitude of the Hohenzollern empire in Germany. We should never forget that the destruction of the Christian religion, and consequently of true civilization, has ever been the deeply rooted resolve, and the unchangeable aim of Judaism since the establishment of Christianity upon earth. All their power and influence are constantly directed to the final attainment of this central object of their immortal hatred. At the present time the Jews concentrate their united efforts in the west of Europe in the hope of preparing the way, and securing powerful auxiliaries for achieving a more complete and lasting victory in the west of Asia, by the recovery of Jerusalem and the permanent reestablishment of their long-lost dominion in Palestine." (Civilta Cattolica, 1st Art., 18th Nov.,1876)

But as every attempt of the Jews to recover their national autonomy and civil power under the pagan Roman empire invariably ended by an aggravation of their subjection; so their efforts to obtain power and wield influence in Christian nations have always resulted in various disasters to their race, and to all those imprudent Christian governments that have favored their ambitious aspirations. This is a fact of history. We are firmly convinced that Jewish perfidy and arrogance shall, as ever before, be completely baffled by the heavenly wisdom and victorious power of Christianity. Modern Jews are in various ways prostituting their material wealth, and abusing their actual power and influence to the injury of the Church of Jesus Christ. We may therefore confidently expect that by a very wise disposition of divine Providence they shall soon be deprived of these abused advantages in a manner that will astonish the world. We believe that the most crushing defeat and humiliation ever experienced during the last fifteen hundred years by that stubborn race, involving their general bankruptcy, will, sooner than many imagine, be the inevitable punishment of their audacity and their attempt against the holy religion of Jesus Christ.

"Christus vincit; Christus regnat; Christus imperat." We have full faith in his divine promises, and the testimony of history corroborates our confidence ....Our main object, however, and the limits prescribed to us by our subject permit only a few authentic extracts, which we intend to give in the next chapter after a brief account of THE "ECCE HOMO" CHAPEL AT JERUSALEM

It was in the year 1842, when the funeral rites of the Count de la Ferronays were being celebrated in the Sant' Andrea delle Fratte, that a Jew of Strasburg by the name of Alphonse Ratisbonne received the light of Faith. This miraculous conversion is well known, and how nobly the convert responded to an after call of grace is likewise a public fact. He joined his worthy brother, who was already a Catholic priest, and they both resolved to devote themselves entirely to the conversion and instruction of their Israelite brethren. Rev. Father Alphonse made the Holy City his home, and there laid the foundation of a work which bears the stamp of true Christian charity.

By a special design of Providence, an Arab made known to Father Ratisbonne the possibility of purchasing the ruins of Pilate's Pretorium, profaned for eighteen centuries, and then in the hands of schismatics. An offer of 15,000 francs was made to them for the building, and this price was at first accepted, but moved by avarice, they afterwards raised the price to 70,000 francs. Father Ratisbonne secured the place, however, notwithstanding the exhorbitant price, for his zeal was nobly supported by souls as generous as they were Christian. An edifice was erected in 1862, and the Daughters of Sion, a religious community founded by the good priest, took up their abode in Jerusalem. Since then the work has grown and prospered.

The *Ecce Homo* Chapel, situated in this convent, is one of the chief attractions of the Holy City. Divine service is celebrated there with heaven-inspired fervor. Who would not be moved to tears at the sight of a once obstinate Jew offering the Holy sacrifice for the conversion of his unhappy brethren! He prays that the Blood of Jesus may be upon the Jews and their children as a dew of mercy and salvation. *Rorate coeli desuper.*

What feeling must take possession of the heart in that chapel! Here the first scenes of the Passion took place; here it was that the Jews, struck with blindness, demanded the iniquitous sentence, and called down upon themselves and their children the curse of the Redeemer's blood. Here it was that Pontius Pilate, when presenting Jesus crowned with thorns to the populace, exclaimed *"Ecce Homo!"*

The explanation of Jewish perfidy is thus accomplished on the very spot of reprobation, and at the place of the anathema stands an altar of reconciliation. To hear Father Ratisbonne pronounce in the name of the Jewish nation the solemn act of amendment dictated by his own fervent heart must cause joy in the highest heaven. He is said to be so moved when reciting it that one would think he could never finish. The good religious also partake in his emotion, when, chanting three times, each time raising their voices a little, the words of our Savior on the cross: *"Pater, dimitte illis: nesciunt quid faciunt.* Father, forgive them: they know not what they do."

CHAPTER XIII

THE SYNAGOGUE IS CROWNED WITH THORNS

"Every tree is known by its fruit. For men do not gather figs from thorns; nor from a bramble bush do they gather grapes." (Lk. 6:44)

We have learned from St. Bernard, that our divine Lord was crowned with thorns by his cruel stepmother, the Jewish synagogue. *"Coronavit eum noverca sua corona spinea."* We should reflect that by its nature and form this crown spreads its prickly thorns in two opposite directions. Some of the thorns naturally diverge to the interior of the circle, and pierce the adorable head of our Lord. Others shoot forth exteriorly to punish and repel all his malicious enemies. Among the enemies of our Savior the Jewish synagogue has ever shown itself the deepest in malice and the most stubborn in obstinacy. We cannot then be surprised to see her entangled and tortured in the thorny bush of her own plantation and growth. *"For,* as St. Paul says, *what things a man shall sow, those also he shall reap."* (Gal. 6:8) Moreover we have heard the voice of eternal truth declaring that; *"Men do not gather figs from thorns, nor from a bramble bush they gather grapes. Every tree is known by its fruit.*

1. *Every tree is known by its fruit.* Religious prejudices are generally most deeply rooted in the human mind. The reason is because sentiments of religion have their origin from sources superior to human nature, and tend to a preternatural end. Real sentiments of the true religion are infused by God into the heart of man; and religious prejudices are inspired and fostered by the malice of the devil. Since his horrible fall Lucifer has never ceased from exciting and perpetuating religious hatred in the mind of his dupes whether fallen angels, or men. He caused the prevarication of our parents, Adam and Eve; and provoked religious dissensions among their immediate children,

which have been perpetuated ever since in human society. This has been the origin of all schisms, heresies and idolatry in the religious world.

We can never sufficiently deplore the antagonism existing between the different religious sects of modern times. A little cool and calm reflection would show that all this animosity proceeds from some diversity of opinion about a few religious dogmas of faith and in some instances, among the sects, this difference is confined to mere matters of ecclesiastical discipline, and to the form of church government. All these Christian denominations are, however, united in the fundamental tenets of the Christian religion. They believe in the dogma of revelation and in the divine inspiration of the Bible. They believe in the original fall of man, in the mystery of the Incarnation, in the mercy of our Savior's atonement, in the establishment of the Christian religion for the eternal salvation of mankind. In short, almost all Christian sects unite in reciting the general formula of Christian faith contained and expressed in the Apostle's Creed. Nevertheless, in spite of all these uniform points of contact, and strong ties of union, we are unhappily kept asunder by few points of difference in belief, or discipline.

This deplorable difference having formed a brazen wall of separation in the Christian Church for more than three hundred and fifty years, between Catholicism and Protestantism, and above a thousand years between our faith and the Greek and Russian schism, how can we Christians hope to find sentiments of religious sympathy in the mind and heart of the Jewish Synagogue, essentially and diametrically opposed to the very idea and nature of the Christian religion? ...Judaism and Christianity are incompatible in the aggregate of the religious idea. The Synagogue, in principle, at least, will ever be opposed to the Christian Church. The Jews expect the Messias to come in future with great power and glory to restore their lost material dominion upon earth. We Christians believe and are bound to believe that the Messias and universal Redeemer of Mankind came upon earth nineteen centuries ago in extreme poverty, deep humility, dying upon a cross in excessive sufferings. *"We preach Christ crucified, to the Jews a stumbling-block, and to the Gentiles foolishness. But to them that are called, both Jews and Greeks, Christ is the power of God and the wisdom of God."* (1 Cor. 1:23) But the proud spirit and the stubborn mind of the Jews will not believe this fact, and they prefer to await for him whom the Christian World fully and firmly believes to have come nearly two thousand years ago. We appeal in vain to the promises and prophecies which they are bound to know and to believe in the Old Testament. They refuse to listen to the account given in the New Testament of the manifold and stupendous prodigies that preceded the birth, accompanied the life, death, and glorious resurrection of our Divine Redeemer. St. Paul, after his miraculous conversion from Judaism, addressed a most magnificent epistle to the Hebrews in which he demonstrates, beyond the possibility of contradiction, the coming of the Messias, his death and resurrection, the imperfect nature of Judaism, its necessary abrogation, and the superior excellence of the Christian religion. But all in vain. The grand and stupendous fact of the Christian church, standing like a huge mountain before the nations of the earth, with more than four hundred millions of believers and worshipers, is by the self-conceited Jew treated as an insane delusion, and horrible idolatry. In his opinion we Christians are worse than anathematized Pagans, whilst he considers himself the genuine Israelite, and the only privileged worshiper of the God of Abraham, Isaac, and Jacob. He is unhappily under a fatal delusion; but so long as this criminal delusion continues in his mind, we cannot expect him to look favorably on Christianity. On the contrary he will in force of his own erroneous principles be sternly opposed to it, because the admission of the truth and reality of the Christian religion is the inevitable abrogation of Judaism.

2. There is another practical obstacle in the way of the conversion of the Jewish race. Their admission of the truth of Christianity necessarily demands their belief in the divinity of Jesus Christ and in all the mysteries of his incarnation, birth, life, passion, death and resurrection. They should have to acknowledge that their forefathers nineteen centuries ago impiously rejected the Messias, most bitterly persecuted him, had him scourged at a pillar like a slave, crowned him with thorns as the king of ignominy and sorrows, postponed him to Barabbas a murderer, demanded his crucifixion from Pilate, the Roman governor, mocked and blasphemed him during his agony upon the cross whereon He finally died ....

The Jews before their conversion should have to study and learn the history of Christianity and deplore the willful blindness of their predecessors in cruelly persecuting all the apostles and disciples of our Divine Lord, stoning St. Stephen to death and killing the holy apostle St. James. They should have to condemn the bitter spirit of hatred and persecution with which their race has ever been animated against Christians during nineteen centuries. Finally they should have to acknowledge their own errors, and bitterly deplore their former obstinacy in rejecting the Christian religion. All this requires a miracle of grace which must be obtained through deep humility and fervent prayer.

In order to prove that in what we have stated about the Jews as a body, we were not and are not animated by religious bigotry, we shall have to give some authentic historical facts.

3. *"Men do not gather figs from thorns,"* our Lord says. The illustrious Cardinal Baronius, no less eminent in piety and learning than in dignity, in his voluminous annals of the Church, has often occasion to reprobate the conduct of the Jews against Christians. They are taught in their synagogues by their rabbins, and at their domestic hearth by their parents to anathematize and curse Jesus Christ as an abominable idol. They are urged to commit this impiety every time they pass before a Christian church, or behold in any place his sacred image. The writer of these lines, has repeatedly heard the confirmation of this fact from a sincere and trusty convert from Judaism, from the tribe of Levi. He was taught to act in this manner from his childhood, and was urged to this practice by the words and example of his Jewish father who invariably uttered a curse when passing before a Catholic church, or before the image of our crucified Savior, spitting, when unobserved, contemptuously against them.

Not being satisfied with words of blasphemy they proceed to more horrible facts. Baronius relates that on many occasions the Jews were guilty of awful sacrileges against our divine Lord in the Sacrament of the Holy Eucharist. He states that in the city of Berytus, or Beiroot in Phencia, the Jews nailed to a cross a picture of our divine Savior from which flowed a prodigious quantity of blood. Very celebrated is the fact testified to by the great Patriarch of Alexandria, St. Athanasius before the fathers of the general council of Nicea which occurred about that time, when the Jews pierced with arrows a wooden figure of our crucified Lord, from which such a quantity of blood miraculously flowed that it was distributed to many Christian churches in different parts of the world. *"Fuit tanta sanguinis copia, ut ditaret omnes ecclesias."* (Baron. Ann. 787. No. 23)

We are far from approving any persecution against the Jews or indeed against any other class of men, merely for their private religious opinions when their conduct is not injurious to public morality, and does not disturb the peace of society. There is no doubt, however, that the Jews, when sufficiently strong, have in different countries and at various times often provoked the just indignation of God and man. Here we could now describe their present conduct in Europe, and more especially in the Austrian Empire, and in Italy, where they wield a powerful influence through their mammon of iniquity, and through the press. The public policy of Austria, through the connivance of anti-Catholic ministers, and infidel officials of the masonic stripe, is shaped to promote the material interests of wealthy Jews and in favor of their anti-Christian prejudices. In Italy and more especially in Rome with their proverbial ingratitude, these men are the most bitter and active foes of the Papacy by which their ancestors have ever been protected and favored. But for various reasons we perfer to allow history to speak in relation to former events.

4. After the death of the Emperor Constantine the great, and of his three sons, their unworthy relative Julian, an impious apostate from the Christian faith, was raised to the imperial throne. Reason and experience shows that apostasy from Christianity perverts the mind, corrupts and embitters the heart of man more thoroughly than any other public crime. Julian was endowed with many natural talents, and possessed remarkable qualities for government. But his scandalous apostasy and horrible sacrileges poisoned them in their very roots and withered all their branches. At the beginning of his exaltation to the imperial dignity by the unanimous voice, and strong, brave arm of his faithful Christian subjects, Julian hypocritically affected a show of moderation, and in words he declaimed any intention of interfereing with their religious and political rights. But as soon as he found himself firmly established on the throne, he with consummate malice sought by every foul and indirect means to undermine the faith, and sap the very foundations of the Christian religion. He revived, and with great zeal encouraged the exercise of pagan worship throughout his vast dominion. This ungrateful wretch dismissed from his military service those faithful and brave Christian officers who refused to follow the pernicious example of his apostasy. Julian excluded from the public schools all Christian professors who were very numerous and clever, substituting in their place pagan teachers. Free Christian schools were forbidden by him, and the children of Christian parents were by his impious and tyrannical laws obliged to receive their education from pagan or heretical masters. The most eminent Catholic patriarchs and bishops were banished from their sees and churches, and heretical Arian ministers thrust into them by military force, or by the brutal violence of mobs, encouraged and supported by his inperial satraps and minions in office.

107

In writing these lines towards the end of this nineteenth century, we scarcely know whether we copy the records of the fourth age of Christianity, or we chronicle the conduct of modern apostate governments in Europe and in many parts of America. The likeness between the two portraits is so very striking that the illusion is natural, and almost inevitable. The hypocritical impiety of Julian about religion and his wily and tyrannical policy against Catholic schools is very closely imitated by too many modern civil governments. The final end shall be like unto his. Some kings and emperors have already found out this truth by sad experience, which should serve as a timely warning to other potentates and governments that abuse their power in oppressing the conscience and by violating the sacred rights of their faithful Catholic subjects. But let us return to our main point.

One of the most malicious and diabolical designs of the apostate emperor, Julian, was to invent some means to frustrate the accomplishment of the prophecies made in different parts of the old testament, and more recently confirmed by our divine Lord in the gospel, about the utter destruction of the famous temple of Jerusalem.

The holy Prophet Daniel foretold this destruction, and its principal cause, in the following clear and explicit words. *"After sixty two weeks Christ shall be slain; and the people that deny·him, shall not be his. And a people with their leader,* (The Romans under Titus) *that shall come, shall destroy the city, and the sanctuary, and the end thereof shall be waste; and after the end of the war, the appointed desolation ...And there shall be in the temple the abomination of desolation; and desolation shall continue even to the consummation and to the end."* (Dan 9:26) Our divine Lord confirmed this prophecy, which he had originally inspired, in the most explicit and positive language, as three of four evangelists testify. St. Mathew says, *"Jesus, being come out of the temple . . . his disciples came to show him the buildings of the temple; and he said to them: Do you see all these things? Amen, I say to you there shall not be left here a stone upon a stone that shall not be thrown down."* (Mt. 24:1)

Julian then was determined to render void this remarkable prophecy, and thus attempt to deny the divinity of Jesus Christ. By this clever stroke of human wisdom, the apostate imperial philosopher presumed to expose the pretended imposture of Jesus of Nazareth, and consequently the falsity of the Christian religion. Had Julian succeeded in his cleverly conceived scheme it would, without doubt, have proved a severe blow against Christianity.

In the year 361, the apostate emperor assembled the principal and most influential persons among the Jews, and spoke to them with affected compassion for the political and religious condition of their people. He exhorted them to return to Palestine, rebuild their famous temple in Jerusalem, and reestablish their ancient public worship, promising them his generous concurrence towards carrying the work to a speedy completion. The Jews received the warrant with inexpressible joy, and were so elated at it, that flocking from all parts of the world to Jerusalem, they began in their unquenchable hatred against the Christians to scorn and insult them, killing several of them, burning and demolishing their churches, and threatening to exterminate them very soon with the cooperation of the empeor. This imperial monster gave orders to his royal treasurer to furnish money and everything necessary for the undertaking. He drew together the most able workmen from every part of the empire, and apointed as overseers persons of the highest rank placing at their head his intimate friend Alypius, who had been formerly prefect or governor in Britain (England.) The Jews of both sexes entered into the enterprise with wonderful enthusiasm. The Jewish women stripped themselves of their most costly ornaments of gold and jewels to contribute to the expense of the building. They helped to dig the ground and carried out the rubbish and and earth in their aprons and skirts of their gowns. All things were now ready to begin the building of the temple. Immense heaps of stones, bricks, timber, and other materials had been collected with enormous labor and expense. The old foundations of the temple were removed, thus unwittingly concurring to the literal and perfect accomplishment of the prophecy of our divine Lord, which they impiously presumed to belie and render illusory. They were doomed, however, to find out, at their own expense and deep humiliation, that *"There is no wisdom, there is no prudence, there is no counsel against the Lord."*

When these perfidious men began to dig the foundation for the intended new temple, and thousands of busy laborers were at work in it till very late at night, on returning to their work early on the following morning, they found that a miraculous earthquake during the night had thrown back into the trenches all the earth removed the previous day. Alypius, the imperial commissioner and the governor of the province, deeply disappointed and excited at these mysterious events, pressed and urged on the work, when, behold! horrible balls of fire issued out from the foundation, which scorched and blasted it.

The workmen fled away in terror and dismay. The work having been suspended, the miraculous fires ceased. But as soon as the Jews attempted to renew their labors the flames burst forth more fierce than ever. They leaped over the immense heaps of timber, and wood of every discription accumulated in the immediate vicinity and produced an awful conflagration. The heat of the fire was so intense as to split the largest stones, melting all the iron, destroying the thousands of spades, picks, axes and all the implements used in the work. A terrible whirlwind scattered the burning cinders in every direction; the lime and sand prepared in immense heaps were blown out of sight and heavy loose materials were by an invisible power miraculously dispersed and carried away. Frightful crashes of thunder and blinding flashes of lightning terrified all the Jews and Pgans, whilst they wonderfully confirmed the faith, and roused the hope of Christians. These two opposite effects became more thrilling when miraculous crosses appeared perfectly well formed on the clothes of the perfidious Jews and obstinate pagans who lingered about the place of the intended building in the vain hope of being soon able to resume their impious undertakings. These miraculous crosses were so admirably executed, as to exceed in art and elegance any painting or embroidery ever seen by human eyes. In vain did these obstinate Jews attempt to wash them off from their clothes, the more they strove to remove from them the sign of salvation, the more clear it became, and moreover, when they changed one suit of clothes to wash the other, the miraculous crosses were formed on both.

On the same evening there appeared over Jerusalem a luminous cross as large as that seen by Constantine and by his entire army over the city of Rome, shining very brightly and accompanied by a halo or circle of light, like a most beautiful rainbow, the hopeful emblem of approaching peace and calm for the faithful persecuted Christians. More prodigies occurred on this memorable occasion which have been recorded by numerous and trusty Christian, Jewish and Pagan writers. We conclude with St. Gregory Nazianzen, "what could be more proper than to close this tremendous scene, or to celebrate this decisive Christian victory over Jewish perfidy, and Pagan impiety, than the miraculous apparition of the cross triumphant, encircled with the heroic symbol, and with the glorious crown of conquest." (St. Greg. Naz. Orat. 4, 8, 9) Thus the Jews and their impious protectors and abettors were severely punished by God in their wicked attempts against the Christian religion. We have however some other facts to relate.

4. *"From a bramble bush we do not gather grapes."* Cardinal Baronius states that about the year 982, a frightful plague was desolating the eastern parts of Europe and Asia Minor. The inhabitants of the ancient city of Sparta in their dire affliction, being destitute of human help, had recourse to prayer and implored the assistance of Heaven. They also sent a delegation, to a very holy hermit, called Nicon, requesting him to visit their desolate city. He very kindly received the messengers and promised to grant their petition, and obtain the discontinuance of the pestilence, if they promised to banish from their city the Jews who contaminated their practices and by their religious rites. The delegates acknowledged their error, promised to comply with the direction of the servant of God, and the plague ceased immediately after the expulsion of the Jews from their city and territory.

Benedict Fernandez in his commentaries on the thirty-fifth chapter of Genesis, relates, that our divine Lord appeared to Simon Gomey, a person of eminent sanctity and doctrine. In this vision the servant of God saw our blessed Savior horribly scourged at the pillar, and crowned with thorns. Our Lord said to him, "In the kingdom of Portugal the king, princes, and principal persons, exalt, honor and enrich those who have so cruelly scourged and deeply dishonored me. Who could dare to harbor, feed and cherish in his house, a traitor who had most severely beaten and wounded his king with a heavy stick, and who obstinately refused to acknowledge his royal dignity and authority? Who could be so perverse and disloyal as to gild all over the bloody stick with which the king was barbarously struck and mortally wounded? Surely this man should be severely punished, and his house should be razed to the ground. Now this is the way in which my enemies are honored, exalted and enriched in Portugal. It is on this account that I am forced to punish the king and the kingdom;" The prophetic vision was soon realized. The Portuguese army was completely routed in Africa by the Moors, King Sebastian was killed, the kingdom was reduced to the brink of ruin and desolation. All these chastisements were inflicted by God upon the kingdom of Portugal, because the Jews were favored and honored in it. *"Omnes in Lusitania judaicae nationis homines honorati et florentes viverent."* (Paciuchellus De Pass. D.N.Lib. 3. Discuss. 6)

We are not preaching a crusade; neither do we wish to foment any persecution against the Jews: but we relate historical facts, which show that God has punished, and continues to punish, the malicious perfidy of these people, in rejecting their Messias and persecuting him even unto the death of

111

the cross. We believe that among the Jews, there are many well disposed individuals; their obstinacy in error, however, and the nature of their religious belief, make them the natural enemies of Christianity. Moreover, as they perceive that the very essence and life of genuine Christianity, is found only in the catholic Church, so by logical instinct, they, as a class, hate deeply our holy religion. If they do not openly persecute, they are found, however, always ranked on the side of our enemies. From their forefathers they have learned to employ three weapons against us which they used with fatal success against our divine Lord and master; namely, hypocrisy, calumny and money. Our Lord often reproached them for their hypocrisy; their calumnies against him are well known; surely they bribed with money Judas who betrayed him; and the soldiers who witnessed his glorious resurrection. The same means are used by their successors at the present time. The modern Jews not only refuse with characteristic obstinacy to believe in their crucified Messias; but in the different Christian countries as in Italy, Austria, Germany, France, they are most active and bitter foes of the Catholic Church. It is not sufficiently observed that almost every influential Jew is a member of the worst secret societies in existence of which they are the soul and life. The Jews at least in Europe have the monopoly of the telegraph, of the press and of financial transactions. Through the telegraph and press they spread calumnies against the Church, Pope and against his most faithful ministers, friends, and supporters. They maliciously suppress from public knowledge whatever may be favorable to the Catholic religion. Through their financial power, they bribe governments, and hire Judases against Jesus Christ and his Holy Faith. As their forefathers, by their hypocritical intrigues and seditious clamors, forced the Roman Governor, Pilate, to confirm and execute their sentence of death against our blessed Lord, so the more powerful and influential Jews, of the present day, stimulate and urge *modern Pilates,* in civil power, to oppress and persecute his Vicar in Rome, and all faithful Catholics. These are known facts that cannot be contradicted. We Catholics, however, who suffer through their malice will strive to imitate the meekness and charity of our crucified Savior; we will excuse their ignorance and pray to God for their conversion, *"Father forgive them, for they know not what they do."* May these modern Sauls become Pauls. May the Immaculate Mother of our blessed Redeemer, multiply the miracles of grace, for the speedy conversion of the Jews; as she mercifully did in Rome with the youthful Ratisbonne. Amen.

CHAPTER XIV

PILATE AND THE CROWN OF THORNS

"Pilate saith to him; Speakest thou not to me? Knowest not that I have power to crucify thee, and have power to release thee?" (Jn.19:10)

During his Passion, our divine Lord had to endure three different kinds of sufferings, namely, anguish in his mind, torture in his body, humiliations in his soul. The first was most severe in the garden of Gethsemani, where he was sorrowful even unto death; the second was on the cross; the third in the city of Jerusalem. In all these three stages of his Passion, our suffering Savior gave us the brightest examples of virtue, and the soundest lessons of wisdom.

In the garden of Gethsemani, he was perfectly resigned to the adorable will of his Heavenly Father, and taught us how to pray. On the cross, he was patient and full of charity. In his profound humiliations in the city of Jerusalem, our divine Lord and Master was the most perfect model of meekness and the teacher of wisest maxims to every class of persons; but especially to those in high dignity. The High Priest Annas, the supreme Pontiff Caiphas, King Herod, Pontius Pilate the Roman Governor, received important lessons from his examples, words and silence. This last was perhaps the most instructive of all. There is often great power in silence, especially before personages in high dignity, when our life is dependent on their will. Such is now the condition of our Lord, before the Roman Governor, which we will examine in this chapter.

1. *"Pilate saith to him: Speakest thou not to me?"* We have already remarked, and shall have again to observe, that the Roman Governor, Pontius Pilate possessed, many good natural qualities. He was a shrewd and intelligent judge of human character. To a great extent he understood the dispositions of the Jewish people, and of their civil and ecclesiastical leaders.

Pilate very soon perceived that in their bitter persecution against our dear Lord, these men were animated by the passion of envy and hatred. He promptly discovered the innocence of out Savior. Several times he boldly proclaimed it before the assembled multitude. Pilate was evidently anxious, to save the life of our persecuted Lord, in short, he was naturally well disposed towards truth and justice. In his heart, however, were concealed two dangerous obstructions, namely, the rock of ambition, and the sand-bank of pusillanimity, whereon, during the present storm, he drifted and was miserably shipwrecked.

2. To all persons in dignity and power, the Holy Ghost says: *"The greater thou art the more humble thyself in all things and thou shalt find grace before God, for great is the power of God alone, and he is honored by the humble."* (Eccli. 3:20) Pilate was ambitious, and coveted dignities and power. On this occasion in his behavior towards our blessed Lord, the Roman Governor showed himself proud of his authority. Having heard from the chief priests, and Jewish magistrates, that our Lord *ought to die; because he made himself the son of God;* he abruptly left the balcony, and re-entering the hall of his palace; hastily interrogated our Savior, saying: *Whence art thou?*...Our dear Master wishing to teach Pilate, and all earthly magistrates, whatever their dignity might be, that justice should be done to every man, whatever his origin and condition is, gave no answer to his inopportune question. By this silence our Lord intended also to teach the Roman Governor, and all civil magistrates, that the knowledge of and judgment of theological matters and theological facts, belongs by right, to a higher and more competent ecclesiastical tribunal. This unexpected silence of our divine Lord gave offense to Pilate, who with an air of haughty indignation; sharply said to him: *"Speakest thou not to me?...knowest thou not that I have power to crucify thee, and I have power to release thee?"*

These words evidently manifest the high opinion that Pontius Pilate had of himself, and of his dignity. He believed himself a very great and superior being, to whom even a person, like our Lord, who claimed divine prerogatives and rights, should show deference, and pay homage....Moreover, the Roman Governor in these words expressed notions and ideas about human power and authority, which are radically wrong and pernicious. He spoke as if he were to exercise his magisterial power, in favor of, or against any of his subjects, independent of their personal merit, or demerit, just as he could distribute his personal gifts to favorites refusing them to any person he disliked. He seemed to believe that the authority and power given him was not intended for the common good of his subjects; but to promote and secure his own personal honor and profit. Pilate spoke to our divine Redeemer as if he were absolutely free to use his supreme power of life and death as arbitrarily as he pleased: *"Knowest thou not, that I have power to crucify thee, and I have power to release thee?* As if he meant to say: Know, Jesus of Nazareth, that I have power of life and death, I can save thy life from the hands of thine enemies, and I can condemn thee to the death of the cross, whether thou be guilty or innocent. My sentence will be favorable and thou shalt be acquitted if thou be respectful to me; otherwise I shall condemn thee to the death of the cross. Take care then to be more obsequious and respectful to me, and promptly answer all my questions."

These proud and presumptuous words, subversive of the true idea and real nature of authority and of legitimate power, afforded a favorable opportunity to our divine Master for confuting and correcting a most erroneous and pernicious maxim, too commonly admitted, and too often acted upon by many of the potentates of the earth .... In their foolish pride, and arrogant presumption, they attribute power to themselves independently of God, refusing to recognize him as the first orgin and source of all human authority. This impious notion has been the main cause of the worst despotisms, and most cruel oppressions, that have afflicted human society. The history of the world, and the annals of Christianity, demonstrate this truth by innumerable facts. Hence our divine Master, and supreme Lord of heaven and earth, of angels and men, seized this opportunity given Him by the words of the Roman Governor, Pilate, to teach a most essential lesson of jurisprudence to all persons in power and dignity. Standing before the representative of the greatest power upon earth, with a Crown of Thorns upon his adorable head, with a purple garment upon his bleeding shoulders, and holding in his manacled hands a reed as his sceptre, our divine Lord and Master in a calm, solemn and dignified manner, said to him; *"Thou shouldst not have any power against me, except it were given thee from above."* Know, Pilate that *"there is no power but from God."* (Rom. 13:2) *"Give not thy mouth to cause thy flesh to sin, and say not before the angel: there is no Providence; Lest God be angry at thy words and destroy all the works of thy hand...For he that is high hath another higher, and there are others still higher than these. Moreover there is the King that reigneth over all the land subject to him."* (Eccles. 5:5) But above governor, presidents, kings and emperors there is the most high and omnipotent God who is above all and who will one day summon to the bar of his dread tribunal all persons in power to give a strict account to him of their administration of law and justice among his people. Know, Pilate, that by condemning me to the death of the cross thou wilt become guilty of an enormous abuse of thy delegated power. There is not, and there cannot be any human power against me, because I am the incarnate Son of the living God. I am eternal love, truth and holiness as I am essential justice. Did I wish it, I could in an instant withdraw myself from the reach of every human and created power. But I came upon earth, and became man to redeem and save mankind from eternal misery, through my voluntary humiliations, sufferings and death. I wish to suffer, and to die in obedience to my eternal Father. My passion and death will redound to his greatest glory, and to my personal honor during an endless eternity. My temporary suffering and death, will be the salvation of mankind. ...Woe, however, to those, who abuse against me their delegated authority and power. This disorder O Pilate, shall speedily be punished in thee by the loss of thy dignity, by exile, and by death. But the crime of the chief priests, and Jewish magistrates, who have delivered me to thee; without any cause on my side, and so obstinately insist on urging thee to condemn me, innocent as I am, to the death of the cross, is by far more heinous; so their punishment shall be the more severe. Take notice Pilate, and remember well my words: *"Thou shouldst not have any power against me, except it were given thee from above. Therefore, he that hath delivered me to thee, hath the greater sin."* (Jn. 19:11)

3. Our divine Master in these words, gave some very important lessons to the Roman Governor, and to all persons in authority. He teaches them very plainly, that all authority, and power must come from God. *"For there is no power but from God."* This fundamental principle is numberless times repeated in the sacred Scripture, in order that no person in authority, believing in revelation, may be ignorant of its import. A few extracts will be useful on this occasion. They are principally selected from acknowledgements made by personages in high authority.

"The Lord is terrible and exceeding great, and his power is admirable. Glorify the Lord as much as ever you can; for he will yet far exceed, and his magnificence is wonderful." (Eccli. 43:31) The pious and zealous King Josaphat glorified God when, *standing in the midst of the assembly of Juda and Jerusalem, in the house of the Lord, said: O Lord God of our*

fathers, thou art God in Heaven, and rulest over all the kingdoms and nations. In thy hand is strength and power; and no one can resist thee." (2 Paralip. 19:6) Holy King David, a short time before his happy death, repeated in substance the praises of God which he had so often sung in his psalms during his holy life. *"David the King, rejoiced also with great joy and he blessed the Lord before all the multitude and said: Blessed art Thou O Lord, the God of Israel, our Father from eternity to eternity. Thine, O Lord, is the magnificence, and power, and glory and victory and to thee is praise. For all that is in heaven and earth, is Thine. Thine is the kingdom, O Lord, and thou art above all princes. Thine are riches and thine is glory; thou hast dominion over all. In thy hand is power and might; in thy hand greatness and the empire of all things. Now therefore, our God, we give thee thanks and we praise thy name."* (1 Paralip. 29) We shall close these sublime extracts with the royal proclamation made by one of the most powerful pagan monarchs of antiquity. *"Then King Darius wrote to all the people, tribes and languages dwelling in the whole earth: Peace be multiplied to you.*

It is decreed by me that in all my empire and my kingdom all men dread and fear the God of Daniel. For he is the living and eternal God forever; and his kingdom shall not be destroyed, and his power shall be everlasting. He is the deliverer and Savior, doing signs and wonders in heaven and on earth; Who hath delivered Daniel out of the Lion's den." (Dan. 6:25)

Those who see and feel the pressing need that in this degenerated age of pride and selfishness we have of these fundamental principles on the origin of power and on the nature of human government, will not disapprove of these rather long quotations from the Bible. We leave to more learned and more competent authors the fuller developments of these great principles. We firmly believe that their ignorance or perversion by persons in authority and power has reduced modern society to the verge of inevitable ruin. When the supreme authority of God is discarded by men in human legislation and government; then no respect for civil authority, no obedience to human law, can be logically claimed, or lawfully enforced. Without the support of God no authority can stand. Power contrary to God's will is tyranny. Law without God's sanction has no validity. *"Counsel and equity is mine,* eternal Wisdom says: *Prudence is mine, strength is mine. By me kings reign and law-givers decree justice."* (Prov. 8:14)

117

Human society must speedily return to those fundamental principles, or it is doomed soon to perish in anarchy, blood and fire ...He will be recognized, praised, and honored as a wise teacher and great benefactor of mankind who has the ability, zeal and courage to announce and propagate these divine doctrines to the nations of the earth. The most holy and zealous of earthly Kings is in search of such apostles of order; *"Who shall declare,* holy David asks: *Who shall declare the powers of the Lord? who shall set forth his praises? Blessed are they that keep judgment and do justice."* (Ps. 105:2)

Our divine Master desires to have these maxims announced to the world: *"All power, he says, all power is given to me in heaven and upon earth. Go ye therefore and teach all nations ...teaching them to observe all things whatsoever I have commanded you and behold I am with you all days, even to the consummation of the world."* (Mt. 28:18.)

When all Christian nations shall understand and appreciate the grand maxim that all authority and power emanate from God through Jesus Christ, and that they are communicated to superiors for the general welfare of society, then we shall be blessed with wise and just magistrates, and with respectful, obedient and happy subjects. This is what our divine Lord taught the Roman Governor with those significant words: *"Thou shouldst not have any power against me, except it were given thee from above."* Our blessed Savior was fully aware that Pilate was very anxious to keep his high position in the Roman Empire as Governor of Judea, and that for this end he was courting the favor and approbation of the chief priests, Jewish magistrates and people. Hence he plainly told Pilate that authority and power emanated from above and not from below and consequently that he should study and strive to deserve the approbation and favor of God by his upright conduct, and strict administration of justice, if he wished to be protected by his divine Omnipotence, and be raised by his divine Majesty to higher honors and to everlasting glory. For justice exalts superiors, as humility exalts individuals. *"The greater thou art humble thyself the more in all things, and thou shalt find grace before God. For great is the power of God alone, and he is honored by the humble."* But Pilate in his pride, considered himself wiser than our divine Lord, the incarnate wisdom of God, and relied for support more on the favorable dispositions of the Jews, than on the approbation and protection of the Almighty. He shall soon have to deplore his fatal mistake. From the rock of his pride and ambition Pilate was stranded on the sandbank of his pusillanimity upon which he was finally wrecked.

4. *"Seek not to be made a judge unless thou hast strength enough to extirpate iniquities; lest thou fear the person of the powerful and lay a stumbling block to thy integrity."* (Eccli. 7:6) A firm determination to administer justice to every person without fear or favor is an essential duty of all superiors. Civil magistrates are elected for the general good of the people; they are armed and protected in the exercise of their important office with the whole strength of executive power; hence, they should be strict and firm in administering justice to all. They should in a special manner defend the weak and protect innocence and virtue. A true magistrate worthy of his name, and position, should be superior to the influence or dread of faction, and above the suspicion of bribery. Civil magistrates are upon earth the representatives of the God of justice, who is no acceptor of persons, and who will most certainly and very soon summon them to appear at the bar of his dreaded tribunal, against which there is no possibility of appeal...

"Hear ye kings and understand. Learn ye that are the judges of the ends of the earth. Give ear you that rule the people and please yourselves in multitudes of nations. For power is given you by the Lord, and strength by the most High who will examine your works and search out your thoughts; because being ministers of his kingdom you have not judged rightly, nor kept the law of justice, nor walked according to the will of God. Horribly and speedily will he appear to you. For a most severe judgment shall be for them that bear rule. To him that is little, mercy is granted, but the mighty shall be mightily tormented. Because God will not accept any man's person, neither will he stand in awe of any man's greatness. For he made the little and the great and he has equally care of all. But a greater punishment is ready for the more mighty." (Wis. 6)

From these sublime doctrines of divine revelation and legislation, written for our instruction at the command of God by the wisest of inspired monarchs, we ought to learn how serious is the responsibility of all judges, and civil magistrates of every degree, from the lowest to the highest, in relation to the respective duties of their office and dignity. From these divine words we hear how strict shall be the account demanded of them by the sovereign Lord of the Universe, and Universal Judge of mankind; and lastly, we hear how terribly severe shall be the punishment inflicted by an offended God on the unfaithful *ministers of his kingdom, who have not judged rightly, and have not kept the laws of justice.* Justice being equality to all, the violation of this fundamental virtue by persons in authority to the injury of the least and last of men, must be rigorously punished by God, who is just and whose judgment is right. *"Justus es Domine et rectum judicium tuum."* Because *God will not accept any man's person, neither will he stand in awe of any man's greatness: For he made the little and the great, and he has equally care of all. "Et nunc reges intelligite; erudimini qui judicatis terram, servite Domino in timore."* And now, O ye kings, understand; receive instruction you that judge the earth. Serve ye the Lord with fear. (Ps. 2:10)

If, however, the God of eternal justice will punish with rigorous severity the injury done by unjust judges and by corrupt and cowardly magistrates to the least of mankind; what punishment shall be inflicted upon those iniquitous judges and magistrates, who not only refused to do justice to his most holy Son, but who condemned him to be scourged at the pillar like the vilest of criminal slaves, who permitted him to be crowned with thorns, and who at last condemned him to the infamous death of the cross? Having considered the punishments inflicted on the chief priests and Jewish magistrates, we must now give our attention more immediately to the Roman Governor, Pilate.

At the beginning of our Lord's Passion, Pilate was well disposed in his favor. He discovered his eminent wisdom and virtue; proclaimed his innocence and pleaded with the chief priests and Jewish magistrates for his acquittal .... But gradually yielding to the solicitations and threats of the Jews, the Roman governor allowed our dear Lord to be scourged at the pillar, to be crowned with thorns, mocked, derided, outraged, and finally condemned him to die the cruel and infamous death of the cross .... He who has the sad misfortune of yielding to the first assault of temptation must, through his fall, become weaker. From one sin he will rapidly pass to a greater one. The habit of vice shall soon be formed, which will drag the unhappy soul to the abyss of misery and to final impenitence .... The Roman governor, Pilate, was weak and vacillating through false motives of human policy. Being anxious to preserve his dignity in Jerusalem as governor of Judea, he studied to conciliate the favor of the chief priests and Jewish leaders. He feared to offend the Jews by protecting our innocent Savior, and somewhat dreaded the indignation of God if he condemned him to death. Pilate had just been entreated by his wife to do no injury to our Savior, because he was a just and holy man, as had been miraculously

120

shown to her in a vision, in which she experienced that morning great uneasiness of mind, fearing some dreadful punishment for her husband, if he had the weakness to yield to the clamor and threats of the Jewish people. Bewildered and confused, knowing not what to do, when Pilate heard the chief priests and Jewish officers insisting upon the crucifixion of our Lord, he with an expression of disgust and indignation, said to them: *"Take him you and crucify him, for I find no cause in him."* The weak and vacillating policy of the Roman Governor, made these wicked men, bolder, and more arrogant in their demands. In a threatening attitude of defiance they replied to him. *"We have a law, and according to the law, he ought to die; because he made himself the Son of God."* These words made a deep impression upon his mind; but his vacillation increased with his timidity. Pilate abruptly left the balcony, re-entered the hall, and with evident marks of uneasiness, asked our Lord; *"Whence art thou?"* Our divine Master wishing to teach the Roman Governor and all earthly magistrates, that justice is equality to all men and that their origin, or the accidental place of their birth or condition, cannot change the essence of this fundamental virtue, gave him no answer, but kept a profound and dignified silence. This mysterious and eloquent silence of our Lord displeased Pilate, who, with an air of disappointed pride, said with a haughty tone of voice: *Speakest thou not to me? . . . Knowest thou not that I have power to crucify thee, and I have power to release thee? . . . * What depth of pride and injustice do these words betray? . . . Speakest thou not to me? Hast thou, O Jesus of Nazareth, no regard for my dignity of Roman Governor? Hast thou no dread of my authority and power? Knowest thou not that I, Pontius Pilate, have power to crucify thee, and I have power to release thee? Oh! Pilate! Pilate you know not to whom you speak. You know not, and are unable and unworthy to understand the dignity, power, wisdom and holiness of Jesus of Nazareth, standing as a reputed criminal before your civil tribunal. But as a Roman Governor, you should know, that no innocent person can without a tyrannical abuse of power, and without a glaring injustice, be condemned as a criminal to the death of the cross .... You have publicly proclaimed the innocence of Jesus, the persecuted victim of Jewish hatred and malice; how can you dare now to attempt to overawe him with all the weight of your dignity and power?... If Jesus be innocent you are bound in strict justice to release him. You officially proclaim his innocence and yet you threaten him with crucifixion. *"Knowest thou not that I have power to crucify thee and I have power to* *release thee?"* Pilate! These words are your condemnation. They prove and demonstrate that in condemning Jesus of Nazareth to death, you were not animated by the love of justice, but by ambition of political power. Pride and ambition, oppression and injustice are always, however, severely punished by God. Take the wise and opportune advice of your pious wife Pilate, and have nothing to do with this just than. Protect his innocence, and use all your power as the representative of the great Roman Empire, to save his life.

Pilate is hesitating. The astute leaders of the Jewish people perceive their advantage, and promptly avail themselves of the opportunity. As soon as he attempted to speak in favor of our Lord, they began to shout and cry aloud: *"If thou release this man, thou art not the friend of Caesar. For, whosoever maketh himself a king, speaketh against Caesar."* Political charges of disloyalty to the state are always the last refuge of malicious persecutors against innocent persons. This plea is ever successful with anti-religious politicians. The state with them is above every right of religion and of justice. Power is their supreme law; might, their standard of right; wealth, the idol of their worship. Innocence, virtue and justice must be immolated on the political altar to the friendship and favor of Caesar. Hence, not to lose the friendship of the Roman Emperor, Pilate condemned our divine Lord to the death of the cross. What a sentence! what horrible perversion of judgment and justice! Innocence, virtue, religion and God are sacrificed to ambition for political dignity and power. But God Almighty is stronger than men, and in their impious and insane conflict with Him, they are invariably defeated.

Like too many earthly potentates, Pilate directed all his political sagacity and power to the perpetuation of his authority. The means he justified by the end of his ambition. He condemned to the death of the cross our innocent and most holy Lord, as a clever stroke of state policy, because he thereby expected to secure the good will of the chief priests and Jewish magistrates, and the approbation of Caesar. *"But there is no wisdom, there is no prudence, there is no counsel against the Lord."* (Prov. 21:26)

Pilate soon found out his terrible mistake. A short time after our Savior's resurrection, and ascension into heaven, this Roman Governor disagreed with the Jewish leaders, who turned against him with their proverbial malignity and black ingratitude; they accused him before the Roman Emperor as guilty of malversation in office, and of high treason against his imperial Majesty. He was immediately recalled to Rome, deposed from his cherished dignity, and sent into exile to France, where, in disgrace and infamy, Pilate died, broken-hearted. Behold the folly of political wisdom! Behold the swift punishment of pride, ambition, and iniquity! The Roman Governor lost his coveted dignity and power through the perverse means employed by him to preserve his authority. With some of the Fathers of the Church, we confidently trust that the punishment of Pilate, as we shall see in a subsequent chapter, was only temporary, it was, however, prompt and severe. When shall the potentates of the earth learn true wisdom from this terrible example.

"Et nunc reges intelligite; erudimini qui judicatis terram."

CHAPTER XV

RESPECT FOR THE CROWN OF AUTHORITY
BY OUR LORD

"Thou shouldst not have any power against me; unless it were given thee from above." (Jn 19:11)

The words and actions of the Roman Governor, Pilate, have afforded an opportunity, for studying the origin and nature of authority. From the doctrine and example of our divine Master, we should learn our duties towards all our legitimate superiors. In the foregoing chapter, having had occasion to make some general reflections, about the obligations of persons in dignity, now'justice demands, that we should also make some few remarks about the principal duties of Christian subjects, towards their respective superiors.

Superiors, though powerful for good, or for evil, are comparatively few in number; whilst, the vast majority of mankind, has ever been, and ever shall be, in a condition of subjection to authority. Many persons are occasionally raised to some temporary dignity or office; but they have to live in subordinate position for the rest of their life. Moreover, even those who actually occupy places of dignity and power have higher superiors above them, to whom they pay homage and obedience. *"For,"* as the wise man says, *"he that is high hath another higher; and there are others still higher than those. Moreover, there is the king that reigneth over all the land subject to him."* (Eccles. 5:8)

Finally, above all earthly dignities and powers, above magistrates, governors, presidents, kings, emperors, autocrats, there is the supreme sovereign of heaven and earth, the Most High and Omnipotent God, the real source and center of all dignity and power, before whom every knee must bow in heaven, on earth, and in hell. We must therefore make some remarks on the duty of respect and obedience, which the vast majority of mankind owe to superiors .... Jesus Christ crowned with thorns will be our Master and Model.

FIRST SECTION

RESPECT OF JESUS FOR THE AUTHORITY OF HIS HEAVENLY FATHER

The great Apostle Paul says: *"Let every soul be subject to higher power; For there is no power, but from God, and those that are, are ordained of God."* (Rom 13:1) All those who understand well this sublime maxim of order and subordination become the most pious souls towards God, and the most humble and docile subjects towards their respective superiors.

Our divine Savior knew this principle in speculation, and practised it with greater perfection, than any other person has ever done upon earth. The first and principal object of his incarnation was to make known to the world the power and dignity of his Heavenly Father; and to lead men by his example and doctrines, to honor his divine Majesty, and to obey his commands. Coming into the world, Jesus said: *"Sacrifice and oblation Thou, O Father, wouldst not; but a body Thou hast fitted to me. Holocausts for sin did not please Thee, then I said: Behold I come to do Thy will O God."* (Heb. 10:17) During his whole life upon earth, our divine Savior kept constantly in view, the honor and homage due to his heavenly Father, and in all his actions, he studied and strove to accomplish his adorable will. This was the real meaning of the words which, at the age of twelve, he addressed to his holy Mother in the temple of Jerusalem, in the presence of the learned doctors of the law, and which these men were unable to understand: *"Did you not know that I must be about the things that are my Father's."* (Lk. 2:40) The will of his heavenly Father was the element and food of his life upon earth. *"My food is to do the will of him who sent me, that I may perfect this world."* (Jn. 4:34) He solemnly protested that he would not move a hand, or foot, or utter a single word, except in conformity with the will of his Father, and to promote his honor and glory. *"I can do nothing of myself...because I seek not my own will, but the will of him that sent me."* (Jn. 5:30) As the will of God was the food of our Savior's life; so He made it the chalice of his passion, the drink of his agony, and his Viaticum in death. In his mortal agony in the garden of Gethsemani, he said: *"The chalice which my Father hath given me, shall I not drink it."* (Jn. 18:2) *"Father not my will, but thine be done."* (Lk. 22:42) Finally, we learn that our divine Lord and Master sacrificed his life upon a cross, to do homage to his Father's supreme dignity; and in perfect obedience to his adorable will. *"Jesus,* St. Paul says, *Jesus was obedient even unto death of the Cross."* (Philip 2:8) Behold here a most perfect model of piety and devotion towards God.

SECOND SECTION

RESPECT OF JESUS FOR THE DIGNITY OF HIS MOTHER

Our parents, in the order of nature, are next to the Godhead, from whom all paternity in heaven and on earth is derived. (Ephes. 3:15) Parents being the fountain-head of human society, are the first visible and living representatives of God-Creator upon earth; they are the first created source of dignity and power among men. The Eternal Son of God, wishing to become *the Son of man,* selected for himself a mother upon earth. We may be sure that he will honor her. It was in respect for her dignity, that he chose her from the noblest royal dynasty that has ever exalted and illustrated human nature.

He wrought, in her honor, the most surprising prodigies. More wonderful than the miraculous opening of the Red Sea or the suspended course of the river Jordan, this divine Son, in regard for the future dignity of his chosen mother, opened for her the tide of life; and rolled back the muddy wave of original sin. She came forth all fair, and in perfect holiness, whence all the children of men are defiled, and born in sin, "How beautiful art thou, my love, how beautiful ... thou art all fair, O my love, and there is no spot in thee." (Cantic. 4) He enriched her pure soul with his choicest gifts, and replenished her immaculate heart with all the graces of his filial love. From the first instant of her miraculous conception, Mary became the dearest object upon earth of the adorable Trinity, and each of the three divine Persons vied with the other in the manifestations of their affection. The highest Archangel proclaims her praises, and salutes her with words never heard before by human ears. In admiration of the sublime dignity of the Mother of God, to which

126

this humble Virgin of Nazareth is now going to be raised, the Archangel in the most respectful manner says to her: *"Hail, full of grace, the Lord is with thee, blessed art thou among women .... thou hast found grace with God, because he desires to become thy Son ... Behold thou shalt conceive in thy womb, and shalt bring forth the incarnate God as thy true Son, and thou shalt call his name Jesus. He shall be great, and shall be called the Son of the most high and the Lord God shall give unto him the throne of David, his Father, and he shall reign in the house of Jacob forever, and of his kingdom there shall be no end ... The Holy Ghost shall come upon thee, and the power of the most High shall overshadow thee. And therefore, also the Holy One that shall be born in thee shall be called the son of God ... And Mary said: Behold the handmaid of the Lord; be it done to me according to thy word."* (Lk. 1:28) Thus, the humble handmaid was honored before angels and men, with the highest dignity possible for any creature upon earth, or in heaven. More happy than St. Paul, Mary, on this glorious occasion, is elevated to the clear contemplation, and the ravishing enjoyment of the beatific vision of the Divinity.

While the angelic intelligences admire in heaven the sublimity of this truly divine dignity of Mother of God, Saint Elizabeth praises and honors it upon Earth. Being visited at her house in Judea, by her most holy cousin, soon after she had been raised to the dignity of her divine maternity, Elizabeth was filled with the Holy Ghost, and her infant leaped in her womb, through supernatural joy, and she cried out with a loud voice, and said *"Blessed art thou, O Mary, among women and blessed is the fruit of thy womb. And whence is this to me, that the mother of my Lord should come to me? ... For behold, as soon as the voice of thy salutation sounded in my ears, the infant in my womb leaped for joy. And blessed art thou that hast believed, because those things shall be accomplished that were spoken to thee by the Lord. And Mary said: My soul doth magnify the Lord, and my spirit hath rejoiced in God my Savior. Because he hath regarded the humility of his handmaid: For, behold, from henceforth all generations shall call me blessed."* (Lk. 1)

This prophecy has been verified ever since. Her divine Son, who inwardly inspired these words, began to realize them at his birth. Being lovingly clasped in the arms of his mother, and sweetly nestling upon her virginal bosom, the incarnate Son of God brought legions of angels from heaven to sing his praises, and to honor her, from whom he was made the Son of man. He called the poor and the rich, the low and the great, shepherds and kings, Jews and Gentiles to the grotto of Bethlehem to adore his Incarnate Divinity, and to venerate his immaculate Mother. It is his will that all generations should call her blessed. Thanks to Jesus' filial piety this august Mother is praised, honored and venerated in the Catholic Church in every part of the world. Hence these humble pages could not remain silent.

As this most dutiful son *"advanced in age, wisdom and grace before God, and before men,"* so he gave new proofs of affectionate respect for his worthy Mother. To screen her from the very shadow of unjust suspicion, he had most wisely provided her with a most holy, most noble and affectionate husband. Joseph was the protector of her virginal purity, and the greatest admirer of her extraordinary sanctity. He was the faithful companion of her travels, and the most careful provider in all her wants. Our Lord, to perfect and reward their virtue, and to honor their dignity, but more especially that of his virginal Mother, passed thirty years of his human life in their happy company; and spent only three in his public ministry, for the rest of mankind. His uniform conduct, during the thirty years of his private life, is described in few words, by the inspired Chronicler of his infancy and childhood. *"He went down with them, and came to Nazareth, and was subject to them."* (Lk. 2:51) This divine child went down, indeed, in humility to be subject to his earthly parents; who was profoundly adored by all the angels of heaven. But the more deeply Jesus humbled himself, the more he exalted the dignity of maternal authority. In respectful homage to the charitable wishes of his Mother, and at the slightest indication of her secret desire, this dutiful son wrought a more stupendous prodigy than that of Josue when he stopped the course of the sun and moon; (Josue. 10:12) or that not less astonishing miracle of the prophet Isaias who pushed *the sun back ten degrees.* (Is. 30:8) This our Lord did at the Marriage Feast of Cana, when to please and honor his Mother he accelerated the time fixed by the eternal decree of his heavenly Father, to work his first public miracle, by changing ordinary water into the nature of exquisite wine (Jn. 2:3) On the cross of Calvary, this loving Son forgot his own sufferings, to honor his afflicted and sorrowful Mother. Lastly, after her death, he suspended in her behalf the common laws of nature, and anticipating in her honor the joys of her resurrection, raised his most holy Mother from the grave; and in body and soul brought her in triumph, to the highest throne of glory, in the eternal kingdom of heaven.

Behold, then how the Incarnate Son of God, and child of Mary, honors his Mother. He has constituted her Queen of heaven and earth, of angels and men; and all generations shall call her blessed in her divine maternity.

We will close our humble but sincere tribute to the divine Son and Virgin Mother, by the more authoritative, and eloquent words of St. Bernard: We should not be surprised, he says, to learn from revelations, that God the Father has generated God the Son; for it is natural to him, by the act of his divine intelligence, to produce a Word in every respect equal to himself, God of God. But it has been, and it continues to be a most wonderful prodigy, that a woman should conceive, and bring forth a divine son. This event demanded that this privileged Mother should, in a certain manner, be raised to a kind of equality with the divinity, by an infusion of immense graces and perfections never granted to any other creature. Hence, I believe that no human, or angelic intelligence, has ever been able to fathom the bottom of that immense ocean of all the supernatural gifts of the Holy Ghost, that were poured down upon the Blessed Virgin Mary, when she conceived in her immaculate womb the Son of God ... Mary the blessed, by her free consent to become the mother of the Eternal Word, merited more than all angels, or men combined together, can merit in all their good thoughts, pious words, and virtuous actions. These could only merit the reward of eternal glory according to their various states and degrees. But this thrice happy Virgin, by her admirable consent, has merited to obtain the total extinction of every incentive to sin; the primacy and dominion over the whole universe, the plenitude of all graces, of all virtues, of all gifts, of every blessing, of all the fruits of the Holy Ghost; the perfection of all wisdom, the knowledge of all languages, the spirit of prophecy, the direction of spirits, and full power of working miracles. By this consent Blessed Mary has deserved her fecundity in the virginal state, and the maternity of the Son of God. She has merited to be made the Star of the Sea, the Gate of Heaven, and above all to be called, and to be in reality the Queen of Mercy. Hence, Solomon justly said: "Many daughters have gathered together, in riches, thou hast surpassed them all." (Prov. 31:29) (St. Bernard, 1. Conclus, 61 art 1. Cap 12 A Lapide, in Cap. 38) We are fully satisfied with this magnificent eulogium, which shows how the Incarnate Word of God honors and rewards the dignity of his most holy Mother. We have expatiated at some length upon this subject partly because we desire to concur in the full realization of the prophecy, *that all generations shall call Blessed,* the divine Mother of our thorn-crowned King, to whom we have dedicated this humble volume. We feel most confident, that both Mother and Son will be pleased with our good intention.

Our second motive for extending our remark has been to offer all Christian children, the most perfect model of filial respect towards parents, that we could find. As parental authority is the first and most sacred in human society, so we are fully and firmly convinced that loving, respectful and obedient children, will grow up into law-abiding and useful citizens. Domestic dicipline is the first and best school in Christian society. We must now return to our divine Master.

THIRD SECTION

RESPECT OF JESUS FOR THE PRIESTLY DIGNITY

As parents, in the *order of nature,* are the first dignity and authority, claiming the respectful homage of children; so the true ministers of God, are the first and highest dignity in the spiritual and supernatural order upon earth. If parents are the loving representatives and agents of God's creative fecundity, and the hand of his beneficent providence; the sacred ministers of God are the eye of his wisdom, the voice of his law, the vessels of his holiness, and the living channels of his graces to mankind. The priests of God are to human souls, what parents are to human bodies. They are our spiritual fathers. Speaking of the Christian priesthood, St. John Chrysostom says: "Consider the priestly dignity. A priest is a man upon earth; but he is elevated to the sublime rank of a divine agent. He lives and works among men, and for men; but his actions are supernatural and divine. The priestly office is not, and cannot be of human institution. The wise philosophers, and the most enlightened statesmen, the greatest generals, with the most powerful monarchs, cannot constitute an order of men, like that of the Christian priesthood. No man upon earth, no saint in heaven, no angel, no archangel, no heavenly power, no creature whatever, can institute such sublime dignity and office; that those who live in a body of flesh upon earth, may exercise a greater than an angelic ministry." (St. John Chrys.

130

De dignit, sacerdotis Lib. 2.) It is evident, that God alone can communicate to his sacred ministers, the power of consecrating the body of his incarnate Son, and of absolving well disposed sinners from all their sins.

We are taught to measure the height of a building, from the length of its shadow. From the long and large shadow of the Jewish priesthood, we may form some imperfect idea of the sublime dignity of the Christian priesthood. In the sixth chapter of this book, we had occasion to allude to the institution of the Aaronic priesthood, when we remarked how severely God punished those ambitious men, who attempted to usurp this dignity and office. In a subsequent occasion, King Saul, by the command of God, was deprived forever of his royal dignity, because once only he attempted to offer a sacrifice, which belonged, by right, to the priestly office. When King Ozias presumed to offer incense in the sanctuary of God's temple in Jerusalem, the High Priest, Azarias, accompanied by eighty zealous priests, bravely withstood the sacrilegious king, and said to him: *"It doth not belong to thee, Ozias, to burn incense to the Lord; but to the priests ... who are consecrated for this ministry."* Because, however, the king in his pride and arrogance, insisted in attempting this profanation, God miraculously covered him on the spot with leprosy, when he was thrust out of the temple; and died through this loathsome and humiliating disease. (2 Paral. 26:18) The superiority of the priestly dignity, to that of earthly potentates in the spiritual and supernatural order, is shown in the Bible from the fact, that in the old law, the High Priest Samuel, by the command of God, made Saul, king; and deposed him for presuming to perform, once only, one single act of the priestly office, and on that occasion, he selected and annointed as king over Israel, the youthful David, son of Isai. (1Kings 15 & 16) By the command of God, priests alone could minister at the altar, and offer sacrifice to him. They were constituted the teachers, interpreters and judges, of God's holy laws, for every class of persons. The people were strictly commanded to listen respectfully to their voice, as the visible angels and ambassadors of God. *"For the lips of the priest shall keep knowledge, and they,* (the people,) *shall seek the law at his mouth; because he is the angel of the Lord of Hosts."* (Malach. 2:7)

Let us see now, how our divine Lord and Master has honored the dignity, and respected the authority of the priesthood. We should beforehand observe, that he is the first source and center of all priestly dignity and power. Jesus is the supreme and eternal Pontiff, according to the order of

Melchisedech; and he became man to abrogate the Aaronic priesthood of the old law, and to substitute for it a more exalted dignity, and a more extensive, and effective power. (Heb. 7 & 8) Nevertheless, he manifested on every occasion great regard for the Jewish priesthood. He honored the Jewish priesthood, by selecting from it his mother, a near relative of Elizabeth, who was of the daughters of Aaron. (Luke 1:5 & 36) His first visit upon earth, soon after his incarnation and several months before his birth, was to the house of Zachary, *a priest of the house of Abia.* (Lk.1:5) Hence, this holy Jewish priest learned the great mystery of the incarnation, and the arrival of the expected Messias even before Saint Joseph, the virginal spouse of his immaculate Mother. At his birth, our Lord sent a miraculous star to invite kings to his cradle; but he wished to be carried in person to the temple of Jerusalem to honor the Jewish priesthood. If our most holy Redeemer could not approve of the vicious conduct of some of the chief priests; yet he ever paid respect to their sacred office, and dignity; and exhorted his hearers and disciples to carefully distinguish the personal behavior, from the official dignity of the priests of God. The faults of a priest are personal acts; but his dignity and office are gifts and privileges of God. Our divine Savior knew and foretold that the Jewish priests had conspired against his life. He knew that they were his mortal enemies, and would be the principal authors of his greatest sufferings, deep humiliations, and cruel death on the cross; nevertheless, though he refused to speak to King Herod, he readily answered, during his trial, every question of the high priest, Caiphas; and in this unworthy man, our blessed Lord respected the sacredness of the priestly dignity.

If the very shadow of Peter is honored we may justly conclude that higher honors, and greater respect will be shown for his real person. We may begin to learn the grave nature and sublime dignity of the Christian priesthood, from the length of preparation required by our divine Lord, before he consented to confer it upon man. The Eternal Son of God has assumed human nature, that he may purify, may sanctify, and elevate it to the sublime dignity of the Christian priesthood. He defers this, the most important of all his divine actions upon earth, to the very last day of his life. Who can tell the care our divine Master used; the trials he had to undergo; the patience he exercised in preparing during more than three years, his disciples and apostles for the grand dignity of the Christian priesthood? ...

This most High God, this great Lord of heaven and earth, is satisfied with a stable at his birth; he contents himself to love and work like an humble mechanic, in the carpenter's shop of his adopted father. During the three years of his apostolic life through Palestine, he cheerfully embraces every opportunity of practising poverty, and of exercising his cherished virtue of humility, and self-abasement. But when the memorable evening arrived, on which Jesus intends to raise men to the sacred dignity of the Christian priesthood He cannot consent to go to a stable or a shop, or even to an ordinary house. He will use one of the most magnificent halls that can be procured in the royal city of Jerusalem. Our divine Lord desires to perform his first ordination in a richly carpeted hall, in order that, through the unusual magnificence of the place, the apostles may begin to perceive how sublime is the dignity to which they are going to be raised on that ever memorable night. On this occasion our Savior procured *"A dining room furnished."* (Mk.16:15) Adorned with green boughs and fresh flowers and splendidly lighted. (A Lapide ibid) It was on this solemn occasion, that our blessed Lord celebrated his first High Mass, at which he consecrated bread and wine; and by the most wonderful prodigy changed them into the substance of his Sacred Body and Blood. It was at this grand High Mass, that the twelve apostles were raised to the sublime dignity of the Christian priesthood; when they received from our divine Savior, the power of offering the same Sacrifice, of consecrating, as he did, and of ordaining other priests who should continue to offer daily, this divine and august Sacrifice to the end of the world.

These great truths we learn from the first three Evangelists, and from St. Paul, who says: *"I have received of the Lord that which also I delivered to you, that the Lord Jesus, the night in which he was betrayed, took bread, and giving thanks, broke and said: Take ye, and eat; this is my body, which shall be delivered for you, do this for the commemoration of me. In like manner also, the chalice ... Saying, this chalice is the new testament in my blood, this do ye, as often as you shall drink it, for the commemoration of me, for as often as you shall eat this bread and drink this chalice you shall show the death of the Lord until he come."* (Cor. 11:23) *"Immensa infinita Sacerdotis dignitas,"* (exclaims St. Ephraim De Sacerdotio) From the example and doctrine of this great Apostle of the Gentiles, we learn that this sublime dignity, power and office of the Christian priesthood, was through the Apostles of our Lord, communicated to other men. In fact

St. Paul was not present with our Lord in the supper room. His conversion took place three years after. But he tells us that he and other bishops and priests, offered the same sacrifice like the rest of the apostles. *"The chalice of benedictions which we bless, is it not the communion of the blood of Christ?And the bread which we break is it not the partaking of the body of the Lord?* (Cor. 10:16.) And in another place he says: *"We have an altar, whereof they have no power to eat, who serve the tabernacle"* (Heb. 13:10) The continuation of the Christian priesthood is essential to the Church of Jesus Christ, wherein, according to the repeated commands of our Lord, the holy sacrifice must be offered daily, and Sacraments must be administered to men, to the end of time. *"Do ye this,* our Lord said, *in commemoration of me."* ... *"For as often as you shall eat this bread and drink this chalice, you shall show the death of the Lord until he come."* From other Epistles of the holy Apostle we learn that bishops, priests, and deacons, were instituted wherever Christians were established. He wrote to Titus, whom he consecrated bishop, *"for this cause I left thee in Crete, that thou shouldst set in order the things that are wanting, and shouldst ordain priests in every city, as I also appointed thee."* (Tit. 1:5) "Ingens et divina dignitas," says Dionysius (De Eccles. H. Cap. 3) We must now return to our divine Lord, who has other honors and privileges in store for his sacred ministers. Besides the sublime power of order, through which he conferred on his priests the divine prerogatives of consecrating his sacred Body and Blood, he communicated to them the most extensive jurisdiction over the souls of men.

In the person of St. Peter our divine Lord conferred the sublime and extensive power over the souls of men to the Pope, the supreme visible head of the Church. *"Thou art Peter, and upon this rock I will build my Church; and the gates of hell shall not prevail against it; and I will give thee the keys of the kindom of Heaven; and whatsoever thou shalt bind upon earth, it shall be bound also in heaven: and whatsoever thou shalt loose upon earth, it shall be loosened also in heaven."* (Mt. 16:18) This grand promise was fulfilled by our Savior after his glorious resurrection, when he commanded Peter to feed his sheep and lambs. (Jn. 19:15) To the rest of the Apostles, and to all the bishops and priests of his Church, our Lord said: *Amen, I say to you, whatsoever you shall bind upon earth, shall be bound also in heaven; and whatsoever you shall loose upon earth shall be loosened also in heaven."* (Mt. 18:18)

After his resurrection, our Divine Master confirmed this power and more fully explained its object. *"As the Father hath sent me, so I also send you. When he had said this, he breathed on them, and he said to them: Receive ye the Holy Ghost; whose sins you shall forgive, they are forgiven them; and whose sins you shall retain, they are retained,"* (Jn 20:23) Here is the divine commission, stamped by the broad seal of heaven, by virtue of which the pastors of Christ's holy Church absolve repenting sinners, after their humble and sincere confession.

St. John Chrysostom says: "The Eternal Father has given all power to his Son, who says, *'All power is given to me in heaven and earth.'* (Mt. 28:18) But I see that the same power is communicated to his priests by God the Son ...These sacred ministers possess now more power than Almighty God has ever been willing to grant to his angels or archangels in heaven." (Lib. 3 de Sacerd. Cap 3) St. Bernard styles priests the parents of Jesus Christ, "Parentes Christi." St. Augustine exclaims: "Oh, truly venerable dignity, in whose hands the Son of God is incarnate. The most blessed Mother of Jesus opened heaven, and brought the eternal Son of God once only in her virginal womb; but the priest brings him upon the altar in every Mass. In the womb of Mary the Son of God was passible and mortal; but in the hand of the priest, he is immortal and impassible." These are the words of St. Bernardine of Sienna. All this is amply sufficient to show, how highly our most holy and divine Master has honored the dignity of the priesthood, in the old and new testament. Our duty is to imitate his example.

We must now proceed to consider, how our divine Lord has honored and respected civil authority.

FOURTH SECTION

RESPECT OF JESUS FOR CIVIL AUTHORITY

All power and authority emanating from God, it follows, as a necessary consequence, that all those who devoutly honor God, will invariably honor and respect all persons, that have by God been raised to any position of dignity and power upon earth. Devout children will always honor, love, respect, and obey their parents.

Pious Christians have always a profound respect for the sacred character of the ministers of God. And, because civil superiors are also in a lower sphere than the ministers of God's power and justice; so every sincere

Christian, and practical Catholic, will respect their authority, and do homage to their dignity. St. Paul says: *"Let every soul be subject to higher powers; For there is no power but from God; and those that are, are ordained of God. Therefore he that resisteth the power resisteth the ordinance of God. And they that resist, purchase to themselves damnation ... For he is the minister of God to thee for good. But if thou do that which is evil, fear; for he beareth not the sword in vain. For he is the minister of God, an avenger to execute wrath upon him that doeth evil. Wherefore be subject of necessity, not only for wrath, but also for conscience sake."* (Rom. 13:1)

These sublime and solid principles of Christian jurisprudence and morality, were dictated to the Apostolic Doctor of the Gentiles by our Lord, Jesus Christ. But according to his maxim, and uniform conduct, our divine Master ever practiced, what he intended to teach. Let us see then, how he showed, in practise, his respect for civil authority.

1. On the very threshold of the palace of civil dignity and power, we should reflect that all power and authority emanated from him, *to whom all power is given both in heaven and upon earth.* For whatever good quality, whatever dignity or power come from God to man, must be transmitted by, and through our Lord Jesus Christ ... *who is the head of all principality and power.* (Coloss. 2:10) *"For he is above all principality and power and virtue and dominion, and every name that is named, not only in this world, but also in that which is to come."* (Ephes. 1:21) Whatever, therefore, may be the civil dignity, power, or title of any potentate upon earth; it should by Christian faith be considered a badge of honor conferred upon him by *the King of Kings, and Lord of Lords.* (Apo. 19:16) By the selection of his blessed mother, and adopted father, from a kingly race, our divine Lord manifested his high regard for the dignity of man. Even before his birth, he recognized the authority of the Roman Emperor Augustus, when in obedience to his decree, he inspired his Virgin Mother and St. Joseph, to undertake a long journey from Nazareth to Bethlehem, in the very depth of winter. His birth in a stable, was an admirable act of obedience, in homage to the civil authority of a pagan monarch. The holy name of Mary, of Joseph, and very likely of Jesus, on the roll book, or imperial register, testify our divine Savior's respect for civil authority, and his ready obedience to human laws. *"And it came to pass that in those days there went out a decree from Caesar Augustus, that the whole world should be enrolled ... And all went to be enrolled, every one to his own city. And Joseph also went from Galilee*

out of the city of Nazareth into Judea, to the city of David, which is called Bethlehem, because he was of the house and family of David, to be enrolled with Mary his espoused wife, who was with child. And it came to pass, that when they went there ... She brought forth her first-born Son, and wrapped him in swaddling clothes, and laid him in a manger; because there was no room for them in the inn." (Lk. 2:1) Behold how soon, and with what inconvenience to himself, and to his young mother, and adopted father, our Infant Savior manifests his respect for civil authority.

Moreover, we are informed by the illustrious Cardinal Baronius, on the authority of Suida and Nicephorus, that soon after our Savior's birth, our Blessed Lady appeared to Caesar Augustus in the Roman Capitol, holding the Divine Infant in her arms. The proper name of this emperor was Octavius; he was a nephew of the famous emperor, general, and historian, Julius Caesar. Octavius had been supernaturally informed of the imminent birth of our Divine Lord, who was to silence all pagan oracles, and destroy the idols. In memory and honor of this apparition, this most happy and best of Roman Emperors that reigned before Constantine, had a magnificent altar erected on capitol hill, with this inscription *"Ara primogeniti Dei,"* namely, "This altar is dedicated to the Incarnate Son of God." A little above three centuries after the remarkable event, the Emperor Constantine erected on the same site a large church in honor of our Blessed Lady, which still exists at the present day, under the ordinary title of *"Ara Coeli."* (A Lapide in Luc. 2:1)

Behold, the holy bishop St. Fulgentius exclaims, *behold, O impious King Herod,* that there is no danger to thy kingly dignity in the birth of this heavenly child. He does not wish to be thy successor on the throne, but he desires to have faithful believers in every part of the world. *"Nec ideo natus est ut tibi succedat, sed ut in eum mundus fideliter credat."* (Serm. 5 De. Epiph.) If the instances we have given could only be used as a favorable interpretation of the respectful regard of an ordinary man for human authority, we should reflect that the divine infant of Bethlehem is the incarnate wisdom of God, whose every act is full of important signification. We possess, however, more explicit proofs of our Savior's respect for civil authority in his more advanced age. St. Matthew relates, that on a certain occasion the hypocritical Pharisees consulted among themselves how to ensnare our divine Master in his speech. For this malicious object, they sent some of their disciples with several officers of King Herod, to our Lord saying to

137

him: *"Master, we know that thou art a true speaker, and teacher in the way of God, in truth; neither carest thou for any man; for thou dost not regard the person of men. Tell us, therefore, what dost thou think; is it lawful to give tribute to Caesar, or not ? ... But Jesus knowing their wickedness said: Why do you tempt me, ye hypocrites? Show me the coin of the tribute. And they offered him a penny. And Jesus said to them: whose image and inscription is this? They say to him, Caesar's. Then he said to them: Render therefore to Caesar the things that are Caesar's, and to God the things that are God's.* (Mt. 22:15) Such are the maxims of this divine teacher of Christian jurisprudence. It is impossible to find any other more wise, more just, more solid, more comprehensive. But, the first part should never be separated from the second which is the most essential. Our duty to civil authority cannot dispense us from our higher obligations to God; but on the contrary, this is the foundation and support of the other. We will respect human authority in proportion as we respect the authority of God.

Action however, is the most evident proof of our convictions. Many persons are as prompt and eloquent in propounding theories, as they are remiss in practicing them. But our divine Master did not belong to this class of teachers. He was generally very concise in announcing theoretical principles, but very exact and perfect in acting upon them. He even taught more by his example, than by his words. *Coepit Jesu facere et docere.*

The following was one of his first maxims. *"Whosoever shall do and teach, the same shall be called great, in the kingdom of heaven."* (Mt. 5:19)

According to the assertion of Orosius, assented to by the learned Cornelius A Lapide: Our Lord Jesus Christ became a Roman citizen, by the fact that his parents and himself, were after his birth, enrolled in Bethlehem in the Roman register. *Christus dicendus civis Romanus census professione Romani.* (Oros. Lib. 6 Cap. 2. ex A Lapide in Lk. 2:3) As the King of Kings and Savior of the world, our Lord was not bound in justice to pay any tribute to any earthly monarch. Moreover he was so poor that he did not possess the necessary amount of money demanded. But he works a miracle, rather than fail in giving this practical proof of his subjection, to human authority and obedience to civil laws. This fact is related in all its beautiful simplicity by St Matthew in the following words: *"When they were come to Capharnum they that received the didrachma; came to Peter,*

138

and said to him: Doth not your master pay the didrachma? He said yes.
And when he was come into the house, Jesus prevented him saying: What
is thy opinion Simon? Of whom do the kings of the earth take tribute, or
custom, of their own children or strangers? And he said of strangers. Jesus
said to him: then the children are free. But, that we may not scandalize
them, go thou to the sea, and cast in a hook; and that fish which shall first
come up, take; and when thou hast opened its mouth, thou shalt find a stater:
take that and give it to them for me and thee." (Mt. 17:23) How many
instructive lessons are contained in this fact! In his extreme poverty our
divine Lord works a miracle to pay the head, or personal tribute not only
for himself, but also for his Apostle Peter. He works a miracle to avoid
giving any occasion of scandal, and this is charity. He consents to pay a
tribute to which he is not bound in strict justice. This is an admirable act
of respect for civil authority. In paying the tribute, he equals himself to
his humble disciple, a poor fisherman. Is this not profound humility? ...
In this humility however, our Lord teaches us the honor due to Peter, whom
he equals to himself, and also the respect due to the Roman Pontiff, his
vicar upon earth. But we must return to our main subject.

Words in praise of authority are good; tributes for the support of
its dignity are better: but the best proof of our profound respect for it is
to suffer and die, when necessary in obedience to its laws. This is what
we have now to consider in our divine Master and Model.

Let us return to the palace of the Roman Governor. Pilate is the
legitimate representative of the Roman Emperor Tiberius, as governor of
Judea. As man our Lord is now placed under his jurisdiction by the chief
priests, senators and magistrates of the Jewish people. Look at our Blessed
Redeemer and Master, and consider his behavior.

We read in history, that the emperor Alexander the Great, having
been severely wounded in battle by an arrow, and a painful surgical operation
being required, was asked by the military surgeon, to allow himself to be
bound for a short time. His answer on this occasion has been highly extolled.
He said with an air of dignified haughtiness: "It is beneath the dignity of
an emperor to be bound with cords. When the pious and dethroned King
of France, Louis XVI, was by his rebellious subjects brought to the scaffold
for public execution in Paris; he firmly refused to have his hands manacled
and his arms pinioned before being beheaded; and prepared to repel the
brutal executioners saying: "I will never allow it to be said that a King

of France consented to be bound with cords like a coward, and manacled like a vile criminal." It was only when his faithful, brave, and prudent confessor proposed to the saintly monarch, the example of our divine Lord, and warmly exhorted him to imitate it, that King Louis devoutly raising his eyes to heaven, heaved a deep sigh, and extending his hands, mildly consented to endure this public humiliation.

But Jesus Christ is the King of kings, and Lord of lords, supreme Sovereign of heaven and earth, of angels and men. He is a God of infinite majesty, and of omnipotent power. Countless millions of angels are in adoration before him ... with an act of his omnipotent will he could destroy all his enemies, and annihilate the whole world ... Yet ... behold, Christian reader, behold this incarnate Son of God, meekly standing before the Roman Governor, bound in chains, like the lowest and worst of malefactors. Look at this divine prisoner. His hands are manacled, his arms pinioned, a rope is fastened around his neck. *"When morning was come,* St. Matthew says: *all the chief priests and ancients of the people held a council against Jesus to put him to death. And they brought him bound and delivered him to Pontius Pilate, the Governor."* (Mt. 27:1) The conduct of our innocent Savior, before the Roman Governor, was very different from that of some great political criminals in the presence of their legitimate judge, when they attempted to justify their treason and rebellion, and boldly despised and denied the authority of their lawful superiors. Some superficial Christians, imbued with the modern spirit of insubordination, too often metamorphose this iniquitous behavior into an heroic act of patriotism, worthy of all admiration and praise. But all good Catholics prefer to follow the example and the doctrines of their Divine Master. Our Lord recognized the authority of the Roman Governor, Pilate, and respected his dignity. He declared that his authority had a divine origin and came to him from above. He mildly answered the Governor's questions. He promptly obeyed all his commands. Our Lord went to the balcony, or retired therefrom, at the least intimation of the Roman Magistrate. Though perfectly innocent, yet when condemned to the cruel punishment of the flagellation at the pillar, the divine Lamb of God humbly submitted to that unjust and degrading chastisement, and bore the scourge without a word of complaint.

See him standing before the Roman Governor, with that horrible Crown of Thorns torturing his adorable head. Does he complain? does he even allude once to his agonizing sufferings? Not a word escapes from his mouth. He, the incarnate Son of the most High, is postponed to the bloody murderer, Barabbas, and bears the insult in silent meekness. He is condemned to the barbarous and infamous death of the Cross, and bows his head in humble submission ... He cheerfully takes upon his shoulders, the heavy instrument of his crucifixion, and carries it to Mount Calvary. There, at the least intimation of the presiding officer of justice, Jesus strips himself, and meekly lays down upon the cross, extending his divine hands and feet, that they may be fastened thereon, with large and rough nails. All this is done in a spirit of obedience, and respect for authority not only divine, but also human; *for there is no power, but from God, "he humbled himself, becoming obedient unto death, even the death of the cross."* (Philip. 2:8) Here is our teacher; this is our model; *"Be ye subject, therefore, to every human creature, for God's sake whether it be the king as excelling or to the governors, as sent by him ... For so is the will of God, that by doing well you may silence the ignorance of foolish men ... Fear God, honor the king; servants be subject to your masters, with all fear; not only to the good and gentle, but also to the froward for this is thanksworthy, if for conscience towards God, a man endure sorrows, suffering wrongfully. For what glory is it, if sinning, and being buffeted, you suffer it? But if doing well, you suffer patiently, this is thanksworthy before God. For unto this you have been called; because Christ also suffered for us, leaving you an example, that you should follow his steps."* (1 Peter 2:13)

CHAPTER XVI

CAUSES OF THE CROWN OF THORNS

"Transgressors shall all of them be plucked up as thorns, and they shall be set on fire." (2 Kings 23:5)

1. These are words of inspiration, and refer to the thorny crown of our blessed Lord. They were uttered by holy David in his old age, and are a portion of the last words which this holy king, and prophet pronounced under a special inspiration of the Holy Ghost. *David the son of Isai said: The man to whom it was appointed concerning the Christ of the God of Jacob … The spirit of the Lord hath spoken by me and his words by my tongue. The God of Israel said to me …Trangressors shall all of them be plucked up as thorns."* These words of inspiration evidently refer to the Crown of Thorns of our divine Savior and indicate the causes, which induced him to wear upon his adorable head, this terrible crown of pain and ignominy. This will form the subject matter of this present chapter.

2. Thorns seem to be the natural fuel for fire. Hence the Royal Prophet in this place says: *Transgressors shall all of them be plucked up as thorns, which are not taken away with hands …but they shall be set on fire.* As we have already observed, thorns are the effect of sin, and the most striking figure of sinners. Hence, St. Augustine says: "What do thorns signify but the condition of sinners who, like hedgehogs, are all over bristling with the thorns of sin," *spinae quid significant, nisi peccatores, qui quasi ericiis spinae peccatorum cooperti sunt.* (In Ps. 10) St. Basil says, that whenever he beheld a beautiful and sweet smelling rose, his heart was more deeply pained than his senses were gratified. He reflected that the rose, queen of flowers, is surrounded with sharp and crooked thorns, that bitterly reproached him for his sins, on account of which this earth has been condemned

by the irritated justice of God to produce thorns and thistles. (St. Basil in Exame.) Hence, according to the opinion of this holy doctor of the Church, the rose would have been free from thorns, if sin had never been committed by men. St. John Chrysostom affirms, that God did not originally create thorns upon earth, but, that He only permitted their growth in consequence of sin and as a punishment to sinners. No wonder, then, that sinners, like prickly thorns and thistles, are doomed to be burned up with fire, as holy David says: *"All transgressors shall be plucked up as thorns ... and shall be set on fire."* To fire then we wretched sinners are condemned.

3. But happily for us, there are two very different kinds of fire. The first is the uncreated fire of God's eternal love. The second is the created fire of his irritated justice, prepared, and intended for the punishment of the rebellious angels, and of all unhappy sinners. To deliver us from the fire of hell, our merciful Savior brought with him from Heaven the fire of his divine love. It was in fact of this love, he spoke, when he said:*"I am come to send fire on the earth, and what will I, but that it be kindled?"* (Lk. 12:49) Sinners, he says to us, sinners, like thorns and thistles, you are doomed to be burned with fire. In punishment of your transgressions, you should have to burn in hell, during a miserable eternity in company with the devil, and all his wicked companions. It is however, in my power to offer to you, the blessed fire of my divine love, which burns in the bosom of God from all eternity, in exchange for the terrible fire of hell due to your crimes. Accept my love and I undertake to atone for all your sins. *"I am come to send fire on the earth, and what will I, but, that it be kindled?"*

Behold here *the first formal cause of the Crown of Thorns.* It is the goodness of God: It is the love and mercy of His incarnate Son, who with the Crown of Thorns assumed upon his head, the responsibility of atoning for all the sins of mankind. The great St. Leo, the Pope says: *Causa reparationis nostrae non est nisi misericordia Dei."* (Serm. de jejun. 10. mens.) Origen says, our Lord Jesus Christ assumed the thorns of our sins, infixed upon his head. These are his genuine words: *"In spina illa corona suscepit* (Jesus) *spinas peccatorum nostrorum intexta in capite suo."*(Tract. 35 in Mt. 27:29) The angelic doctor St. Thomas says: "These bloody thorns of our Savior's crown are intended to signify the stings of sin, with which our conscience is wounded. Our merciful Lord accepted these thorns as our substitute, because he undertook to suffer and die for our sins. (St. Thom. in Chap. 27 Matt.) He is truly the Good Shepherd who thrusts his head and body within a thorny bush in order to disentangle the suffering sheep from its prickly branches by which she is surrounded, and held captive, in pain and hunger. Prompted by his love, he endures the pricks of the thorns in his effort to free his beloved sheep from suffering and death. His love and mercy was then the moving cause that induced our blessed Savior to endure the painful and ignominious Crown of Thorns. *"In his love and in his mercy the prophet says: He redeemed them, and he carried them and lifted them up."*

4. The second cause was the source of sin. Three conditions are essential to sin. Sufficient matter, full knowledge, and deliberate consent. Whatever may be the matter of sin, no sin can be committed without the necessary knowledge of its malice, and the free deliberate consent of our will. Now knowledge is a prerogative of our mind, as consent is the free act of our will. Sin therefore is committed first in our mind, when, with full knowledge and deliberate consent we form in our head the resolution of doing anything morally wrong. Hence, St. Augustine says "that it is with the will that we do wrong, as it is with the will that we do good." *"Voluntate peccatur, et bene agitur."* All sins originate their malice in our mind. Sin is first conceived in the head, and consented to in the soul. *"Every man is tempted, being drawn away and allured by his own concupiscence. Then, when concupiscence hath conceived it bringeth forth sin."* (James 1:14) Our divine Master expressly teaches: *"that it is out of the heart of man that originate, and proceed evil thoughts, murders, adulteries, fornications, thefts, false testimonies, blasphemies, which defile with sin the soul of man."* (Mt. 15:19) The organs, senses and members of the body are only the instruments used by the soul in her operations and external deeds. Hence, the external action, as theft, murder, adultery, blasphemy is not the cause, but it is the consequence and the effect of the internal sin of the heart. In short, sin is committed with the mind, and with the will. Every sin is an internal rebellion of the soul against God's eternal law. Now the brain is the organ of human intelligence and will. The head is the workshop of the mind. The brain is the laboratory of the soul. This head, this human brain deserved therefore a special punishment. Behold here the other cause of our Savior's Crown of Thorns. Like a wise and skillful physician, he applied the remedy to the seat of the complaint, to the very root of the evil. Having become our Redeemer, he applied to his innocent, most holy and adorable head, the painful Crown of Thorns as a full atonement, and most effective

cure for our sins. Moreover, man fell off from God, through pride. *"The beginning of the pride of man is to fall off from God ... For pride is the beginning of all sins."* (Eccli. 10:14)

Pride being the origin of every sin, it was necessary that humility should become the general remedy of all evil. Now, we have seen in the previous chapter, what profound humility our divine Lord practiced at his crowning of thorns. Thus the Crown of Thorns on the head of our Lord, becomes the general remedy of sin. May the contemplation of this crown enlighten the mind of men, to understand the malice of sin and especially the internal sins of thought and affection.

5. Many persons make little account of internal sins. But besides the fact, that all sins are essentially committed by the mind, and will of men, we should, moreover, observe that the greater number of our sins are by their nature accomplished in the soul. All bad thoughts, and sinful affections belong to this category. The Holy Ghost says: *"Perverse thoughts separate from God."* (Wis.1:3) In fact evil thoughts and sinful affections by their nature, corrupt more immediately the heart, and defile the soul more directly than bad external actions. For, as we have observed, the malice of sin is derived from the knowledge that the mind has of the evil, and from the consenting of the will to it. All this mischief is perpetrated in the sacred cabinet of the soul.

We should, moreover, observe, that for the accomplishment of exterior actions many external circumstances of time, place, persons, and means are required, which are not necessary for the commission of internal sins. Again sinful external acts naturally, and often bring upon the sinner temporal losses, disgrace, infamy and many other human and physical punishment, to which internal sins cannot be subject. Hence both reason and experience force us to conclude that internal sins are without comparison more frequently committed, than exterior evil actions. We cannot venture to form any calculation, but the knowledge of human nature induces us to fear that thousands of internal sins are committed before one external crime is perpetrated. But what idea shall we be able to form of the awful amount of interior sins committed, when so many exterior sinful actions are witnessed in human society?

Reflect, now, that all these sins were fully known to our divine Savior. He knew all past, present and future sins of mankind. He saw them all committed in the soul, through the understanding and will. He observed

145

the vast majority of sins accomplished in the mind. To offer to his Eternal Father an adequate satisfaction for them our merciful Savior consented to bear the painful and ignominious Crown of Thorns. "The Crown of Thorns, Theophilatus says, is the figure of our sins which Jesus Christ abolished by his divinity, represented by his head." (Com. in St. Matt. 27:29)

6. Reflect then, Christian reader, that our divine Savior is crowned with sharp thorns, to punish on his own head all your sinful deeds, but more especially the wicked thoughts, by which you have offended God, and have defiled his divine image impressed upon your soul. Numerous thorns pierce, and torture his divine head, because we have harbored in our mind many bad thoughts of different kinds. Our thoughts against faith and against hope, our thoughts of presumption, or despair, impious and blasphemous thoughts against God, have produced the longest and sharpest thorns that torment the most holy head of our divine Savior. Our habitual dissipation of mind, our forgetfulness of God's holy presence, our voluntary distractions in prayer, are the reeds with which, like his cruel executioners, we strike and more deeply press his thorny crown. Uncharitable thoughts against our neighbors, rash judgment, envy and jealousy against our fellow Christians, are the cruel thorns that torture our Savior's head. Those frequent thoughts of pride, ambition, vain-glory; that hypocrisy, that habitual disposition to overreach, and deceive our fellow men, so common in human society at the present time, those desires of revenge, sensuality and lust, have produced that terrible thorny bush from which the Crown of Thorns has been formed, that pricks and torment the head of the incarnate Son of God.

Whilst, Christian reader, you are considering the sufferings of your Savior crowned with thorns, enter into your heart and examine therein what are the evil thoughts that more frequently occupy your mind. Conceive a sincere sorrow for them. Ask with profound humility your Savior's pardon; and firmly resolve for the future to watch over your heart, and promptly to banish from your mind every imagination or thought that may be displeasing to God, and calculated to increase the sufferings of your loving Redeemer, crowned with thorns as the King of Sorrows. It is only in this practical way that we can render our spiritual reading, or our meditation on the Passion of our dear Lord, pleasing to his Sacred Heart, and profitable to our souls.

146

CHAPTER XVII

CONTINUATION OF THE SAME SUBJECT—JESUS IS CROWNED AS THE SAVIOR OF MANKIND

"We see Jesus ... For the suffering of death, crowned with glory and honor." (Heb. 2:19)

1. A crown is an object of human ambition. The reason may be because a crown, by its very nature and form represents the idea of perfection and of endless duration, having neither beginning nor end. Moreover a crown is always associated with the idea of honor, dignity, power and glory. Several crowns have been invented in different nations for the encouragement and reward for brave deeds and glorious achievments. The Pagan Romans, however, surpassed every other nation in inventing, and, in awarding these honorable distinctions. Different writers mention seven as the principal crowns bestowed upon deserving persons as a reward for their meritorious deeds.

The *first* and most illustrious was the *Triumphal Crown*. This was a golden crown placed on the head of the Emperor, or of some very distinguished general of the army, when he was received in triumph in the city of Rome, after having obtained some great victory over the enemies of the country.

The *second* was the *Crown of Deliverance* awarded to a general, or officer who delivered a city, or fortress from a seige by forcing the enemy to withdraw from it. This was a golden crown with a beseiged city engraved on its front.

The *third* was the *Mural Crown* which was given by the emperor to any officer, or soldier, who was the first to scale the wall of a city or fortress of an enemy during an assault made upon it. This was another golden crown with a walled city or fortress being assaulted and scaled, engraven on it.

147

The *fourth* was the *Camp Crown* awarded to the soldier who was first to enter the enemy's entrenched camp during a battle. This crown was also made of gold and had a military encampment engraven on it.

The *fifth* was the *Naval Crown* made of gold having a ship engraven upon it. This crown was given to the sailor who during a naval engagement was the first to board an enemy's ship.

The *sixth* was the *Civic Crown*. It was formed of small boughs of holm and oak trees, carefully entwined in a garland, with which was publicly crowned any person who had saved the life of a citizen.

The *seventh* was the *Poetic Crown* formed of laurel leaves, and awarded to poetic genius.

2. These crowns were highly esteemed by the ancient Romans. No man upon earth deserved all these crowns more than our divine Savior. But as he came to redeem man from the curse of sin, and thorns being the most expressive figure thereof, so he selected for himself a Crown of Thorns. By this choice, our Lord wished to announce to us, that he came to remove from earth the malediction pronounced against it by God on account of the prevarication of our first parents, Adam and Eve. These are the sentiments of the great and glorious martyr, St. Cyprian, the eloquent Bishop of Carthage in northern Africa. In his sermon on the passion and cross of our Lord, St. Cyprian says: "In order that you may understand the deep mystery of the Crown of Thorns, you should know that our Savior not only came to take away sin from the world, but also to remove the curse from the earth which God pronounced against it in punishment of the sin of our first parents when He said: *"Cursed is the earth in thy work ... Thorns and thistles shall it bring forth to thee."* Hence, Jesus our Lord, is crowned with thorns to the end that this first sentence of condemnation may be removed. *"Propterea ergo spinis coronatur Jesus, ut prima illa condemnationis sententia solvetur."* (St. Cypr. Serm. de Pass and Cruce Domini). As this first sentence of condemnation was pronounced by God against the first man, who was the head and representative of mankind; so our divine Redeemer as the head of the church, and the first of the elect wished to have his adorable head crowned with thorns, to teach us that by so doing he, as God, removed the curse which had been pronounced against us. For the head of Jesus represents his divinity. *"Corona ex spinis peccata sunt; quae Christus sua Deitate consumit. Per caput enim Deitas praesignatur."* (Theophil. in Matt. 27:29)

3. *Jesus is crowned as a victim.*

It was a general custom among Jews and Gentiles to crown the victims intended for sacrifice. This crown laid on the head of the victim was a public profession of profound respect for him to whom the sacrifice was offered. Sacrifice strictly speaking being, by its very nature offered to God alone, hence, to him should always be offered the most perfect, the most worthy and select victims. Now a crown was placed on the head of the animal to declare it to be the best victim found for the occasion.

We have a remarkable illustration of this in the Acts of the Apostles. St. Paul and St. Barnabas being in the city of Lystria in Lycaonia, miraculously cured in an instant a poor man who had been born lame, and never could walk. When the multitude had seen this prodigy they all lifted up their voice saying: *"The gods in the likeness of men are come down to us ..."* Then the priest of Jupiter, bringing oxen and garlands would have offered sacrifice in honor of the two Apostles, had he not been strongly rebuked for it by St. Paul. (Acts. 14:12) Now Jesus our Lord was truly the most worthy, indeed he was the only worthy victim fit to be offered to the supreme majesty of God. He was to be offered to God for the four principal objects for which victims are immolated, namely in recognition of the supreme dominion of God over all creatures; as the most perfect act of adoration of his divine majesty; as the most complete act of atonement for sin; and lastly, as the most powerful and effective prayer to obtain every grace and blessing from Almighty God for time and eternity.

Moreover, in the person of our Savior sacrificed on the Altar of the Cross on Mount Calvary, all the victims and sacrifices of the old Testament were contained in a most eminent degree of perfection. *"For if the blood of goats and of oxen, and the ashes of a heifer, being sprinkled, sanctify such as are defiled, to the cleansing of the flesh; how much more shall the blood of Christ, Who, through the Holy Ghost, offered himself without spot to God, cleanse our conscience from dead works, to serve the living God? And therefore he is the mediator of the New Testament; that by means of his death for the redemption of those transgressions, which were under the former Testament, they who are called may receive the promise of eternal inheritance."* (Heb 9:13) Surely this great, this glorious, this divine Victim of the cross deserved to be crowned before sacrifice. Behold here another cause of the Crown of Throns.

5. *Jesus is crowned as our model.*

We have seen above that our divine Lord has been crowned with thorns in order to atone for our sins, and thus satisfy divine justice. The holy and learned Pope, Innocent III, concludes from this fact our individual duty of doing penance. The Crown of Thorns is intended, he says, to teach us that we should surround our head, or rather our mind with deep sentiments of sorrow and penance for our sins according to the words of the Royal Psalmist who says: *"I am turned in my anguish whilst the thorn is fastened. I have acknowledged my sins to thee."* (Ps. 31:4) By these words: *"I am turned in my anguish whilst the thorn is fastened,"* may be expressed the intensity of the Royal Prophet's sufferings, who could not enjoy any rest; but they may also signify the salutary effect produced in his soul by these intense pains which become the happy cause of his perfect conversion and turning to God. Let us imitate his good example.

Sin being committed by the understanding and will, our conversion should begin from a full understanding of the malice of sin, passing then to sorrow of heart, and to the detestation of sin by the will. All this we shall learn and accomplish, if we meditate deeply on the mystery of the Crown of Thorns.

Moreover, from our thorn-crowned Savior, we should learn the duty of penance, because, as St. Bernard says, we should be ashamed to be delicate members of Jesus Christ crowned with thorns. *"Sub capite spinoso pudeat membrum esse delicatum."* Thorns and thistles represent the sorrows, trials and sufferings of this life. Let us learn from our divine model to bear them with perfect patience and full resignation to the will of God. *"Not my will, but thine be done."* The holy Martyr St. Agapitus having red hot coals put upon his bare head exclaimed with joy: "I can cheerfully bear to have my head burned with fire, which will be crowned in heaven with glory. These burning coals will be changed into precious stones to adorn and enrich my crown. Oh! how glorious that crown will be for my head tormented for love of Christ. An habitual dislike for suffering, and a constant yearning for the amusements and pleasures of this world, are essentially opposed to the spirit of Jesus Christ, the King of Sorrows. How can loving and faithful subjects crown themselves with flowers, when they behold their king crowned with thorns on account of their sins? Saint Clement of Alexandria says: *"It is contrary to reason and to common sense for a Christian who has heard the history of the Crown of Thorns of our Lord, to wish himself*

150

crowned with flowers. This is a mockery and an insult to our thorn-crowned King." (Lib. 2 Poer, Chap. 8)

The famous ecclesiastical historian, Baronius relates that about the year 167, the Emperor Marcus Aurelius, on a certain occasion of general rejoicing, commanded all his soldiers to wear a crown of laurel leaves in sign of joy. Observing however that one of them had no crown, he asked the cause of it. The brave soldier calmly and respectfully answered: *"Sire, it is not proper for a Christian to wear during this present life a crown of pleasure. Non decet Christianum in hac vita coronari."* Worldlings may wish to be crowned with roses, but they renounce thereby the crown of eternal glory. Those who wish to be crowned with Jesus in heaven, must be willing to share his Crown of Thorns upon earth. The pious king of Jerusalem, Godfred de Bouillon, constantly refused to wear a crown of gold in that city wherein our Lord, the King of Kings, was crowned with thorns.

6. *Jesus is crowned as our King.*

Jesus Christ, being the incarnate Son of God is consequently by creation, preservation, and redemption, the Lord, Master and King of the Universe. But, because upon this subject some reflections will be made in the following chapters, we wish here to consider him as our King in relation only to his Crown of Thorns. Through his passion and death our Savior has conquered sin, death and hell.

First. He wished to be crowned with thorns and thistles, both being the emblem and the punishment of sin. Our Lord, through his thorny crown, shows to all the world that he has removed sin from mankind, and the curse of God from the Earth. Through the punctures of the Crown of Thorns, our crucified Lord has removed from the penitent sinner the sting of conscience, and the pang and danger of despair. Moreover as the Crown of Thorns caused copious streams of blood to flow from our Savior's head down on the inferior members of his suffering body, so, through this sacred crown he obtained for all his elect, who are the mystical members of his body the Church, all the graces, blessings, and gifts of God. As sinners we were thorny, noxious and barren trees destined to be cut down to the ground, and doomed to eternal fire. But since our Lord has been crowned with the thorns of our sins, he has removed the thorny branches, and by engrafting his prolific holiness upon us through his Sacraments, has enabled us to bear abundant fruits of virtuous actions. These are in substance the words of Clement of Alexandria, *"Coronatus est Christus spinis, ut nos*

151

qui antea spinei et infructuosi eramus, fructum bonae arboris apportemus."
(Epist. ad .Oceanum)

Second. Through his Crown of Thorns our heavenly King has conquered death. By removing sin our Savior has taken away its terrible sting from death. *"Death is swallowed up in victory. O death where is thy victory? O death where is thy sting? Now the sting of death is sin. But thanks be to God who hath given the victory through our Lord Jesus Christ."* (1 Cor. 15:55) Our Lord, then having obtained the victory over sin and death, deserved to receive a crown. The crown which he was pleased to choose was that of thorns.

Reflecting on this glorious victory the servants of God rejoiced at the hour of death. Gerard, the pious brother of St. Bernard, feeling that he was dying, intoned aloud with a cheerful voice the psalm; *Laudate Dominun. "Praise ye the Lord from the heavens; praise him in the high places; Praise ye him all his angels."* (Ps. 148:1) St. Bernard says: "I was called to witness this prodigy. I saw this man exulting in death, and defying its terrors. *"Accitus sum ego ad id miracculi, videre exultantem in morte hominem, et insultantiem morti."* (Serm. 26. in Cantic.)

In his last agony the seraphic Patriarch, St. Francis, was singing sacred hymns and psalms, together with his religious. Being somewhat chided for this by Brother Elias, the dying Saint mildly answered: *"Dear brother, I cannot help doing this, knowing that I shall soon be with God."*

Blessed Reginald, a Dominican friar, being near death, was exhorted by his religious brethren to prepare himself for his last combat by receiving the Sacrament of Extreme Unction. "I desire, my dear fathers," he said, "to receive all the Sacraments of the Church, because through them all the merits of our Savior's Passion are applied to our soul, and because the grace that we have received through them is by them increased. However, I have not the least fear of death; on the contrary, I am expecting it with great joy. Christ our Lord has overcome death and has taken away from it its sting. Through the Crown of Thorns he has blunted the sting of death. Death, my dearest brothers, is life for those for whom the passage to heaven is opened through the sacred side of our crucified Savior. Do then, very dear fathers, in your charity, administer to me the Sacrament of Extreme Unction." This dying servant of God having received this last Sacrament with the most lively faith and devotion, sweetly slept in the Lord. *"Obdormivit in Domino."* (Malvenda, Annals O. P.)

Third. Through the Crown of Thorns hell has been conquered. Sin and death being overcome, the devil can no longer have any power over our soul. The infernal serpent is defeated by those very thorns which he sowed upon earth, through the sins of our first parents, and the malediction that on his account God pronounced against this earth, rebounds with terrible effect upon his proud and malignant head. The Crown of Thorns, on our Savior's head is the impenetrable hedge with which he surrounds and protects the vineyard of his Church, and every one of his elect. Through this hedge the friends of Christ are defended, and the infernal enemy of their soul is excluded. *"Hoc diadema spinarum, inimicum iis, qui insidiantur, eos prohibet; iis autem qui in ecclesia simul versantur, amicum, eos circumsepit et munit."* (Clement Alexand. Lib. 2 Poen. Cap. 8)

Fourth. Lastly the Crown of our Savior is the infallible pledge of our diadem of everlasting glory. Sin, death, hell being overcome, heaven is secured to us. It was in a special manner through his Crown of Thorns, that our Savior has merited, for his faithful servants the crown of immortal glory, *"Be thou faithful unto death and I will give thee the Crown of Life."* (Apoc. 2:10)

Dionysius the Carthusian says: Jesus has been crowned with thorns, that we may be crowned in heaven with a crown of precious stones. *"Therefore they shall receive a kingdom of glory and a crown of beauty at the hand of the Lord.* (Wis. 5:17) *Spinea corona capitis Jesu diadema regni adepti sumus,"* St. Jerome says.

CHAPTER XVIII

THE MYSTERIES OF THE CROWN OF THORNS

"In that day the Lord of hosts shall be a crown of glory and a garland of joy to the residue of his people." (Is. 28:5)

In two different ways, namely, in a merely human, or in a truly Christian point of view, can we consider the sufferings and humiliations of Jesus, our Lord. If we look at them, with a merely human eye like the carnal Jews, and the proud Pagans, we shall like them, incur the danger of being scandalized at their apparent foolishness. The excess of the sufferings of our dear Redeemer, the depth of his humiliations, his apparent complete helplessness, have often been a stumbling block of scandal to proud men. Hence St. Paul could say: *"We preached Christ crucified, to the Jews a stumbling black, and to the Gentiles foolishness."* (1 Cor. 1:23) If, however, with the enlightened eye of Christian faith we try to penetrate into the deep mysteries of our Savior's passion, we shall discover the wonders of God's power, and the merciful designs of his divine wisdom. *"To them that are called, that is, to sincere and reflecting Christians, Christ is the power of God, and the wisdom of God."* (1 Cor. 1:24) In the light of Christian faith we will therefore consider the mysteries of the Crown of Thorns. In the present chapter we shall have an opportunity of admiring the designs of the wisdom and mercy of our divine Lord. We shall soon be able to discover important meanings, and learn practical lessons from the thorns, reed, and mockeries used by his cruel and malicious enemies against our Savior.

FIRST SECTION

THE CROWN OF THORNS

The thorns, with which the adorable head of our Lord was crowned, were not planted upon earth by the paternal hand of God, but they were maliciously sowed by a treacherous enemy. From the Gospel we learn that this enemy was the Devil, and the sin of our first parents, Adam and Eve was the noxious seed. The curse of God made them grow long and sharp. These thorns and thistles were more intended to prick the sinner's conscience than the callous hand of the industrious laborer. This is the wise reflection of St. John Chrysostom; "when God said to our fallen parents: *Cursed is the earth in thy work; thorns and thistles shall it bring forth to thee.*" He intended to signify; thy conscience O sinner, shall never cease producing thorns and stings which will prick thy guilty soul. (St. John Chrys. in Mark 10:19) The thorns of this accursed earth are therefore the figures of our sins. They are the brand of God's malediction impressed on the forehead of sinners. Even the learned protestant Grotius discovered this truth and said; "The curse of sin was the origin of thorns." *"Maledictio in spinis Coepit."* (Grot. comm. in Mark 15:17)

Now our Lord Jesus Christ, being the second person of the most adorable Trinity, essential holiness in human flesh, *Verbum Caro factum* and the most cherished object of the eternal predilection of his heavenly Father, could never be defiled by the least shadow of sin and consequently he never could be subject to the malediction of God. In his infinite mercy he could however consent to experience the temporary effects of both. Jesus could assume and wear for our sake the infamous badge of sin. He could in mercy for us taste and drink the loathsome bitterness of the cup filled up to the brim with the gall and vinegar of God's malediction.

Our divine Redeemer did in fact consent to wear during his whole mortal life, the sinner's garb and he daily drank in large doses the disgusting potion squeezed from the corrupted hearts of sinful men as from sour grapes by the weight of God's anathema. But because the large and deep vessel containing the poison of sin was not exhausted, being daily and hourly replenished by new crimes; so our dear Lord was obliged to make a most painful effort in order to drain it all at once and completely during his bitter passion. This heroic act was accomplished in the garden of Gethsemani wherein he was so copiously drenched with the large chalice of sin that he was cast into a deadly swoon and his life's blood was forced out from every pore of his agonizing body.

Now we should attentively observe that the same plan was followed by our merciful Redeemer in wearing the filthy badge of sin. Having once assumed it in his incarnation with our human nature, he had to wear it continually during his whole mortal life. At the time, however, of his passion our Lord had to be publicly and solemnly installed as the King of Sinners and Sorrows. Oh! the grand and sublime mystery of the Crown of Thorns.

It was then in the city of Jerusalem, the capital of Judea, it was in the hall of Pilate, the Roman Governor, that our divine Lord chose to be crowned with thorns and to assume the full uniform of sinner and the infamous wreath of sin. It was on this memorable occasion that the great and eternal Son of God the Incarnate Word was installed as the King of Sinners and consequently as the man deepest in infamy and greatest in sorrow: "Despised and the most abject of men! ..." Our sins are Jesus' Crown of Thorns. *"Corona ex spinis pcccata sunt."* (Theopil. in Matt. 27) Thorns being the offshoot and the stigma of God's malediction against sin, hence, by consenting to be crowned with thorns, our merciful Lord voluntarily became the responsible head and the willing victim of God's anathema directed and intended for sinners only. It is thus according to St. Paul that *"Christ hath redeemed us from the curse of the law, being made a curse for us."* (Gal. 3:13) Hence, by wearing the Crown of Thorns, our most holy Redeemer received upon his adorable head the curse pronounced by the irritated justice of God against our sinful race, and through this act of mercy he shielded us from its terrible blow. *"In corona spinea maledictum solvit antiquum,"* says Origen.

Our merciful Savior effected still more in our behalf. Thorns and thistles, as we have remarked, are the principal offshoot of God's curse against sin. Now by consenting to take these sharp thorns upon his adorable head, he removed this malediction and changed it into a blessing for mankind. In this way our Lord Jesus Christ diminished the quantity and the intensity of our temporal sufferings; and through his blessing, grace and example, he rendered all our labors and toils meritorious of eternal reward. Children of sinful parents, conceived and born in sin, we have indeed much to suffer yet; but had not our blessed Lord come to our relief our temporal sufferings should have been by far more numerous in quantity and more intense in quality as daily experience testifies among Infidel and

Pagan nations. Moreover we should have been condemned to pass from temporal to eternal misery. Through his merciful Crown of Thorns our Savior has removed from mankind the brand of everlasting infamy and has secured for his faithful servants the diadem of heavenly glory. *"In that day,* the prophet Isaias says, *the Lord of Hosts shall be a crown of glory, and a garland of joy to the residue of his people."* (Is. 28:5) Hence St. Jerome could with reason say that: Through the merit of the thorny crown of Jesus' head we have acquired a right to the diadem of the heavenly kingdom. *"Corona spinea capitis ejus diadema regni adepti sumus."* (In Marc. 15)

In all our sufferings then let us look up to the King of Sorrows crowned with thorns. This should be done more especially when by irksome neuralgia, and severe head-aches, we are invited to bear a share of the thorny crown of our divine Master. St. Bernard justly remarks that: *"Christians should be ashamed to be too delicate members of a divine head crowned with thorns."* We should however acknowledge that persons afflicted with these sufferings deserve more charitable compassion than they do generally receive. These afflictions being internal and invisible do not excite to commiseration those especially who had never experienced their painful and saddening effects. We should also reflect that head-aches are often caused by an overflow of blood to the head which produces a flush on the face and this is mistaken by many superficial observers for a sign of vigorous health. Hence compliments are offered which to the ears of the sufferer sound like irony. Moreover these painful attacks of the head are naturally the cause of mistakes and of awkward failures, which bring upon their victim ridicule and undeserved humiliations. The best and perhaps the only comfort and consolation on these mortifying occasions, will be a devout glance at Jesus crowned with thorns and mocked in the hall of Pilate. He is fully aware of our sufferings and trials. He suffered more than we do both in physical pain and in humiliations. Our Lord can compassionate our misery and will abundantly reward our humility, meekness and patience.

In the lives of the Fathers of the Desert, we read that St. Pacomius towards the end of his life, while suffering intense pain in his head and oppressed with interior anguish of mind, had recourse to prayer to obtain some relief and consolation from God. On this occasion our Lord appeared to him accompanied by many holy angels and wearing a Crown of Thorns but at the same time shining with dazzling glory. Surprised at the heavenly vision the suffering servant of God prostrated himself with his face to the ground when one of the angels very affectionately raised him up and informed him that Jesus Christ had come to console him in his affliction. Our Lord then spoke to Pacomius words of heavenly comfort encouraging him to bear his trials and sufferings with resignation, assuring him that they were intended for the purification of his soul, and for a great increase of merit which was soon to be crowned with corresponding glory and bliss for all eternity in heaven.

SECOND SECTION

THE SCARLET CLOAK

"They put a scarlet cloak about him." (Mt. 27:28)

We will now proceed to examine for a short time the meaning of the scarlet cloak which the malicious enemies of our Lord, Jesus Christ threw in derision over his bruised and bleeding shoulders.

In order to understand the mysterious significance of this extraordinary event, we should reflect that our first parents in the terrestial paradise had no need of any material dress so long as they were clad and adorned with the beautiful robe of original grace and innocence. The same should have been the happy condition of their posterity, had they persevered in their state of holiness. Innocent childhood alone partially enjoys this privilege now, and this only for a very short space of time. But the prevarication of Adam and Eve caused the rebellion of the flesh against the spirit and produced a general feeling of shame. All this combined with their expulsion from the Garden of Eden, and their perpetual exile to this cold region of the earth, imposed upon mankind the necessity of external dress. Dress then should be considered both the badge and the punishment of sinners. Here we may begin to understand the profound meaning of the scarlet cloak thrown over the shoulders of our divine Savior. Being essential holiness he could not assume the guilt, nor, strictly speaking feel the remorse of sin. But in his infinite mercy he could assume its appearance, and experience its temporal effects. Hence our Lord was first stripped of that sacred garment which he had received from the immaculate hands of his most holy Mother. Thus he was in appearance deprived of the essential attribute of his inseparable holiness. Then a soiled and worn out red cloak of a Pagan soldier was temporarily cast over his sacred shoulders. This cruel and humiliating insult was permitted by divine Wisdom to enable us to understand that our merciful Savior wished, through this action, to signify that he consented to assume the filthy dress of sin, deeply dyed in the blood and crimes of mankind during the long period of four thousand years. This is the admirable expression of the great Origen who said: *"Suscipiens Dominus clamydem coccineam in se, sanguinem mundi, idest peccata suscepit."* (Homil. 35 in Matt. 27:29)

In assuming and wearing before heaven and earth the degrading livery of sin, our dear Lord had also to bear the burning shame and confusion due to all sinners. He had moreover to endure a special mortification, and to feel a deep blush at the conduct of those worldly persons that boldly carry vice in triumph in the extravagance of public luxury in dress, in the ridiculous whims of modern fashions, and in the scandalous immodesty of unblushing vanity. Oh! If Christian men, and more especially if Christian women were able to reflect occasionally on the deep shame and confusion their criminal vanity and extravagance in dress caused our suffering Savior: they should remember that at the Baptismal font they were solemnly pledged to renounce worldly pomps and empty vanities and bound to appear in public, as St. Paul directs, *"in decent apparel, adorning themselves with modesty and sobriety, and not with plaited hair, or gold, or pearls, or costly array."* (1 Tim. 2:9) But alas! That modishness has affected the brain, and corrupted the heart of modern society, which disdains to listen to the voice of truth ...

Some courage and firmness of determination is certainly necessary to withstand the frothy, sweeping current of modern fashion, which carries away headlong so many thoughtless victims to the abyss of temporal ruin and eternal misery. But let more serious Christians reflect that our Lord Jesus Christ, by the shame and ignominy which he underwent in Pilate's hall, has sanctified modesty and has acquired for Christian society the necessary grace and strength for resisting the seductions of worldly vanity. By bearing the humiliation and the blushing shame of the old scarlet cloak, our blessed Savior has hallowed evangelical poverty, simplicity, humility and modesty in dress. This is one of the principal reasons why the poor, humble and modest habit of religious persons is generally honored and respected not only among real Christians but also by Pagans and by savages as daily experience teaches. Let us conclude with the opportune words addressed by the Prince of the Apostles to all Christian women. *"Considering your chaste conversation with fear: whose adorning let it not be in the outward plaiting of the hair, or the wearing of gold, or the putting on of apparel; but in the hidden man of the heart, in the incorruptibility of a quiet and meek spirit, which is rich in the sight of God."* (1 Pet. 3:2)

The Fathers of the Church in their enlightened zeal frequently inculcated these salutary lessons with such warmth of eloquent power, that made a deep and lasting impression on the minds of their Christian auditors. The effects of their sermons were evident on the modesty of Christian society. All our female saints and great servants of God, have been remarkable for their strict modesty and evangelical simplicity in dress. The bright example of the holy Empress, St. Pulcheria, the daughter, sister and wife of an emperor, that of St. Elizabeth, Queen of Portugal, of St. Margaret, Queen of Scotland, of St. Elizabeth of Hungary, of St. Bridget, Duchess of Sweden, of St. Frances of Rome, in short of all Christian female saints should convince us that modesty in dress is the most valuable ornament of a Christian lady. *"Favor is deceitful,"* the Holy Ghost says, *"and beauty is vain: The woman that feareth the Lord, she shall be praised. Give her of the fruit of her hands; and let her works praise her in the gates."* (Prov. 31:30)

May all men of the present frivolous age understand and appreciate the worth and beauty of Christian modesty. It will adorn them in life, it will comfort them in death, and finally it will·clothe them with a mantle of glory during an ever blessed eternity, *"when the Lord will reform the body of our lowliness, and make it like the body of his glory,"* as St. Paul teaches. (Philip 3:21)

THIRD SECTION

THE REED IN THE HAND OF JESUS

They put a reed in his right hand. (Mt. 27:29)

As the scarlet cloak was the figure of our sinfulness, as the thorns were the sign of our barrenness and sterility; so the reed is a striking emblem of human frailty, emptiness and inconstancy. A reed is an empty, hollow, frail, light and inconstant plant. It has no solidity. It is moved about in every direction by the least breath of wind. This despicable plant was never more honored than when it was in derision put in the divine hand of our Lord.

What an admirable figure is this of our fallen human nature! What can be more hollow and empty than the reed of a poor sinful man? Sin strips him of every supernatural grace, virtue and merit. Like the merchant

160

of Jericho, he is robbed of all his wealth and he is left prostrate upon the ground wounded and bleeding to death. Like the eminent man of the Apocalypse who in his greedy and ridiculous vanity flatters himself that he is rich, wealthy and wants nothing, sin has made him "wretched and miserable, poor, blind and naked." (Apoc. 3:17)

Then what is more weak and frail than a sinner? Stripped of the supernatural strength of grace, left to his own innate weakness, urged by temptation, impelled by his own evil passions, he totters and falls at every step. Like a frail reed he bends to every whim of fancy and to the slightest whisper of seduction. Such is the reed of fallen human nature left to itself.

But since our Blessed Lord took this reed in his hand it has been completely changed; its hollowness has been filled with the solidity of his grace and love. In the hand of our Savior we become firmer and stronger than the cedars of Lebanon. Through faith and confidence in him we can resist the most violent temptations of hell and the fiercest storms of human persecutions. By assuming our frail nature the Son of God has endowed us with the power and strength of his divine Omnipotence, and we like St. Paul *"can do everything in the power of him who strengtheneth."* (Phil. 4:13) St. Ambrose says: "Our Lord has taken the reed of our humanity in his hand in order to hinder the frailty of our fallen nature from being tossed by every wind of false doctrine and to render it firm and steady by the truth of faith and solid by the fullness of virtuous works." (S. Ambrose. com. in. S. Matt. chap. 27) So long then as we remain in the hand of Jesus we are invincible. He changes us from frail and empty reeds into golden scepters of his power. With these scepters, if we remain faithful, he will make us kings of his heavenly kingdom as Origen says: *"Pro calamo illo priori, dedit nobis sceptrum Regni caelestis."* (Orig. Homil. 35 in Matt.)

FOURTH SECTION

JESUS IS MOCKED AND OUTRAGED

The insults and mockeries of the Crown of Thorns remain to be considered. St. Matthew says: *"And bowing the knee before him, they mocked him saying: Hail King of the Jews. And spitting upon him, they took the reed and struck his head."* (Mt. 27:30). From these words we learn

161

that our divine Lord received on this memorable occasion four different marks of contempt.

First. These impious men bowed the knee in derision before him.

Second. They saluted him in mockery, King of the Jews.

Third. They struck his thorn-crowned head with a reed.

Fourth. They spat upon his face.

These are the four kinds of insults that the majesty of God daily receives from men and which our suffering Savior on this occasion undertook to expiate.

1.The first insult is offered to God by Pagans in their idolatrous worship, when they bow their knees to abominable idols. Reason alone is capable of seeing, and able to demonstrate that there can be but one God, self-existent, eternal in duration, infinite in his perfections, immense in his nature, Creator of the world, supreme Lord and absolute master of all creatures. For this one and only God, Pagans have substituted an endless variety of dumb and material idols which they have shaped with their own hands according to the suggestion of their whims and fancies. Before them they bow their knee, these they worship, to them they offer incense and immolate their victims. It is evident that by so doing, Pagans discard the true living God, and they insult his divine majesty by every act of their idolatrous worship. It is no less evident that some condign expiation is demanded by the offended majesty of God. A divine victim only can duly expiate outrages offered directly to God, in his highest attribute of supreme Lord of Creation. Behold then what our most holy Savior is doing now in Pilate's hall. Reflect that Pilate is a Pagan, his soldiers are Pagans, like himself, This hall is turned by these men into a temporary temple. The hard and cold stone, upon which our Lord is seated, serves as his altar. Victims of sacrifice are by Pagan hands garlanded with roses about their heads. Jesus is, by them crowned with thorns. They bow down their knee before him in mock worship. That this act was intended by the Pagan soldiers as derisive and ironical worship towards our Lord, we learn from St. Mark who expressly says: *"that bowing their knees, they worshipped him."* (Mk. 15:19)

Jesus being the Person of the Incarnate Word of God by whom all things were made, truly deserves divine worship. But by receiving impious mockeries and sacrilegious insults, instead of adoration, he fully expiates before his eternal Father for all the impieties of Paganism, abolishes more effectively Pagan idolatry, and through his profound humiliations, merits for all idolaters the light of faith and the grace of conversion to Christianity.

2. The second insult offered to our Savior was to salute him in derision *King of the Jews.*

Jesus was by every right and title the true King of the Jews. He was their supreme Lord in his divine nature. He was their King by divine appointment because God bestowed the kingdom of Judea on the descendants of David, and our Lord in his human nature belongs to the family of David. Moreover the angel said to Mary his Mother: *"The Lord, God shall give unto him the throne of David, his father, and he shall reign in the house of Jacob forever, and of his kingdom there shall be no end."* (Lk. 1:32) But the Jews have repudiated him. They have just protested before the Roman Governor, that *they have no king but Caesar.* (Jn. 19:15) Our blessed Lord heard these words. Now the Pagan soldiers to humble and degrade him more, and to gratify the Jews who witnessed these outrages with immense satisfaction, ridicule and mock him by ironically saluting him, *King of the Jews.* By rejecting Jesus as their King, the Jews reject him as their Messias. Because in his person these two titles are inseparable. By rejecting the Son they reject the Father, because the Son and the Father are one. (Jn. 10:30) The Jews have arrived at this depth of impiety by performing their religious acts of worship in the temple, in their synagogues and on every other occasion without any spirit of devotion but by mere routine in a mechanical and material way. As St. Paul says they stuck to the letter, which killeth, and abandoned the true spirit of religious worship which alone can give life to the individual soul and to the entire nation. In bearing these humiliations and insults, our blessed Lord expiates the irreverences of the Jews in their acts of religion towards God, and for their rejection of him as their Messias and King. It is through these sufferings and deep humiliations that he confirms to the Jewish nation the privileged honor of the Apostolate; for all the apostles were selected exclusively from them. He merits and obtains for many thousands of them the grace of conversion to Christianity as the first fruit of his Passion; and towards the end of the world he will see prostrate at his feet like the penitent Magdalene the entire Jewish nation worshiping him, *in spirit and in truth,* in deep sorrow and sincere repentance as their true Messias and only King.

3. The third outrage offered to our Lord was the striking of his thorn crowned head with a reed. This represents the malice of heretical Christians.

Heresy is essentially an individual choice in belief. Heresy necessarily rebels at least indirectly against the authority of the Church. Obedience and heresy is a contradiction in terms. No heretic as such has ever been found in practice docile to the decisions of the Church of God. The authority of the Church has by Jesus Christ been concentrated in the person of Peter when he said to him: *Thou art Peter, and upon this rock I will build my Church.* (Mt. 16:18) *Feed my lambs, feed my sheep.* (Jn. 21) Heresy changes lambs into rams that butt against the Shepherd. All heretics rebel against the Pope and make war against his authority. Hence they strike Jesus on the head. And as we have learned from St. Paul, *the head of Christ is God*; so our suffering Lord had also to atone for this insult and merit for many deluded heretics the grace of their return to Catholic faith and unity.

4. The last and most shocking insult offered to our Savior crowned with thorns was that of spitting upon his sacred countenance. St. Gregory remarks that we know a person by his face. This vulgar insult comes then from those who know our Lord. These then are bad Catholics. They spit upon his face by their bad example by which they scandalize their fellow-Christians, they dishonor their religion and make the enemies of God blaspheme his holy name. This terrible insult is in a special manner offered to our Lord by those hypocritical Catholics who practice some external acts of religion through human motives, self-interest and vain-glory. But above all, those truly spit upon our Lord who receive him, like Judas, sacrilegiously in Holy Communion with mortal sin in their souls. As our most merciful Lord suffered and prayed on the cross for his executioners, so in the hall of Pilate he prays and atones for these unworthy members of his Church. These are the principal mysteries of the Crown of Thorns. They are mysteries of the wisdom and power of God. We have so far considered the wonders of our Savior's wisdom and mercy in the mystery of his crowning with thorns. In the next chapter we will admire the triumph of his divine power.

CHAPTER XIX

TRIUMPHS OF JESUS THROUGH THE CROWN OF THORNS

"I saw, and beheld a white horse and he that sat on it had a bow, and a crown was given to him; and he went forth conquering that he might conquer." (Apoc. 6:2)

This mysterious vision was seen by St. John in the island of Patmos. The white horse signifies the innocent and holy human body assumed by the Eternal Son of God at his incarnation. *The bow* with which he fights is that of truth. He goes forth fighting with humility and patience that he may conquer the pride and sensuality of the world. We have seen above that according to St. Bernard, four crowns were given to our blessed Lord. We are now considering the triumph achieved by him through his Crown of Thorns.

Our Lord having by his enemies been accused to the Roman Governor of making himself a king, Pilate asked him whether he was the King of the Jews. *Jesus answered: My kingdom is not of this world. If my kingdom were of this world, my servants would certainly strive that I should not be delivered to the Jews. But now my kingdom is not from hence.* Pilate from these words of our Lord logically concluded that he was a king; therefore he replied: *Art thou a king then? Jesus answered: thou sayest that I am a king. For this I was born, and for this I came into the world, that I should give testimony to the truth. Every one that is of the truth heareth my voice.* (Jn. 18:36) We Christians professing to be of the truth, should therefore listen to the voice of our divine Master and study the lessons which he imparts to us.

1.The first truth our Lord teaches on this solemn occasion is that *he is a King*. We learn this fact from his words to Pilate: *"thou sayest that*

I am a king," which is equivalent to saying: I am a king as thou sayest. This is an *Hebraism,* or a mode of affirming commonly used by the Jews, as Pilate well knows. We must observe here that in his answer to the Roman Governor our Lord claims a higher dignity and a more extensive power and dominion than that ever possessed by any Jewish king. He is interrogated by Pilate, whether *he be the king of the Jews* ... He answers that he is a king implying that he is a greater monarch than a mere Jewish king could be. Jesus in fact is the *King of Kings, and the Lord of Lords.* (Apoc. 19:16) *He is a great King over all the earth ... He shall reign over the nations.* (Ps. 46) Jesus will most certainly reign over the nations of the earth. But what are the laws by which he proposes to govern this vast empire? What promises does he make to men to draw them to his standard? What reward will he give to his faithful followers? His laws, his promises, his rewards are of an opposite nature to those of earthly monarchs. Human laws are in modern times chiefly directed to the promotion of material progress. Modern civil legislation seems so intent to advance the accumulation of material wealth as if this were the main end of human society. But the laws of Jesus, promulgated in the Gospel condemn riches as most dangerous to the eternal salvation of man and bless voluntary poverty, as the surest guarantee for obtaining the kingdom of heaven. We are warned against the allurements of earthly prosperity, and strongly exhorted to make friends of the mammon of iniquity by large alms to the poor that they may receive us in the eternal tabernacles which are their legitimate inheritance; because the kingdom of heaven is awarded to the poor in spirit. Glory is promised to the humble, power to the meek and eternal bliss to the virtuous sufferer. The promises of Jesus are principally confined to the next life. In this present life he promises to his followers the privations of poverty, the contempt of the world, the calumnies of malice the persecutions of tyranny. He invites his disciples to follow him in the constant practice of self-denial, willingly carrying their cross to Mount Calvary, to be crucified in his company, to suffer and to die in contempt for his sake.

Our divine Master and model gives in his person a specimen of these humiliations and sufferings. At his installment in the hall of Pilate, his throne is a cold and hard stone, his diadem is a crown of sharp thorns. But this throne and this crown, which are the most convincing proofs of his enemies' cruelty and hardness of heart, are at the same time the fittest insignia of his dignity and power. What more solid throne than a stone can be found for the Monarch of the Universe? What better diadem than a Crown of Thorns for the King of Sorrows? By sitting upon a stone he takes actual possession of the whole earth. Being now installed, a crown is due to him as a king. But a crown of gold would make Jesus of Nazareth appear a mortal king with a limited kingdom like other earthly monarchs whose principal strength consists in the power of their perishable riches to support their tottering dignity. A crown of flowers would designate him as a voluptuous and self-indulgent man, the king of an effeminate race of subjects. A laurel crown would suit a victorious conqueror of nations whose sword is crimsoned with the blood of innumerable victims of his ambition. Any of these crowns would no doubt appear more honorable in the eyes of carnal men, but in reality it would be a sign of weakness, and a badge of infamy for our divine Lord, because it would make him appear a mere man elevated to an earthly kingdom like other monarchs of this world by material instruments and human means. A Crown of Thorns then is the most honorable for Jesus Christ. It makes him indeed the King of Sorrows. It makes him an object of derision and contempt for the impious, for the wicked, and the proud. But in spite of them Jesus draws more numerous, more sincere and nobler courtiers round this cold stone, crimsoned with his blood than the monarchs of the earth can ever hope to see near their thrones of gold enameled with precious stones. Jesus crowned with thorns beholds daily scores of millions of earnest worshipers who adore him in spirit and in truth, who love and serve him with devoted hearts. While the monarchs of the earth must have recourse to forced conscription to enroll soldiers for the defense of their drooping standards, three hundred millions of true believers are ready to shed their blood at the foot of the Cross in defense of their Faith and of the laws of Jesus Christ, their thorn-crowned King. But his glory and power is more fully manifested in heaven, where countless millions of angels and saints serve, praise, love and worship him as their Lord and God. This Crown of Thorns then, which has been pressed upon his sacred head to afflict, humble and degrade him, has been changed into *a crown of gold, wherein holiness is engraved, a badge of honor, a work of power, delightful to the eyes of Faith for its beauty.* (Eccli. 45:13) Such are the triumphs of the Crown of Thorns. Jesus crowned with thorns is become the King of Kings and the Master of heaven and earth.

With these sentiments of Faith in his Christian heart the truly noble Godfrey de Bouillon, having through his bravery and military skill contributed much to the recovery of Jerusalem, was declared king of the re-conquered holy city and territory. But in his humility he would never consent to wear a crown of gold, because as he said, "Jesus our Lord had worn in Jerusalem a Crown of Thorns."

2. In the second place Our Lord said to Pilate: *My kingdom is not of this world.* These words should not be distorted in favor of the modern sacrilegious robberies of the States and other property of the Church in many parts of the world. Jesus did not say that his kingdom was not *upon earth.* Because as we have seen, he is the *King of Kings,* and surely this means that he is the sovereign Lord, and king of all earthly monarchs. *He is the great King over all the Earth.* He became man to save and govern all men. He makes us pray daily that his kingdom may be established upon the whole earth, and that he may reign over all nations. *"Thy kingdom come, thy will be done on earth as it is in heaven."* When our Lord said to Pilate: *My kingdom is not of this world,* he intended to teach men that *the origin* of his supreme power and dignity is not from the earth but from heaven, not from men, but immediately from God. He wished us to understand that the means and instruments which he uses for the establishment, extension and perpetuation of his kingdom, are not material and human, like those of earthly potentates, but of a very different nature. He has omnipotence as an essential attribute of his divinity. Hence he has no need of powerful armies with numerous squadrons of trained cavalry, supported by large parks of modern artillery. He builds no navy because he has no need of it. The bark of Peter is sufficient for him. All these engines of war serve only to demonstrate the utter weakness of earthly governments that are obliged to use them to keep their discontented subjects in forced obedience to their laws, and to repel the invasions of external foes. Jesus is the God of truth and recruits his subjects through the maxims of the Gospel. He is the Prince of Peace, and draws his followers through the charms of Christian charity. No man is forced into his service against his will. In the kingdom of Christ every person is free. In his army all are volunteers without pay, and without any other promise of bounty, except an eternal reward, if they remain faithful to him until death, *Be thou faithful unto death and I will give thee the crown of life.* (Apoc. 2:10) In the school of Jesus the wise according to the flesh are taught to become fools for his sake, and to subject the boasted light of their reason to the authority of Faith. In the company of Jesus, the ambitious and proud in high honors and dignities are humbled; and the low

and humble in spirit are raised above them. The rich are taught lessons of poverty, thc vigor of youth and the strength of manhood are weakened by labor and voluntary penance. All the wealth, power and success of his followers are confined to humble, fervent prayer. These are the means, and the instruments which our Lord Jesus Christ employs for the establishment, extension and perpetuation of his kingdom upon earth.

Now, what scepter could have better and more strikingly expressed the apparent weakness of these instruments, than the hollow, light and frail reed which was placed in the right hand of our Savior crowned with thorns? Yet, it is with this empty reed that he has established the great kingdom of his Church upon earth. How empty and poor, ignorant, weak and frail were the apostles, the first instruments our Lord selected for the preaching of his Gospel! ...St. Paul says: *See your vocation, brethren, that not many are wise according to the flesh, not many mighty, not many noble. But the foolish things of the world hath God chosen, that He may confound the wise, and the weak things of the world hath God chosen that he may confound the strong. And the mean things of the world, and the things that are not, that he might destroy the things that are.* (1 Cor. 1:26) Before St. Paul wrote these divine truths, they had been forcibly expressed by our Redeemer and Master, through a reed in his hand in Pilate's hall. It is with instruments as frail and hollow as a reed that he has succeeded in a short period of time in establishing his kingdom in all the principal nations of the world. Wise philosophers, like Dionysius the areopagite and St. Justin, eloquent orators like Cyprian and Augustine were captivated by the folly of the cross. The high and the noble of the earth came down from their lofty dignities and honors to the lowliness and obscurity of the Catacombs, and the wealthy embraced the poverty of the Gospel. Kings, like Clovis, and emperors like Constantine bowed their heads under the yoke of Christ, and raised his cross over their standards and upon their imperial diadems. So long as they held their scepters of power in the name of Jesus, and wielded them for the promotion of his holy kingdom, they were always victorious, respected, and prosperous. But when the potentates of the earth abused their material power to oppress his Church, to persecute his followers, and to harass his Vicar in Rome, their scepters of gold were changed into hollow and frail reeds, which in their insane and impotent efforts broke and wounded their hands, while their thrones were shivered to pieces, and scattered as rubbish over the face of the earth. So foretold the best of prophet kings: *"Thou shalt rule them with a rod of iron, and shalt break them in pieces like a Potter's vessel. And now, ye kings understand, and receive instruction you that judge the earth. Serve the Lord with fear ... embrace discipline, lest at any time the Lord be angry, and you perish ... when his wrath shall be kindled in a short time, blessed are all they that trust in him."* (Ps. 2:9)

When his wrath shall be kindled in a short time. The materials for a general conflagration are ready in the universal discontent of mankind, against modern rulers and governments. These have impiously abdicated the Christian character of their mission, and direct all the energies of their waning power to paganize their subjects. They wield their scepters with a heavy hand upon the people, overwhelming them with an unbearable burden of taxes, oppressing their bodies with military conscription, perverting their minds with the impious doctrines of godless schools, and tyrannizing over their consciences with unjust and anti-Christian laws. They persecute the ministers of religion, interfere with the freedom of divine worship, rob them of their churches, imprison, or exile Catholic priests and bishops, suppress religious houses and confiscate their legitimate property. An impious conspiracy has been formed *"among the kings of the earth, and the princes have met together against the Lord, and against his Christ, the venerable pontiff of Rome ..."* What wonder if according to the warning of the royal Prophet, these discontented subjects say: *"Let us break their bonds asunder, and let us cast away their yoke from us. He that dwelleth in heaven will laugh at our tyrants, and the Lord shall deride them. Then he will speak to them in his anger, and trouble them in his rage."* (Ps. 2) Through his Vicar, the infallible Pope, Jesus has already spoken and his *syllabus* has troubled the mighty kings of the earth. Their scepters of gold, through the anger of God, have been changed in their hands of flesh into frail and hollow reeds, without any power for good. Having rejected God's sanction, their authority has lost the respect of their subjects. Deprived through their anti-Christian policy of the respect and love of mankind, they are obliged to surround their tottering thrones with millions of guns and bayonets, which, before the end of this century, by one of God's greatest prodigies, *when His wrath shall be kindled in a short time,* will be turned into weapons for their utter destruction, together with that of their impious counselors and abettors, the sworn enemies and malicious persecutors of God's holy Church. *"The Lord said to my Lord: Sit thou at my right hand, until I make thy enemies thy footstool. The Lord will send forth the scepter of thy power out of Sion. Rule thou in the midst of thy enemies ... The Lord at thy right hand hath broken kings in the day of his wrath. He shall judge among nations: He shall fill ruins: he shall crush the heads in the land of many."* (Ps. 109) Mankind will be surprised at the triumphs of Jesus crowned with thorns, when with his reed, a scepter of derision, he will, as with an iron rod, break as a potter's vessel, the power of all the tyrants of the earth. Men of all nations will then bend their knees before the throne of his majesty and glory, and worship him in spirit and in truth saying: To the king of ages, immortal, invisible, the only God, be honor and glory for ever and ever. Amen. (Tim. 1:17) Hence, that reed, which was an instrument of derision at the end of his mortal life, will become the scepter of his greatest triumph and glory towards the end of time, which is fast approaching, in spite of the incredulity of men, and in just punishment of this incredulity ...

CHAPTER XX

CONTINUATION OF THE SAME SUBJECT

1. The monarchs of the earth, to enhance their dignity surround it with external emblems of power. They live in magnificent palaces; they sit on high thrones of gold; they clothe themselves in purple, they wear upon their heads golden diadems glistening with precious stones, and wield rich scepters in their hands. We have seen that our divine Lord is a prisoner in the hall of Pilate, where he is made to sit upon a hard stone for his throne, as a sham king: a crown of thorns has been placed upon his adorable head, and a reed of derision in his hands. Lastly, a cast off, old and ragged military cloak is thrown with contempt over his bleeding shoulders. These are the ironical insignia of royalty, which his enemies force upon our Lord to insult and degrade him before the people. But the wisdom and power of God turns to the honor and glory of Jesus all the insults and humiliations heaped upon him by wicked men. Had our blessed Lord received from their hands a new purple mantle, adorned with golden lace, and glittering with jewels, this would have made him appear like other kings of the earth, whose scarlet cloaks are often dyed in the blood of wars, oppression, and persecution. Having, however, been covered with an old cloak, cast off by other men, and crimsoned only in his own blood; this demonstrates that Jesus Christ is the only true King, who establishes and propagates his kingdom and saves his subjects by his own sufferings and personal humiliations, and redeems them with his life's blood. This scarlet cloak is a prophecy which announces him as the adored king of millions of glorious Martyrs, who will with truly heroic fortitude, endure all manner of tortures, and gladly shed the last drop of their heart's blood in his holy service, and for his dear sake. These are the noble soldiers of Jesus who fight for the defence and extension of his kingdom, and are always victorious and triumphant with him, not by shedding the blood of his enemies and of their own persecutors; but by

sacrificing their own lives on the altar of his faith and love. *"Venit Jesus non ut pugnet vivus, sed ut triumphet occisus."* (St. Fulgentius serm. 3 de Epiph)

This scarlet cloak indicates another profound mystery of the kingdom of Jesus Christ. The Jewish nation had hitherto been selected by God as the center of his holy Religion. Jesus our Lord was born from, and among the Jews; he lived with them, preached to them his new covenant of grace, wrought miracles for their conversion. But they have refused to believe in his mission, they have rejected with scorn his heavenly doctrines, and finally, they have officially and publicly repudiated him before the Roman Governor, postponed him to Barabbas, and have with diabolical fury insisted that he should be put to death upon a cross. Unhappily for them, their impious request is now accomplished. The Jews have given up the person of our Lord, their true Messias, into the hands of the Roman soldiers. These have scourged him. Behold, now they strip him of that tunic which he originally received from his people. This mystic and miraculous tunic is the figure of the old covenant, which God made with their forefathers. Jesus being stripped of it through the hatred and malice of the Jews, they are now deprived of the rights and privileges of their holy religion, which is taken away from them at the same moment that our Lord is stripped of his garments. But, because the religion of God can never cease to exist among men, hence, it is immediately transferred from the Jews to the Gentiles with the scarlet cloak, which the latter put on the sacred shoulders of our Redeemer. This beautiful explanation is given by St. Jerome, who is recognized by the church as the best interpreter of the holy Scriptures. The following are his words. *"Jesus is mystically stripped of his vestments, the Jews; and he is clothed with a purple mantle which is the church among the Gentiles."* (St. Jerome. Com. in, Chap. 27 S. Matt) In fact St. Matthew says that: *The soldiers of the Governor, taking Jesus into the hall, gathered together unto him the whole band, and stripping him, they put a scarlet cloak about him.* (Mt. 27:27) These words so simple in their historical signification, express most admirably the transition of the true Religion of God from the Jews to the Gentiles. Observe how completely our Lord, the Teacher of all moral doctrines, and religious truths, is in the hands of the Gentiles. At his crowning of thorns, which must be considered his solemn installment as Head of the Church, our Lord is in the hall of the Roman Governor. Consequently in this particular circumstance, he is out of the power and jurisdiction of the

Jews, as he foretold in these words: *they*, the Jews, *shall deliver him to the Gentiles.* (Mk. 10:33) According to the law of nations he is even outside of their territorial possessions, not only because the Jews are now under the civil dominion of the Romans, but because he is actually in the house of the representative of the Roman Emperor. It is in this Roman palace that our Lord is stripped of all the insignia of the ancient covenant made by God with the Jewish nation. It is in this Roman hall that he receives his crown, his scepter, his royal purple. It is in the Roman hall that all the Gentile nations are gathered in the persons of the Pagan soldiers round about him, to offer him their first homage as to the sovereign Lord and King of Christianity. *"The soldiers of the governor, taking Jesus into the hall, gathered together unto him the whole band."* The malicious intentions of those Roman soldiers cannot invalidate the decree and design of his divine will. He makes them act in spite of their actual dispositions, as his ministers and instruments, as the holy pope, and eloquent orator, St. Leo I says: (Serm. 3 de Passione.) St. Jerome also remarks that, "As the high Pontiff Caiphas, contrary to his intention, made a prophecy of our Redeemer, when he said *that one man should die for the people. (*Jn. 11:50) So these cruel Pagan soldiers, in spite of their dispositions, were executing wonderful mysteries of religion and salvation, when they tormented and derided our Savior at his crowning with thorns in the hall of the Roman Governor." (St. Jerome. Com. in Matt. Chap. 27) Holy Bede says the same. *"Milites illudendo nobis operantur mysteria."* (In Joan 10) And Sedulius more expressly affirms: *"Sub regiae imaginis illusione, Magni gerebantur sacramenta mysterii."* (Lib. 3. oper. Paschal) Great mysteries were accomplished when the Roman soldiers derided our Lord as a mock King. As St. Genesius became a real Christian and died a martyr by beginning, as a theatrical buffoon, to mimic in the Roman amphitheater the rite of Christian Baptism before the Emperor Diocletian; so these deluded men actually proclaimed Jesus our Lord, the King of the universe by their mock homage. We should also observe, that the scarlet cloak placed on the shoulders of our Lord was an old mantle cast off by the former owner. Behold here, how strikingly correct is every figure of the mysteries accomplished on this memorable occasion. Reflect, that our blessed Lord did not come upon earth to establish altogether a new religion. Christianity is essentially the same religion as that established by God among the Jews. Our Lord said to them: *"Think not that I am come to destroy the law, or the Prophets. I am not come to destroy, but to fulfill."*

(Mt. 5:17) He came among the Jews to accomplish all the figures and prophecies, and to perfect all that was imperfect. But what is perfected is not destroyed or abolished. This mysterious fact is well expressed in the old cloak placed over the bleeding shoulders of our blessed Redeemer. Had he founded an entirely new religion, a new mantle should have been given him. But, as he came to purify in his sacred blood the old religion, and to make it perfect by assuming, practicing, and divinizing it in his human nature, he would consent to receive only an old scarlet cloak for his royal purple.

Again, this scarlet cloak had been cast away by the owner as useless. What could more fully express the conduct of the Jews, who paid scrupulous attention to superficial practices of their own invention, and neglected the essential duties of their holy religion? *"Woe to you Scribes and Pharisees, hypocrites; who pay the tithe of mint, and anise and cumin; and have left alone the weightier things of the law, judgment, and mercy, and faith."* (Mt. 23:23) After having cast off as an old garment these weightier things of their law and religion, the Jews now reject the Messias, who is the author of their religion and law. But Jesus takes this rejected garment upon his shoulders, purifies and sanctifies it with his divine blood. Thus, purified and sanctified, this sacred cloak of religion is transferred from the perfidious Jews to the Gentiles, and thus Christianity is established among them.

Finally, let us consider the agency through which this most important transaction is executed. This is done by the soldiers of the Roman Governor, Pilate. They strip our Lord, and thus deprive the Jews of their religion. They clothe him with the scarlet cloak which belongs to the Roman army and government, and thus they officially transfer the true religion of God to themselves. *"Mystice vestimentis, idest Judeis, nudatur Jesus: purpura induitur, idest gentili ecclesia."* These are the genuine words of St. Jerome. (Com. in. Matt. 27) Admire here, the wonders of the wisdom and power of God. After the great miracle of our Lord at the resurrection of Lazarus, many Jews who had been present believed in our Savior. *"Some of them,* the Evangelist says, *went to the Pharisees and told them the things that Jesus had done. The chief priests, therefore, and the Pharisees gathered a council, and said: what do we, for this man doeth many miracles? If we let him alone so, all men will believe in him: and the Romans will come and take away our place and nation.* (Jn. 11:48) It was on this occasion, that the high Pontiff Caiphas said that our Lord should be put to death.

He has, in fact, been condemned to death by the Jewish priests and magistrates, and delivered by them for execution into the hands of the Roman soldiers. Now, God makes use of these very soldiers to deprive the Jewish people of their religion, and of their holy city, and nation ... Behold how God turns against His enemies the means they use in opposition to His divine will. Before many years hence, we expect to see a similar, but more magnificent and more complete stroke of divine wisdom and power against the modern enemies of Jesus, the malicious and bitter persecutors of his Church. With scarcely any exception, the powers of the earth have allied themselves with the power of darkness, the secret societies, to fight against the religion of Christ, and against his Vicar upon earth. God will before long use these powerful secret organizations for the destruction of those deluded governments that have hired them as allies in the unholy war, to accelerate in spite of their malice, the inevitable universal triumph of his holy religion, as foretold, by so many of his prophetical seers in the old and new testament. This great triumph must be entirely the work of God: For this end He has permitted the powers of the earth to abandon the protection of His Church. When all human hope has vanished, then the hand of God will in a more striking manner, be made apparent to all mankind. Let the faithful draw nearer to their King, crowned with thorns. Let them cover themselves with the scarlet cloak of his holy religion. Very likely, some of the more worthy members will have to dye and enrich it with the blood of martyrdom. But this blood will be the surest pledge of approaching victory and the prolific seed of a rich harvest of conversions to the Catholic Faith. The triumph of the cross is achieved by humility and suffering. Let us close these remarks with an example adapted to our present subject.

Chosroas, the proud king of Persia, taking advantage of the distracted condition of the Eastern Empire in the reign of Phocas, declared war against him, marched his victorious army through Palestine, and entered the city of Jerusalem, which he sacked, and carried away with him as a trophy the cross of our Savior. The pious Emperor Heraclius, the successor of Phocas, anxious to recover this precious treasure of Christian devotion, made several overtures to the king, who rejected them with scornful insolence. In his distress Heraclius, placing his confidence in God, betook himself to fasting and prayer, fevently imploring the divine assistance. Animated with a lively faith he, with a very inferior army, attacked his powerful pagan adversary, and in three successive battles so completely routed Chosroas as to put him to an ignominious flight, who was soon after killed by his own son. Heraclius recovered the sacred treasure, which his Christian heart so ardently coveted. Full of joy he returned to Jerusalem, where he was received with great triumph. By his order a grand procession was organized. A large number of clergy and religious took part in it with several bishops headed by the Patriarch of Jerusalem. The emperor, clad in his richest and most magnificent robes of state, wearing a golden diadem over his head, and a rich purple mantle on his shoulders, devoutly took the cross, anxious to carry it to the Basilica of the Holy Sepulcher, built by St. Helena on Mount Calvary. But notwithstanding all his efforts the emperor could not move a single step. In the general surprise and consternation caused by this unexpected event the holy Bishop of Jerusalem, Zacharias, moved by the inspiration of God, said to the astonished monarch. "Please, your Majesty, reflect that the gorgeous robes that you wear are too much in contrast with the poverty and humility of our Savior, when, in this place, he carried the same cross to Mount Calvary". This truly Christian Sovereign, struck by the wise remark of the holy Bishop, put aside all his imperial insignia, clothed himself with poor garments, put a crown of thorns on his head, and with bare feet performed the journey with great ease and inexpressible joy of heart. In this manner the holy cross of our Lord was restored to his Church. This glorious triumph, with the previous victories over the enemies of our holy religion, were obtained by prayer and fasting, by voluntary poverty and humility. These are the victorious weapons with which all the enemies of Christ, and of his holy Church are defeated and overthrown. May we learn a lesson from this example.

2. The wisest monarch of antiquity said: "In the multitude of people is the dignity of the king: and in the small number of people the dishonor of the prince." (Prov. 14:28) The magnificence, with which earthly potentates surround themselves, is intended to draw to their allegiance a large number of subjects. This is the general object of human ambition. This is the aspiration of the human heart. Man likes to command. More wars have been waged to gratify this passion of ambitious dominion over multitudes of men, than through any other motive. In our present age this aspiration for power and dominion, though perhaps more sly and cautious, is as strong and intriguing as it has ever been in the human breast. This is the motive power which arms millions of men with the effective weapons of modern warfare, and keeps them, with menacing looks in an attitude of aggression,

striking terror into the hearts of weaker neighbors. The higher this ambition of dominion is, the more profound the homage it demands from humiliated humanity.

Very different, however, is the meekness and humility of Jesus from the ambition and arrogance of proud men. Behold him sitting upon a cold stone, a fit emblem of the dispositions of the human heart towards him, who is the King of Kings. His diadem is a crown of sharp thorns, dripping with his life's Blood. A reed of derision has been placed in his divine hands. An old scarlet rag covers his wounded and bleeding shoulders. A number of Pagan soldiers have been gathered round his Person. But these, instead of homage, heap upon him derision and insults, the most painful and humiliating. They bow their knees before him in mockery, and with sneers salute him *"King of the Jews."* They approach him in turn. Some slap his cheeks, some spit upon his face, one strikes him with his hard fist, another beats down his Crown of Thorns with a heavy stroke, whilst the surrounding multitude of Jews and Gentiles applaud and encourage these horrible barbarities, with shouts of laughter. Not one person is found to say a word in favor of this innocent victim, not a single man raises his hand in his defense. Jesus can now truly say: *I am a worm and no man; the reproach of men, and the outcast of the people. All they that saw me have laughed me to scorn.* (Ps. 21:7)

Strange as it may appear to carnal men, these scorns and reproaches, these humiliations and insults showered down so profusely upon the King of heaven and earth, are in reality the best proofs of his victory, and the most precious trophies of his complete triumphs in his war against the false maxims of this deluded world.

Reflect, dear reader, that the kingdom which Jesus our Lord came to establish upon earth, is that of contempt for the honors and homages of men. He came to establish among men the reign of humility, meekness, patience, forbearance, and forgivness, in opposition to the spirit of pride, ambition, arrogance, oppression, revenge and persecution, which have tyrannized over the hearts of men since the fall of Adam. Such being the object of our Savior's incarnation, such being the end of his mission upon earth; by what means could this great teacher and king make us understand and appreciate better the spirit of this sublime and heavenly legislation, than by receiving slaps, and spittle upon his sacred face as tributes due to his person, by receiving sham adoration, derisions, blasphemies and maledictions, instead of homage, and by bearing all these insults, humiliations and outrages, with unconquerable meekness and superhuman patience? ... The mere sight of our Lord despised, dishonored and outraged by the impious and the wicked, shows at once who he really is, and what is the intended object of his mission to mankind. In beholding Jesus in the hall of Pilate, crowned with thorns, we learn that he is the Messias, the Savior, the King, who ransoms his people from the curse of sin, which made these thorns spring from the earth. In beholding this divine Lord, and sovereign king of heaven and earth, mocked, derided, slapped and spat upon, we learn from his example what virtues are expected from his followers, and what account we should make of the praises, honors and applause of men. In short, when we contemplate Jesus in his humiliations and sufferings, we learn the doctrines of his Gospel, more effectively than when we hear them preached by the most eloquent orators. Jesus, covered with wounds, Jesus crowned with thorns, Jesus defiled with spittle, Jesus bruised and bleeding from the soles of his feet to the top of his head, is the living mirror that faithfully represents to the eyes of Christian faith, the real condition of our fallen human nature, which he came to assume in order to cure and save us from temporal and eternal misery. From the extreme severity of the remedy, we practically learn the desperate condition of our spiritual malady. Our souls must have been frightfully wounded, and horribly degraded by sin, when it became necessary for our Redeemer to be scourged at the pillar, crowned with thorns, pierced with nails, mocked, derided, buffeted, spat upon in order to heal and cure them, and to lift them up from the trough of their degradation. *"He became their Savior, the prophet says, in his love and in his mercy he redeemd them, and carried them, and lifted them up."* (Is. 63:8)

Our merciful Lord having as we have seen, transferred his covenant from the ungrateful Jews to the Gentiles, and wishing to establish his Church among them, and unite her to himself as the inseparable spouse of his heart, he consented to assume her deformity represented in his wounds, and wash her in his blood, in order to communicate to her the divine beauty of his grace, and endow her with the immense treasure of his merits.

Hence, St. Paul says: *"Christ is the head of the Church. He is the Savior of his body. He loved the Church and delivered himself for it, that he might sanctify it, cleansing it by the laver of water in the word of life, that he might present to himself a glorious Church not having spot or wrinke, nor any such thing, but that it should be holy and without blemish."* (Ephes. 5:25) Christ is the head of the Church, hence, to make her his spouse and our queen, he consented to be crowned with thorns. To exalt her to this sublime dignity and to merit for her the admiration of mankind, and the profound and sincere homage of his followers, he humbled himself, and meekly accepted in the hall of Pilate the mockeries, derisions, insults and outrages of the Roman soldiers. *He is the Savior of his body.* Hence, to heal the wounds of sin which he found in it, and to cleanse it of the accumulated filth of ages of crime, he subjected his own innocent body to the lashes of the scourge, to the bruises of blows, to the wounds of nails and spear. The blood and water, which issued from them, is the sacred laver, in which he cleanses our souls. The injustice of Pilate, the Roman Governor, and the cruel barbarity of his satellites, could not make him change his determination of establishing his Church among the Gentiles, and of fixing in Rome the throne of his universal dominion. During the painful hours of his passion, in his immediate contact with these Pagan Romans, our Lord has more closely watched their dispositions and character. In the Roman Governor, Pilate, our Lord observed wise maxims of government, foresight, respect for authority, fidelity to his imperial master, love of justice, a conciliatory disposition of character, regard for the rights and demands of the people. If Pilate hesitated in protecting our Lord's innocence, and reluctantly consented at last to his condemnation: it was through fear of offending the leading men of Judea, giving occasion to an apparently inevitable riot among the excited multitude, and a consequent revolution in that fickle and discontented people, and thus jeopardize the Roman authority in that province. If our wise and just Lord could not approve the weak and vacillating conduct of Pilate towards him; yet he understood and made due allowance for the circumstances, and the motives of his policy. Moreover, our Savior, in reward of the favorable disposition of Pilate towards him, had determined to show him mercy, and convert him to his faith. This conversion was accomplished through the prodigies wrought at his death and resurrection. It was according to Tertullian, in consequence and as a proof of his conversion that Pilate sent to the Emperor Tiberius in Rome, an official relation of all the events that took place during the passion, death and resurrection of our blessed Lord. The following are Tertullian's words: *"Ea omnia super Christo Pilatus, et ipse jam pro sua conscientia christianus, Caesari tunc Tiberio nunciavit."* (Apolog. Cap. 21)

It is very probable that, on account of his conversion, and the favorable dispositions of Pilate towards the primitive Christians in Jerusalem and Judea, he was accused by the Jews before the Roman Emperor, deposed by him from his dignity, and sent in exile to Vienne in Gaul, where he died. St. Augustine says that, *"Pilate, like the Magi, entered heaven through his faith in Christ."* (Serm. 3. de Ephiph.) Some other authors are of a different opinion about the conversion of Pilate, but they may have been prejudiced through the bitter statements made against him by the Jewish Historian Josephus.

All agree, however, in admitting the conversion and salvation of his pious wife, Claudia Procula. Lucius Dexter in his chronicle of the thirty-four years of our Lord says: Claudia Procula, wife of Pilate, admonished by a dream, believed in Christ, and obtained eternal salvation. It is supposed that St. Paul mentions her name in connection with the noble Roman senators and holy Martyrs Ebulus, and Pudens, and with the holy Pope and Martyr Linus in these words to Timothy: *"Ebulus and Pudens, and Linus and Claudia ... salute thee."* (2 Tim. 4:21) This truly noble Roman lady, by her conduct towards our Lord, when brought by the Jewish magistrates before the tribunal of her husband, deserved the compassion of his mercy. Claudia believed in the innocence, justice and sanctity of our Lord. She made, at least indirectly, a public confession of her belief at the tribunal of her husband, in the presence of the Jewish magistrates, when she warmly pleaded for the acquittal of our calumniated Savior. Claudia with her husband were the only two persons who spoke in favor of our Lord during his trial. St. Matthew says: *"As he,* Pilate, *was sitting in the judgment seat, his wife sent to him saying: Have thou nothing to do with that just man. For I have suffered many things this morning in a dream on account of him.* (Mt. 27:19) Hereupon, St. Augustine beautifully remarks that; *"Eve, at the beginning of the world induced Adam to commit sin, and thus caused the Passion of our Lord; so now during his trial, Claudia, the wife of the judge, urges her husband to do justice to his innocence, and to protect his character and life from the calumnies and persecutions of his enemies."* (Serm. de Semp. 121) This admirable Roman lady is not only the first and only person who publicly pleads in favor of our persecuted Savior, but she is the first apostle of his holy faith among the Jews and Gentiles. Before both, she proclaims his innocence and sanctity. Converted to his faith, and inflamed with zeal through her heavenly vision, strengthened and emboldened by the sufferings endured for his sake, Claudia exhorts both Jews and Gentiles to be converted to the religion of Jesus Christ. St. Hilary says: Claudia Procula is a noble specimen of the zeal and fervor of the converted Gentiles. After having received the gift of faith she exerts herself to procure the conversion of all unbelievers to the religion of Jesus, her persecuted Master." (St. Hilary Can. 33) The miraculous dream, or rather supernatural vision, of this Roman lady, according to St. Jerome, is a hopeful prelude to a more complete revelation of the Christian faith to the people of the Roman Empire, and to all the nations of the Gentiles. *"Fidei gentilis populi praesagium Fuit."* (A Lapide, com. in Matt. Chap. 27:19)

We may reasonably believe that the good example, position and zeal of Claudia contributed much to the conversion of the Roman soldiers who scourged our innocent Lord at the pillar, crowned him with thorns, nailed him to the cross, or who witnessed his admirable patience and meekness during these frightful sufferings. We learn from St. Matthew that: *"The Centurion and they that were with him watching Jesus, having seen the earthquake, and the things that were done, were greatly afraid saying: Indeed this was the Son of God."* (Mt. 27:54) The learned Cardinal Baronius, in his ecclesiastical history, and many other writers, affirm that the name of this Centurion was Longinus, who is supposed to have pierced our Savior's side with his spear, and who was, converted to Christianity by the prodigies which he witnessed at his death and resurrection. Deeply sorry for the part he had taken in the passion of our Lord as a military officer, Longinus renounced his position in the army, and retired to Cappadocia where he suffered martyrdom for his faith. Metaphrastes wrote his life, and after him Surius who assigns the fifteenth of March as the day of his death. Lucius Dexter, however, states that the Centurion mentioned by the Evangelist was C. Oppius, a native of Spain, but a Roman citizen, who was baptized by St. Barnabbas, then consecrated Bishop of Milan, and was the first to preach the faith of Christ in his native country. (L. Dexter. Chronic. year of Christ 34)

We learn from all this that our Lord attracts his disciples and followers, not by the splendor of his material wealth, but by the squalor of his voluntary poverty; not by the enjoyment, or promises of carnal pleasures, but by patience and meekness in suffering. He obtains the sincere and profound homage and adoration of his loving subjects, not by the overpowering magnificence of his earthly throne, or by the imposing grandeur of his court;

but by his humiliations, by the insults and mockeries that he receives from proud men. That hard stone in Pilate's hall, that scarlet rag on his shoulders, that reed of derision in his hand, that crown of thorns, especially, have made Jesus the adored King of all truly noble souls, and generous Christian hearts. He is more universally honored, he is more profoundly worshiped in heaven and on earth by angels and by men, in proportion as he was more deeply humbled, derided and despised for our sake. The hard stone in Pilate's hall is changed for him into a throne of immense magnificence in heaven, and in every Christian breast his throne is a loving human heart. A million churches have sprung up in every corner of the earth in each of which, Jesus is daily honored and adored in reparation for the outrages he received from a few deluded men in the hall of Pilate. The reed of derision has become the scepter of his universal and everlasting empire. The scarlet cloak is a most precious relic for Christian devotion, which has adorned his temple and altars with the richest silks, and brocades that the industry and skill of man can produce. At least, thirty million Martyrs, bearing triumphantly this scarlet mantle deeply dyed in their blood, surround his altar upon earth, and do homage to our glorified Lord on his heavenly throne.

But the dear Crown of Thorns has conferred more honor and glory on our blessed Lord than any other instrument of the Passion, because it has caused him more intense sufferings and deeper humiliations. This Crown of Thorns that made Jesus the King of Sorrows, has become for him and for us, a crown of glory, and a garland of joy. *"In that day,* the Prophet says, *In that day the Lord of hosts shall be a crown of glory, and a garland of joy to his people."* (Is. 28:5) This Crown of Thorns, intended by his cruel and malicious enemies, as a brand of wickedness, a badge of infamy, and a mark of his utter weakness; has been changed by God into a crown of gold, placed upon his glorified head, wherein the inseparable attribute of his divine Holiness is engraved, an ornament of honor, an emblem of his power, the mirror of his beauty. (Eccles. 45:14) Thus in the joy of his heart our blessed Lord can say. *"I will greatly rejoice in the Lord, and my soul shall be joyful in my God; for He hath clothed me with the garment of salvation, and with the robe of justice He hath covered me, as a bridegroom decked with a crown adorned with jewels.* (Is. 61:10)

No wonder that before the Majesty of this heavenly King the highest angels fall down in profound adoration and casting their crowns before his throne, they exclaim: *"To him that sitteth on the throne, and to the Lamb, benediction and glory, and honor, and power forever and ever. Amen. Worthy is the Lamb that was slain, to receive power and divinity, and wisdom and strength, and honor, and glory and benediction."* Let all saints and angels in heaven answer, Amen. (Apoc. 4, 5)

All the angels lay down their crowns of glory at the foot of the throne of Jesus, because they more fully comprehend the sublimity of his divine Majesty, and the immense treasure of his personal merits. If the potentates of the earth fail to imitate the example of the angelic princes, it is because they have allowed themselves to be deceived by Lucifer, the rebellious spirit of pride. Blinded by self-conceit they understand not the honor that accrues to their dignity by the homage they pay to Jesus, the divine King of heaven and earth. Those monarchs however, who were more enlightened by Christian Faith, and animated by nobler sentiments of piety, have illustrated their history with bright examples of Catholic humility and devotion.

Christianity has been edified in beholding the noble figure of Constantine laying down his golden diadem, and imperial scepter to assume the pick and spade, and in the presence of all Rome, stoop down to dig the foundation of the most magnificent temple erected under the invocation of St. Peter to the worship of Jesus crowned with thorns and crucified.

St. Canutus, the holy king of Denmark, is another illustrious example. Like every true Christian monarch he was a lover of peace, but when necessary he knew how to fight, and how to conquer. He was brave and skilful in the art of war. Attacked by his barbarous Pagan neighbors, principally in hatred of his holy religion, Canutus, with his faithful little army, full of confidence in God, met his enemies on the field of battle, entirely defeated them, and wrested from their hands, three provinces, wherein he immediately established the Christian religion. Returning in triumph to his capital, surrounded by the joyful acclamations of his people, and amidst the glory of his victories, this truly noble monarch prostrated himself publicly in the Church before the altar of his crucified Lord, and in profound gratitude to him for all his favors, laid his royal crown at the foot of the cross, consecrating his person, and offering his kingdom to the honor and glory of the King of kings. May he soon obtain for Lutheran Denmark, severely punished for her apostacy, her speedy return to the true faith, and sentiments of devotion similar to those of her best and most glorious King. May all the great ones of the earth imitate the example of the holy King Canutus.

184

Several others, kings and queens, have through devotion to Jesus, renounced their earthly dignities, and laid their scepters and crowns at the foot of the altar, to assume the monastic cowl, or the religious veil with a crown of thorns for its ornament. One of these was St. Elizabeth of Hungary who would never consent to wear in any church a crown of gold ornamented with precious stones in the presence of our Lord crowned with thorns; immediately after the death of her saintly husband this young widow exchanged the royal robes for the poor habit of the third order of St. Francis of Assisi. Millions more of generous victims have, for the sake of Jesus, crowned with thorns, left, not an earthly crown, but their very heads under the axe of the pagan or apostate tyrant, in exchange for the glorious and immortal crown of martyrdom. Whilst these lines are being written, thousands of Catholic victims suffer in Germany and Switzerland, in Mexico and Brazil, and bravely shed their heart's blood on the soil of Catholic Spain for their holy religion.

But more glorious than all is the noble hero, Gabriel Maria Garcia Moreno, the illustrious President of the Catholic Republic of Equador, who on the feast of our Lord's Transfiguration 1875, expires at the foot of the altar in the church of our Lady, a Martyr to his faith, and a victim of devotion to our holy religion murdered by the secret command, and through the sectarian hands of modern infidelity and freemasonry. Impious and cruel persecutors of the Catholic Church, your defeat is nearer, when you dream of victory. The blood of martyrs is the surest and soundest seed of Christianity. The faith can never be extinguished in an age of Christian confessors. Champions beget heroes, who always lead to victory, and we Catholics have heroes and champions in every country where our Church is persecuted. At the school of our King crowned with thorns, we have learned to expect glory from humiliation, strength in suffering, triumph in contempt, life in death. *Whether we live or die we belong to Christ,* Who is immortal. *"God cannot die"* exclaimed the dying hero and martyr of Equador. In company with the four and twenty ancients, martyred Apostles and Pontiffs of the Apocalypse, we prostrate ourselves before the throne of our glorified, Lord and king to sing with them the pean of triumph: *"Thou art worthy, O Lord, to receive power and honor and glory ... because Thou wast slain, and hast redeemed us to God out of every tribe and tongue and people and nation, and hast made us to our God a kingdom, and priests, and we shall reign on the earth.* (Apoc. 5:9) May this prophecy, through the merits of

185

Jesus crowned with thorns, be speedily and fully realized. *Thy kingdom come, O Lord, our king, and Thy will be done on earth as it is in heaven. Amen.*

HYMN

TO THE MOST HOLY CROWN OF THORNS

Christ's peerless Crown is pictured in
The figures of the Law.

The Ram entangled in the Thorns;
The Bush which Moses saw,

The rainbow girding round the ark
The table's crown of gold;

The incense that in waving wreaths
Around the Altar rolled.

Hail! Circlet dear! that didst the pangs
Of dying Jesus feel,

Thou dost the brightest gems outshine.
And all the stars excel

Praise honor, to the Fathers be
And sole begotten Son;

Praise to the Spirit Paraclete
While endless ages run. Amen.

CHAPTER XXI

HISTORY OF THE CROWN OF THORNS

"The soldiers platting a Crown of Thorns put it upon his head" (Jn 19:2)

Our work would be incomplete without some historical notice of the Crown of Thorns of our Savior. We trust that a brief account of it will be agreeable to Catholic piety and devotion.

In the outset we have to observe that Almighty God in His divine wisdom, deals very differently with Christians from what he was pleased to do with the Jews. These were, by nature, and circumstances more material, and had more need of visible and sensible objects in the practices of their religion. Moreover, being surrounded on every side by idolatrous nations, they were exposed to the temptation and danger of falling into idolatry. For these motives God gave them very explicit and detailed instructions about the nature and form of the objects and instruments of their religious worship, and sacred rites and ceremonies. This is evident to any one who reads *Exodus, Leviticus* etc. Hence, Almighty God, speaking of the Tabernacle and its appurtenances said to Moses: *"Look and make it according to the pattern that was shown to thee in the mount."* (Exod. 25:40) About the principal facts which are the foundation of Christianity, God has given us the most certain, and convincing proofs. Take, for instance, the birth, life, passion, death and resurection of our divine Redeemer, the institution of the seven Sacraments, the holy sacrifice of the Mass and so on. But he has been pleased to leave us in obscurity about many details, which would naturally gratify human curiosity, but are not essential to Christian Faith. We know for certain that our Savior was born, but we know not the exact year. We know not in what month his holy Mother and Saint Joseph had to flee with him into Egypt, or in what year and month they returned thence to Palestine. We are told by the Evangelists that he was scourged, but they do not inform us what were the instruments used on that occasion, and for how long a time this cruel torture lasted. They state the fact of his crucifixion, but they do not describe to us the nature of the wood from which the cross was made; how large it was, nor whether only three, or four nails were used. The holy Evangelists have done the same in relation to our Savior's crowning with thorns. They announce to us that he was crowned with thorns, but they neither mention the quality, nor the quantity of these thorns. This knowledge would certainly gratify a pious curiosity, but it is not essential to our faith, or devotion. One of the principal motives for their reticence may have been to induce us to seek and find out by reading, by studying, or by listening to instructions, what the Evangelists have judged best to entrust to the safe treasury of Christian tradition. Our Lord likes to see his disciples practising humility by acknowledging their ignorance in many things, and evincing their docility by seeking information. Let us try to please our divine Master by the practice of both these Christian virtues.

Many Christians would like to know what was the nature of the thorns with which our dear Lord was crowned by the Pagan soldiers. Upon this subject there are three opinions, which we will state on this occasion, and thus enable the devout reader to select that which best satisfies his mind.

1. Some Christian writers are of opinion that the thorns with which our divine Lord was crowned in the hall of Pilate were taken by the soldiers from a bramble bush, or from the haw-thorn tree. Other able writers sustain that the crown of our Lord was formed of Red Sea bulrushes. (See A Lapide. com. in 27 St. Matt) Both sides have authorities and facts in their favor.

In support of the first opinion we have the well-known fact that in some churches, thorns are venerated by the faithful with the approbation and sanction of the Church, as belonging to the original crown of our suffering Savior, which are not Red Sea rushes, but have been taken from a thorny bush. The great Pope Benedict XIV states that a remarkable relic of *one branch with five thorns* of the crown of our Lord Jesus Christ is devoutly preserved in the Chapel of the Royal Palace in Munich, Bavaria. (De Beot. et Cann. Lib. 4 Part. 2 Chap. 14 No. I5) It is well known that bulrushes have neither branches, nor side thorns.

2. The opinion, however, of those writers who sustain that the crown of our Lord was formed of Red Sea rushes is well supported by facts. The principal portion of the Crown of Thorns preserved and venerated in the holy Chapel in Paris favors this opinion. William Durandus states that he saw this holy crown in Paris composed of Red Sea bulrushes. The pious and learned Cornelius A Lapide, the prince of biblical commentators states

that: "In Rome he saw two of the sacred thorns of our Savior's crown, which by direction of the holy Empress St. Helena were preserved in the Basilica of the Holy Cross. According to his description, these thorns are long and sharp like large needles: *"Sunt illae longae et acutae instar crassarum acicularum."* (Com. in S. Matt. 27:29) Again St. Vincent Ferrer says that the Crown of Thorns of our Lord was formed by the executioners in the shape of a hat, or helmet, which covered his entire head. *"Spinea Domini corona erat ad modum pilei, ita ut totum tegeret caput."* (Serm. In Parasceve)

We know no kind of thorns that could be woven, or platted in such a form, except Red Sea rushes. Whilst the brown thorny points of these rushes are very hard and sharp, the stem itself as the name of rush implies, is sufficiently long and flexible to be twisted and shaped in the form of a cap adapted to the head of a man. This kind of thorny rushes, growing profusely on the shores of the Red-Sea and about Palestine, could easily have been procured by the Roman soldiers. St. Vincent of Lerin testifies that the points of these Red-Sea thorns are so hard and sharp as to pierce through the soles of travelers' shoes.

3. From what we have said we must naturally arrive at a third conclusion. It is pretty plain that the Crown of Thorns of Our Lord was partly formed of the small branches of some thorny bush, round which were woven the Red-Sea bulrushes. In this supposition we embrace both the two former opinions, and are more easily satisfied about the form of the Crown of Thorns mentioned by St. Vincent Ferrer. Cornelius A. Lapide seems to incline to this third opinion. *Forte in ea corona spinas junci spinis rhamni intertextae fuere.* (A. Lapide in Matt. 27:29) We should also remember that St. Anselm, St. Bernard and Tauler affirm that this horrible crown contained a thousand thorns. *"Ipsa corona mille puncturis speciosum caput Jesu devulnerat."* (St. Bernard)

It is generally believed that our Lord was made to wear the Crown of Thorns, during the remaining portion of his passion. This fact is proclaimed by every picture or engraving representing the crucifixion of our Lord. The uniformity of these images expresses the traditional belief of Christianity. Origen and Tertullian explicitly state, that our Lord on the cross wore the Crown of Thorns on his sacred head. This is confirmed by the revelations made to St. Bridget. This great Saint writes, that the Blessed Virgin Mary revealed to her that immediately before the crucifixion, the Crown of Thorns was drawn violently by the executioners, out of the head of our Lord in order to strip him of his seamless tunic. But after the crucifixion, the Crown of Thorns was replaced with inexpressible pain on the head of our Lord, and pressed down to the middle of his forehead. So copious was the blood flowing from every part of his perforated head, that it filled his ears and especially his eyes in such a way, that when our crucified Savior wished to look at his afflicted Mother standing with St. John at the foot of the cross, he was obliged by compressing the eye-lids to force the blood out of his eyes. (St. Bridget. Lib. 1 Revel. Chap. 10)

The Crown of Thorns came in possession of St. Helena, mother of the Emperor Constantine, when she visited Jerusalem in the Spring of the year 326. The object of her journey was to find the cross of our Savior and some of the principal instruments of his passion. Jews and Gentiles had combined in a common effort to conceal from Christian devotion, these venerated relics. It was an invariable custom among the Jews, to bury near the body of a public criminal, whatever instrument had been used at his execution. In conformity with this practice, they buried near the Sepulcher of our Lord on Mount Calvary, the cross and other instruments of his passion. Large numbers of fervent Christians, however, often visited this hallowed spot to commemorate the sufferings of their Redeemer and to venerate, in the best manner they could, the hidden instruments of his passion and death. The heathens, from an aversion to Christianity, did everything in their power to prevent this manifestation of Christian faith and devotion. For this end they heaped on this place a large quantity of stones and earth; and erected near it a temple in honor of the impure Venus, that those who came thither to adore our Lord, might appear to worship, in the marble idol, the false and degrading goddess of Paganism. Pious Christians had addressed many fervent prayers to God, for the removal of these Pagan abominations, and for the public and complete triumph of the Christian religion. Three hundred years of persecution, had well tried the invincible firmness of Christian faith and devotion. God was determined to reward, even upon earth the fidelity of his servants. He miraculously converted the brave and youthful Emperor Constantine to the sacred standard of his crucified Son; and inspired him with the determination of abolishing idolatry throughout all his vast dominions. His pious mother, St. Helena, by word and example urged Constantine to the execution of these good works. Though eighty years of age, this holy empress in the Spring of the year 326, undertook a journey from Constantinople to Jerusalem. The principal object of her pious pilgrimage was to find out the place of our Lord's Sepulcher with his cross and the instruments of his passion and then build there a magnificent church for the worship of the true living God and of his incarnate Son. After her arrival in Jerusalem, St. Helena made every prudent inquiry in order to discover the place of our Lord's Sepulcher. Her Christian piety was horrified when she beheld with her own eyes Mount Calvary and the sepulcher of our Lord profaned by the temple and statue of the impure Venus. Fired with a holy zeal, she gave orders for their immediate demolition and destruction. Under her direction the heap of stones and earth was removed and a large and deep hole was dug until the sacred instruments of our Savior's passion were unearthed. With her heart overflowing with joy and with sentiments of profound gratitude to God for the recovery of these precious treasures of Christian devotion, the holy and generous Empress built in the city of Jerusalem some churches, the most magnificent of which was that of the Holy Sepulcher. This she enriched with a good portion of the sacred relics of our Lords's passion. Some others she sent to Rome, and the remainder she took with her to Constantinople. Among the sacred relics of the passion taken by this holy empress to the latter imperial city, was the Crown of Thorns of our blessed Lord, which she highly valued and deeply venerated. Out of respect for the Chair of St. Peter, she sent to the Pope in Rome; two thorns of the sacred crown. This precious discovery was made May 3rd, when the Church commemorates the finding of the holy Cross. This pious empress was called by God to her eternal crown of glory in heaven Aug. 18, 326.

The sacred Crown of our Lord remained in Constantinople about nine hundred years. Baldwin the II, the Latin Emperor of the East had many and powerful enemies to contend with. The Greek Christians disliked him, and turned against his government. They treacherously enticed the Saracens, or Turks to attack him. Harassed by both parties, Baldwin had serious fears that Constantinople would soon fall into their hands. In his spirit of Christian devotion, being anxious to protect from infidel desecration, the principal relics of our Lord's passion, he sent them to France to his relative, the holy King St. Louis. Baldwin by these sacred presents wished to testify his esteem for the great virtue of St. Louis and his profound gratitude for the magnanimous efforts of the pious King of France in defending the holy places of Palestine and the Eastern Empire. The first relic sent by the Emperor Baldwin to the holy King of France was, according to Genebrard, the Crown of Thorns of our blessed Lord. It was carefully sealed in a rich case and taken by two Dominican Fathers, James and Andrew from Constantinople to Venice. Thence, it was brought through Italy into France. This was in August of the year 1239.

St. Louis accompanied by his pious mother Blanche, by his brother Robert of Artois, and by many princes and prelates,went in procession to meet the sacred treasure fifteen miles beyond the ancient city of Sens. Arrived at the appointed place, the holy king knelt before it in profound veneration, and the remainder of the numerous procession imitated his example. Dressed in sack cloth and in his bare feet, this most Christian monarch with his pious brother reverently took the sacred relic and returned in solemn procession to Sens; shedding tears of devotion through sentiments of religious gratitude to our Lord Jesus Christ, the King of kings. From Sens the holy crown was soon conveyed to Paris, where it was received with extraordinary solemnity and devotion. St. Louis built a beautiful new church for its reception, which on account of the many precious relics wherewith it is enriched, is called the Holy Chapel, *La Sainte Chapelle*. From the holy Crown of our Lord in Paris, some sacred thorns have been distributed to other churches. They are usually very long. (See Butler's Lives of Saints, May 3)

We will close this chapter with another account of the Crown of Thorns, given in the *"illustrated Catholic Family Almanac,"* 1877, from which some other interesting details about this precious object of Catholic devotion will be learned. It bears the following title:

THE CROWN OF THORNS WORN BY OUR LORD JESUS CHRIST

Below we copy an engraving of the crown of thorns from the magnificent work of M. Paul Lacroix, *Military and Religious Life in the Middle Ages.* The crown is composed of a ring of small reeds tied into a bundle, the thorns being no longer visible; it is enshrined in gold and held together by three golden acanthus leaves. The opening is large enough to encircle the head and to fall rather low over the brow. This circlet is the support or foundation, so to speak, of the painful crown of our Lord. The branches of thorns were twined alternately within and without, and twisted across in such a manner, as to form not only a circlet, but a cap, as it were, of torture, which covered our Redeemer's head. The authentic history of this sacred relic is of great interest:

192

In the year 1204 the French and the Venetians, having captured Constantinople, established there as emperor Baldwin, Count of Flanders. On the division of the booty this prince requested for his share the sacred crown of our Savior, which was found among the treasure of the emperors of the East. His successor, Baldwin II, finding his empire in the year 1238, threatened by the Greeks on the one side, and on the other by the Bulgarians, came into the West to seek aid and protection against his enemies. Whilst at the court of France, whither he had gone to entreat the assistance of St. Louis, tidings reached him that the nobles whom he had left at Constantinople, finding their resources completely exhausted, were on the point of pledging the holy crown to the Venetians, for a sum of money. The young emperor, strongly disapproving of this measure, offered as a free gift to St. Louis, the precious relic which the lords of Byzantium were wishing to sell. St. Louis eagerly accepted such a gift as this, and immediately at the same time that Baldwin dispatched one of his officers with letters-patent, commanding the holy crown should be sent to him, the French monarch sent two of the Friars Preachers named James and Andrew, to receive it in his name. On the arrival of the messengers at Constantinople, they found the sacred relic gone from the treasury and pledged to the Venetians for 13,075 hyperperia or about £157,000 sterling. It had been deposited by their chamberlain, Pancratius Caverson in the church of Panta Craton, that of his nation at Byzantium. On receiving the emperor's orders, the Latin lords rearranged the matter with the Venetians, and it was agreed that, if within a reasonably short time, the latter did not receive the reimbursement of the sum they had paid, the sacred crown should become their undoubted property. Meanwhile, it was to be carried to Venice, accompanied by the envoys of the King of France, one of whom, Father Andrew, had formerly been guardian of the convent of his order at Constantinople and, having on several occasions seen the crown, knew its appearance perfectly well. Every possible precaution was taken to secure the identification of the holy crown, which was enclosed in three chests, the first of gold the second of silver on which the Venetian lords affixed their seals, the third of wood which was sealed by the French nobles. On the arrival of the envoys at Venice, the holy crown was at once borne to St. Mark's and there placed among the treasures in the Chapel of the Blessed Sacrament, where reposed the body of the Evangelist, between the two columns of alabaster which are said to have been brought from the Temple of Solomon. At the same time one of the Dominican Fathers set out for France to acquaint St. Louis with the terms agreed upon. These were approved by the king who directed the French merchants to repay the Venetains the sum they had advanced. The sacred relic was then delivered into the hands of the French envoys who after assuring themselves that the seals were intact, started homewards with their treasure on the road to France. Safely arrived in Paris, the crown, amid great solemnities was disposited in the palace chapel. Besides all the precautions taken to render any substitution impossible, we may add that Baldwin, on being required to examine and identify the relic, declared its authenticty in a document written on parchment, which was in existence until the Revolution of 1793, signed with his own hand in Greek characters traced in cinnabar, and having his own seal of lead covered with gold, affixed. On one side of the seal the emperor was represented enthroned, with the inscription: *"Balduinus Imperator Romaniae semper Augustus."* On the other he was on horseback with the inscription in Greek letters: *"Baudoin, Empereur, Comte de Flandre."* It must also be borne in mind that the Venetians, before lending so considerable a sum for such a pledge, would be certain to satisfy themselves beyond all doubts as to its authenticity. It is certain too that a century and a half before the reign of St. Louis, at the time of the First Crusade, all the world admitted that a very large portion of the crown was perserved at Constantinople in the chapel of the Greek emperors. When Alexis Comnenus wished to induce the Christian princes to go to his assistance, he spoke to them of the very precious relics which they would help to save, amongst which he especially designated the Crown of Thorns. Also in the time of Charlemagne, all the West had the certainty that Constantinople possessed this treasure, of which a considerable part was equally known to be at Jerusalem. Towards the year 8oo, according to Aimoin, the Patriarch of Jerusalem had detached some of the thorns which he sent to Charlemagne, who deposited them at Aix-la-Chapelle, with one of the nails of the true cross, and it was these relics which were afterwards given by Charles le Chauve to the Abbey of St. Denis. The existence of the crown is a fact constantly alluded to in the sixth century by St. Gregory of Tours amongst others; and about the year 409, St. Paulinus of Nola knew of its preservation. He writes: "The thorns with which the Savior was crowned, and the other relics of his passion, recall to us the living remembrance of his presence."

For the reception of the crown and other precious relics of the passion, St. Louis caused to be erected in Paris, the elegant Sainte Chapelle, at a cost of about $3,500,000, and there they remained till the Revolution, when this, as so many other churches, was desecrated, the interior being nearly destroyed. Fortunately, the holy treasures belonging to the Sainte Chapelle were rescued, the sacred crown having been deposited in the National Library, where it was preserved with the utmost care by the Abbé Barthélemy. On the 10th of August, 1806, the holy crown was deposited in Notre Dame where it is now.

"The soldiers of the Roman Governor, after having scourged my Son at the pillar, adapted a Crown of Thorns to his adorable head, and, pressed it with such violence that blood was made to gush so copiously from it as to cover his eyes, fill his ears and imbrue all his beard." (Revelations of St. Bridget : Lib. 2 cap. 10)

SECOND PART

CHAPTER I

THE MYSTIC CROWN OF THORNS
IN THE CHURCH

"Rejoice, thou, our mother, because the Lord will give to thy head increase of grace and protect thee with a noble crown." (Prov. 4:9) Mass of the Crown of Thorns.

These words, taken from the fourth chapter of Proverbs, are read by the celebrant in the Mass of the Crown of Thorns, immediately after Communion. They are evidently addressed to the Church, our mother in the supernatural order of grace, and the beloved spouse of Jesus Christ. Her divine Bridegroom, having been crowned with thorns for her sake, it was proper that she should have a share with him in the pain and joy, in the humiliation and glory of this precious instrument of his passion.

Two remarkable facts will show how dear to our blessed Redeemer is the Crown of Thorns. In the life of Blessed Marie Alacoque, a nun of the Visitation in the Convent of Paray-Le-Monial, so well known to the devout lovers of the Sacred Heart, we read that this holy religious had the following vision.

"During the Christmas holidays in the year 1674, and precisely on the Feast of St. John the Evangelist, Blessed Margaret Marie was ravished in an ecstasy, when the Sacred Heart of our Lord was represented to her on a throne of heavenly fire, with flames radiating in all directions, and transparent as crystal. The wound received on the cross was visible. *"There was a crown of thorns round his Sacred Heart,* and a cross rose above it, to make known, as the Redeemer explained, that his love was the source of his sufferings; that from the first moment of his Incarnation, all his passion had been present to him, so that the cross had been as it were, planted in his heart."* (History of B. Margaret Marie Chapter 16 by Father Daniel, SJ) With the cross there should ever be the cherished Crown of Thorns, and, as we learn from this vision, both are preserved in the *glorified heart* of our dear Lord. But still more surprising is what we learn from the life of the admirable Anna Maria Taigi. During forty-seven years, this holy woman was favored by God with a clear and uninterrupted view of a most brilliant sun. Around it were rays emanating from the center, *and a very closely set crown of thorns intertwined, encircling the superior disk of the sun, stood upon the points of the upper rays. Two of the thorns, lengthened on either side beyond the others, descended below the disk, where, crossing one another, they formed with their points a figure like a cross.* In the center was a beautiful figure, clothed with a resplendent mantle, majestically seated with eyes upturned to heaven, as of one enjoying ecstatic repose. From the forehead, two beams of light shot upward, and the figure touched with its feet, the left and lower side of the disk. This figure was never obscured by any shadow or form arising from the lower part of the sun; on the contrary all shadows that rose near it were driven away from it by some irresistible power. No human eye, even the strongest, could bear this brilliant light. Yet Anna Maria could gaze on it for hours together, without pain although her sight was naturally very weak and she was scarcely able to distinguish the nearest object. Some of her spiritual directors, well informed about this extraordinary favor, thought that "The sun was our glorified Lord, the Sun of Justice, come to the world to illumine the souls of men that were in the valley and shadow of death; that the thorns were intended to remind us of the most painful sufferings of the humanity of our Savior, and that the majestic figure was that of Divine Wisdom before whom ages are but a moment, and the most hidden things are made manifest. The servant of God who knew well the meaning of this wonderful phenomenon said that: *The Omnipotence of the divine Wisdom Incarnate was in this sun.* Through the supernatural light of this heavenly sun, Anna Maria could see anything she desired to know, past, present or future.

The meaning of these extraordinary facts are clear enough in relation to the Crown of Thorns. We may remark that the seal of ecclesiastical authority has, by the Pope, been fixed to the revelations of Blessed Margaret Marie Alacoque, about the Sacred Heart of our Savior, by the fact of her beatification, and by the authoritative orders given that the pictures of the sacred heart, exposed to the veneration of the faithful, should be represented surrounded by the Crown of Thorns. The same might be said in proportion about Anna Maria Taigi, who has been declared venerable and who may soon be beatified. We can learn from these divine visions and revelations, how dear the Crown of Thorns is to our blessed Lord, and may therefore conclude that a special devotion to this sacred instrument of his holy passion, will be very agreeable to his loving heart. The two just mentioned are indeed very remarkable events in favor of our devotion to the Crown of Thorns; but our Lord has been pleased to illustrate his Church for our edification and instruction, with a much larger number of them.

We have thought proper to give the first place to the visions and revelations of Blessed Margaret Mary and of Ven. Anna Maria Taigi, because more immediately connected with the glorified humanity of our blessed Redeemer. But during the last seven centuries, our divine Savior has been, we may say, continually promoting in his own admirable way, a special devotion to his cherished Crown of Thorns. In the previous chapter on the history of the real Crown of Thorns, we saw that our Lord in his predilection for the Catholics of Western Europe, made a present to our forefathers of this precious relic. This was in the year 1239. Now it is a remarkable fact that from that memorable epoch to the present day, some favored servant of our Lord has successively, almost without interruption, been in a miraculous manner, impressed with the mystic Crown of Thorns. Hence, without fear of contradiction, we may affirm that, during the last seven centuries, the Crown of Thorns has been supernaturally kept *visibly bleeding* on the head of some saint or great servant of God. We have compiled a list of more than fifty of these privileged persons from the second volume of the Stigmatized, *"Les Stigmatizees,"* Palma d'Oria, published in Paris, 1873, by the celebrated French doctor, A. Imbert Gourbeyre, Professor of Medicine in the College de Clermont Ferrand. This eminent and truly Catholic medical doctor has with great labor been able to gather a catalogue of one hundred and forty-five saints and servants of God, who have received the stigmas of the Five Wounds, the impression of the Crown of Thorns, or who have endured in an extraordinary and miraculous manner, some special suffering of our Savior's passion. He declares that notwithstanding his careful researches, the list is incomplete. We cannot give even this catalogue. The object of our present work confines our selection to those canonized or beatified saints, or eminent servants of God who have been impressed with the Crown of Thorns, or who have supernaturally suffered a share of these mystic thorns in their heads. These will be found amounting to more than fifty. They are distributed in the last seven centuries. Some are living and suffering at the present time. As far as the dates of their births and deaths will warrant, we will classify them within the respective centuries to which these privileged servants of God belonged. For the sake of perspicuity and convenience, we will also divide them chronologically into different chapters corresponding to the respective century. We conclude these preliminaries with the following truly Catholic sentiments of the pious and learned French doctor.

"In this grave question of Supernatural facts, we Catholics are supported by the documents of history, by genuine and solid science, by the doctrines and decisions of the infallible authority of the Church. Resting upon the columns of reason and faith, we can, with certitude and confidence, proclaim the recent decree about miracles of the Ecumenical Council of the Vatican. *"If any one says, that there cannot be miracles, and consequently, that the narrative of miracles, including those mentioned in the Sacred Scripture, are to be relegated among the fables or myths; or that miracles can never be known with certitude, and that the divine origin of the Christian religion never can be rightly proved by them, let him be accursed. Anathema sit."*

CHAPTER II

THIRTEENTH CENTURY – THE CROWN OF THORNS ON THE MEMBERS OF THE CHURCH

In the history of Christianity the thirteenth century is very illustrious for sanctity, learning and active zeal for the propagation of the Christian religion. Several Religious Orders were instituted about this time, and rapidly spread in different parts of Europe, flourishing in sanctity, and producing abundant fruits of holiness and sound knowledge. It is sufficient to mention the two famous Religious Orders, the Dominican and Franciscan, which seem to have been destined by God to illustrate the earth with the burning charity of the Seraphim, and the wisdom of the Cherubim. St. Dominic and St. Francis of Assisi, St Thomas of Aquin and St. Bonaventure, St. Antony of Padua, St. Hyacinth of Poland, St. Raymund de Pennafort, St. Peter Martyr, B. Albertus Magnus, St. Clare, St. Elizabeth of Hungary, St. Margaret of Cortona, were members of these two Orders, and all illustrated this century with their sanctity, and many by their great learning. Forty more Saints who have since been raised to the honors of the altar, could be mentioned at the head of whom we find St. Peter Celestine, Pope, St. Louis King of France, St. Ferdinand, King of Castile, Spain, St. Margaret, Princess of Hungary, St. Isabel, virgin daughter of Louis VIII, King of France. Moreover, there are twenty-four saints and servants of God who, since St. Francis of Assisi, have been stigmatized or received the Crown of Thorns. This splendid galaxy of eminent saints and learned doctors, is more than sufficient to demonstrate, that the thirteenth century cannot be relegated to the gloom of the so-called dark ages.

In mentioning more particularly the Religious Orders of St. Dominic and of St. Francis, we had a special object in view. In the long catalogue of one hundred and fifty or sixty saints and servants of God, who have been honored by our Lord with a particular share of the sufferings of his sacred passion and crown of thorns, we shall find that by far the vast majority belonged to these two illustrious Orders.

We are told that the Seraphic Patriarch St. Francis received from our crucified Lord the impressions of his five wounds in order that through five red tongues of fire, and by the voice of living blood, he should preach to a proud, carnal and selfish world, the sublime mystery of his sacred passion. The Church, in the prayer for the feast instituted to commemorate the impressions of the stigmata of this admirable Saint, on the 17th of September says: *"Lord Jesus Christ, who in this cold world, hast renewed the sacred stigmas of thy passion in the body of the most blessed Francis, to inflame our heart with the fire of thy love; vouchsafe through his merits and prayers to grant that we may ever carry thy cross, and bear worthy fruits of penance."*

In compiling the following list of at least fifty saints and eminent servants of God, the majority of whom, besides the crown of thorns, have also received the stigmata of the five wounds, we make from our heart the same prayer for ourselves and for all our pious readers. May our Lord inflame our hearts with the flames of his divine love and enlighten our minds to understand and appreciate the sublime mystery of his crown of thorns, through the intercession of his holy servants who participated in these special sufferings.

1. *Blessed Emilia Bicchieri*

Blessed Emily or Emilia Bicchieri is the first on the list of those who are known to have received on the head, the miraculous impression of the crown of thorns. She was born May 3rd 1238, about one year before the real crown of thorns of our Savior arrived in Paris. When very young, Emilia became a member of the third Order of St. Dominic. An ardent devotion for the passion of our Lord, and a burning love for penance characterized her life. Blessed Emilia died May 3rd, 1278 being exactly forty years of age. It is a remarkable circumstance that, on May 3rd the date of the birth and death of B. Emilia, the church celebrates the feast of the finding of the holy cross of our Lord. This holy servant of God was born and died in the city of Vercelli, Piedmont, Italy. May she obtain from God the conversion of the present Duke of Piedmont, King of Sardinia, usurper of Italy and the perfect triumph of our holy religion in her native country and in the whole world. (See Bollandist's Acta Sanctorum Appendix. May 3rd)

2. *Blessed Christina de Stumbelle*

The Bollandists, a high authority in these matters, enumerate Christina among the beatified servants of God. She is surnamed de Stumbelle, from the place of her birth, a village about six miles from the ancient city of Cologne on the Rhine, Germany. She was born July 24th, 1242. This great servant of God became a Nun of the Order of St. Dominic. In obedience to Father Peter of Dacia of the same Order, she humbly related to him that, on Thursday in Passion Week, 1267, less than twenty-seven years after the arrival of the real Crown of Thorns at Paris, she received from our Lord the impression of the Crown of Thorns, and on the following Thursday night in Holy Week, she suffered the agony and sweat of blood followed by the Stigmata of the five wounds on the next day, which was Good Friday. These sensible and visible sufferings of the passion were repeated every subsequent year, in Holy Week until her death which occurred in the month of June 1312. The body of this holy religious was burried at Niedeck, and many miracles were wrought through her intercession.

About the close of the sixteenth century, these precious relics were transferred to Juliers, when a new prodigy was discovered. It was found that a *green crown* about an inch large was miraculously formed on the front of her skull and gradually extending right and left round the head, converging towards the occiput. Father Steinfunder wrote to Father Papebrok, the famous Bollandist and editor of the life of blessed Christina, that he went to visit in the year 1685, the head of this wonderful saint, and saw the miraculous crown reaching to the ears. Seven years later, namely in 1692, the same Father returned to Juliers to venerate a second time this sacred relic. The miraculous crown was visibly extending round the virginal head, and it was sprinkled with red drops like blood, which vividly called to mind the Crown of Thorns, which this admirable saint endured during her life. This prodigy is also mentioned in her biography written in the German language by Rev. Peter Lulle, parish priest of Juliers and published in Cologne 1689. (See Bolland. Acta s. s. 2 22d Jun. De Beata Christina Stumbleri etc.) May she pray for her sorely afflicted country, and for the speedy conversion or humiliation of all the enemies and persecutors of our most holy Religion, especially in Germany and Switzerland.

CHAPTER III

FOURTEENTH CENTURY – THE MYSTIC CROWN
OF THORNS

This memorable century was illustrated by more than thirty saints and eminent servants of God who are now venerated upon our altars, illustrious among these we find St. Andrew Corsini, St. John Neupumucen, the protomartyr of the sacramental seal of confession; St. Bridget of Sweden with her angelic daughter St. Catharine and admirable virgin in the marriage state. St. Mectildes, St. Juliana Falconeri and St. Catharine of Sienna belong to this century. During this Epoch at least twenty-three saints and great servants of God, were adorned with the glorious stigmata of the passion or with the mystic crown of thorns. St. Catharine of Sienna claims our special attention.

3. *St. Catharine of Sienna*

This great Saint was born in Sienna, an ancient city of Tuscany, Italy, in the year 1347. She joined the third Order of St. Dominic when very young. This holy religious received the sacred stigmata of the five wounds and the Crown of Thorns at twenty-eight years of age. On this occasion, the saint being sorely afflicted on account of various calumnies raised against her honor and reputation, our divine Savior appeared to her with a crown of gold, all inlaid with pearls and precious stones in his right hand, and holding in his left a Crown of Thorns, and affectionately said to her: know my dear daughter that you must of necessity be crowned some time or other, with one of these two crowns. Therefore take your choice; either the Crown of Thorns in this transitory life, and have the other reserved for your everlasting glory; or take the crown of gold at present and hereafter that of thorns. "It is a long time, O Lord, answered the holy virgin, since I have made an entire renunciation of my own will to follow but yours, and consequently, it is not for me to choose anything. If, however, you will have me to answer, I desire to select that which is most acceptable to your divine heart: and the better to imitate your example, I do most willingly accept the crown of suffering and ignominy." Having said this, St. Catharine took from our Savior's left hand the Crown of Thorns and placed it upon her head, she fervently pressed it down with such force, that from that time this illustrious saint always endured an intense pain in her head, caused by the miraculous hidden thorns which continually pierced it.

During her short life, this admirable servant of God worked hard and suffered much for the welfare of the Church in general, and for her native country in particular. She died in Rome while on her mission of charity, April 29th, 1380, when scarcely thirty-three years old. St. Catherine was cannonized by Pope Pius II, 80 years after her holy death. Her body is preserved incorrupt in the magnificent Dominican Church of Santa Maria Della Minerva in the Eternal City, of which she has been declared by the present Pope Pius IX, one of its principal patron saints. The left hand of this holy religious is kept in a rich reliquary in the convent of St. Sixtus and St. Dominic on the Palatine hill in Rome, and her left foot is preserved as a precious relic in the city of Venice, on both of which members the miraculous impressions of the sacred stigmas are at this moment plainly visible. (Bolland. Acta s.s 55. 30th·April)

4. *Bridget of Holland*

Very little is known of this servant of God. She was a Dominican Nun and received the stigmata of the Five Wounds and the impression of the Crown of Thorns of our crucified Savior. She died in the year 1390. (See Marchese 23rd July)

5. *Maria of Massa*

Maria, called of Massa, from her native town in Tuscany, Italy, became, when young, a Franciscan Nun in the city of Fuligno. Through ardent devotion to the Crown of Thorns, she obtained from our blessed Lord, the privilege of sharing every Friday, during many years of her life, his sufferings in her head, which she endured in the most edifying manner. This servant of God was living in the year 1340. (See Harturas and Hueber 20th, September)

6. *Blessed Ritta of Cassia*

This holy servant of God was born in 1386, at Cassia, a town in Humbria in the States of the Church. In obedience to her parents she consented to be married. After the death of her husband, Ritta entered the convent of the Augustinian Nuns of the strict observance, where she received the impression of the Crown of Thorns. Her death occurred May 14th, 1456. She was beatified by Pope Urban VII in the year 1627. Her body was incorrupt in 1682. (Bolland. Acta s.s 55. 22nd, May)

CHAPTER IV

FIFTEENTH CENTURY – THE CROWN OF THORNS BLEEDING

During this century the Church had to endure severe trials. But She was consoled by more than twenty canonized saints and other eminent servants of God, thirteen of whom received the stigmata or suffered the dolors of our Lord's passion. We enumerate those who are known to have received the impression of the Crown of Thorns in a supernatural manner.

7. *Blessed Magdalene de Parateri*

Magdalene was born at Trino, near Vercelli in Piedmont, Italy. We learn that she became a Dominican Nun. For many years, this holy religious, every Good Friday, was made to pass in a sensible and visible manner through all the stages of our Lord's passion, recived the stigmata of the Five Wounds with the impression of the Crown of Thorns. She died in the year 1503. Having been long venerated by the faithful as a saint, Pope Leo XII declared blessed Magdalene worthy of the honors of the altar in the year 1827. (See her life by father Peter Fondazuca, Milan 1644. Also Marchese 13th October)

8. *Blessed Osanna Andrasia*

God is wonderful in his saints ... and holy in all his works, says the Royal Prophet. As the perfections of God are infinite, and each of his divine attributes is essentially identified with the immensity of his nature; so the way in which God's wisdom can manifest the wonders of his power in any of his creatures, and more especially in his saints, are beyond the comprehension and calculation of created intelligence. Let us then believe and admire. We are taught by St. Paul that *"there are diversities of graces* distributed by the goodness of God to the souls of his elect, *but all these things one and the same spirit worketh, dividing to every one according as he will."* (1 Cor. 12:2)

In Blessed Osanna Andrasia we find an illustration of this principle of mystic theology. This admirable servant of God was born in the city of Mantua, Italy, on the 17th of January 1447. She became a member of the third Order of St. Dominic very early in life. On the 24th of February 1476, when twenty-seven years old, Sister Osanna received the miraculous impression of the Crown of Thorns. In the following year June 7th she was supernaturally pierced in her left side with the wound of the heart. The stigmata in her hands and feet appeared on Thursday in Passion Week of the third year. Her death occurred on June 18th, 1505.

Three years after her burial her virginal body was found incorrupt, and the miraculous wound in the side was as purple as if she were actually living. The other four stigmata in her hands and feet were clearly marked, and could be seen by the witnesses admitted on the occasion by ecclesiastical authority. Sister Osanna was beatified by Pope Leo X and declared, at the request of the people, patron saint of her native city of Mantua. The body of the saint is to this day, preserved incorrupt in the Cathedral Church of that ancient city. In the year 1871, the canons of the Cathedral chapter sent by request a certificate of the incorruptibility of B. Osanna's body to the distinguished French medical professor, A. Imbert Gourbeyere whom we have mentioned above. (See Bolland 55. 18th June)

9. *Sister Clara of Bugni*

This servant of God was born at Bugni, in Italy, in the year 1472, on the same day whereon St. Francis of Assisi came into this world. Through a special devotion towards this saraphic Patriarch, Clara became a member of the third Franciscan Order. She received the wound of the side, whence flowed blood exhaling an admirable preternatural odor. Some time after, this holy religious suffered also the miraculous impression of the Crown of Thorns and the stigmata in her hands and feet. Through her humble and earnest prayer, however, Clara obtained from our Lord the disappearance of the stigmata. But immediately after her holy death they were visible again. She died in the city of Venice in the year.1514, on the 17th of September, being the day on which the Church commemorates the impression of the stigmata of her seraphic father St. Francis.

10. *Vincentia Ferreria.*

Vincentia was born at Valentia in Spain. She was a member of the third order of St. Dominic and she is known to have received the Crown of Thorns and to have died in the year 1515. (See Steill 18th April)

11. *Blessed Stephana dé Quinzani*

Stephana was born on February 5th, 1457, in the town of Soncino, Italy. When very young, she became a Nun in the Order of St. Dominic. A few years after this holy religious received the impression of the Crown of Thorns, and successively the stigmata of the five Wounds. During forty years this admirable servant of God endured with heroic fortitude, every Friday, all the visible sufferings of our blessed Lord. The Crown of Thorns was for her the most painful. On the feast of the Holy Cross, the thorns of this miraculous crown, pressed by an invisible hand, penetrated her skull when, through the vehemence of pain, she was cast into an agony which lasted three days. This holy religious died 2nd January, 1530. (See Marchese and Steill)

12. *Sister Johanna of the Cross*

This great servant of God was born in the town of Cuba, near the city of Toledo, in Spain, in the year 1481. In her youth she embraced the religious state in the Order of St. Francis. Sister Johanna was forty years old when, on Good Friday in Holy Week, she received the stigmata which bled every Friday and Saturday, until the Feast of the Ascension of our Lord, diffusing a most agreeable odor. But in her humility, fearing lest this external manifestation of God's favor might become to her soul, an occasion of spiritual pride or vainglory, she warmly entreated our Lord to conceal them from the eyes of mankind. Her prayer was heard on condition of having the five wounds exchanged for the impression of the Crown of Thorns. During her frequent ecstasies, this holy religious spoke different languages. In Spain she was held in so high an esteem during her life, that she received many visits from persons, desirous of asking her advice. Among these were Gonzalvus of Cordova, Cardinal Ximenes and the Emperor Charles V. Sister Johanna of the Cross died in 1534 aged 53. (See Wading Hueber and Arturus)

Writing these historical sketches in Ameica, we cannot pass from the fifteenth to the sixteenth century without mentioning the name of the celebrated mariner, and eminent servant of God, Christopher Columbus, a native of Genoa, Italy, whose superior genius and ardent zeal, gave a new world to Christianity. By the envy, treachery and and ingratitude of bad men, this grand discovery was platted for him into a crown of deep humiliations and intense suffering. We believe, however, that in heaven, Christopher Columbus has long ago received a brilliant crown from the hands of his Lord and Savior, whom he loved and served so well. We moreover cherish the hope that revived Christendom will soon do full justice to his merits and venerate his eminent virtue. May the whole American Continent, and the numerous islands which he discovered, become a crown of joy to the Church and precious jewels in the diadem of Columbus, who brought to them the standard and faith of Jesus Christ symbolized in his name.

CHAPTER V

SIXTEENTH CENTURY – THE CHURCH CROWNED WITH THORNS

Since the fall of man the knowledge and experience of good and evil, has ever existed in human society: but this experimental truth has never perhaps been so strikingly evident as during the sixteenth century. We should not, however, be surprised if this nineteenth century of ours, before closing its cycle, will make an effort to surpass it both in malice and in goodness, ending in the complete triumph of truth and justice.

During the sixteenth century the two mighty and everlasting foes, evil and good, truth and error, Satan and God, waged a terrible war upon earth. As before the creation of man, Lucifer boldly lifted in heaven the banner of rebellion against God and drew to his ranks, it is believed, about one third of his fellow angels; so in the sixteenth century he succeeded, through his agents upon earth, in exciting a third part of Europe to rebellion against the Church of God. The Church was in dire affliction, and more bitterly than Rachel, she lamented over the loss of millions of her deluded children. The proud and impious leaders of the rebellion boasted of their victory, which was in reality their most fatal defeat and their successors have since kept up the insane shout, to delude their credulous dupes and followers. But the Church of God can never be conquered. She is built upon an impregnable rock, surrounded by hundreds of millions of brave and faithful children, illuminated by the wisdom and defended by the omnipotence of God. Round her thick walls, more solid than granite, more impervious than steel, we daily read the words engraved by the hand of God in shining characters of gold. *The gates of hell shall never prevail against the Church.* Betrayed by the Judases of the sixteenth century, defamed by the Scribes and Pharisees, persecuted to death by Jews and Gentiles, she, as usual, quietly took refuge in the Cenacle chamber of her council, not

211

in Jerusalem but in Trent; not on Mount Sion, but on the higher and more majestic mountains of the Alps, the Citadel of Europe. There the Church defeated her enemy. The true wisdom and virtue of Christianity was concentrated in that august assembly. The Holy Ghost descended upon it. The Church enjoyed a second Pentecost. Floods of heavenly light, and flames of burning zeal, darted from it north and south, east and west, reaching rapidly the shores of the Pacific Ocean and the distant islands of Japan. Her apostles quickly repaired her losses and doubled her numbers, by conquests in Asia, Africa and America.

In Europe, the fervor of her faithful children was rekindled. The illustrious Society of Jesus was firmly established. The spirit of older religious institutions was re-animated. New religious congregations sprang up almost miraculously in every direction. The cloisters were filled with fervent inmates, and the Church flourished in solid learning and heroic sanctity. In this century our holy religion produced about fifty saints and martyrs, raised since to the honors of the altar. Nineteen priests and religious men, after suffering many insults, were put to death on account of their religion on the 9th of July, 1572 at Bril, in Holland by the Calvinists. They are known as the Martyrs of Gorchum, because they were all taken from that town. Pope Clement X declared them Martyrs of the Faith and beatified them in 1674. We do not mention the many thousands of faithful Catholics, who suffered and died for their Faith in this century of persecution, in Germany, England and Ireland.

Among the thirty canonized saints of this century, several were very eminent in virtue and good works. It will be sufficient to mention the names of St. Francis of Paula, founder of the austere contemplative religious order of Friar Minims in Italy, who died in 1507. St. Philip Neri, founder of the Oratorians, Italy. St. Jerome Emiliani, founder of the Congregation of Regular Teaching Clergy of Somascha, Italy. St. Charles Borromeo, St. Andrew Avelino, St. Catharine of Genoa, St. Aloysius Gonzaga, St. Cajetan of Thienna, Italy, founder of the Religious Congregation called Theatines. In Spain we find St. Thomas of Villanova, St. John of the Cross and St. Teresa, the seraphic reformer of the Carmelites; St. Peter of Alcantara, the austere reformer of the Franciscan Friars. St. Louis Bertrand, the great Apostle of South America. St. Francis Xavier, the famous Apostle of the East Indies and Japan, St. Francis Borgia and towering above all, we admire the noble figure of the great founder of the Society of Jesus, St. Ignatius

212

Loyola. In France there is the holy queen St. Jane. Portugal has given to the Church St. John of God, founder of the admirable Congregation of Religious Brothers of the Infirm, who have done and do so much to alleviate the manifold sufferings of humanity.

In this important section, we have extended our remarks and enumerations to put to shame if possible, the arrogant boasting of the pretended reformers. We must now return to our main subject. During this century we find no less than thirty saints or servants of God, who received the stigmata of the five wounds, the Crown of Thorns, or supernaturally shared in the sufferings of the passion of our blessed Savior. We confine our special notice to the Crown of Thorns.

13. *Blessed Christina of Aquila*

Blessed Christina was a native of Aquila in the Kingdom of Naples, became an Augustinian Nun and on a Thursday in Holy Week, she received the miraculous Crown of Thorns. She died Feburary 18th 1543, being 63 years of age. The Bollandists mention her name on the 18th of January among the saints previously omitted. See also the History of the Order of St. Augustine, of the saints, blessed, and other illustrious persons of the Order, by Father Simplician of St. Martin, published 1640.

14. *Dominica del Paradiso*

This great servant of God was born in the city of Florence, Tuscany in the year 1473, and entered the Convent of the Dominican Nuns in her native city when very young. She was only twenty-four years of age, when she received the Five Wounds and the Crown of Thorns. Dominica died August 5th, 1553. Her virginal body is preserved incorrupt to the present day in the Chapel of the Villa Poertilli near Florence. One of her fingers is wanting, having through devotion been taken by the Queen of Etruria. (Marchese, 5th August. Also life of the servant of God Dominica del Paradiso by the Dominican Father Ignatius del Niente, published in Florence, 1625)

15. *Blessed Catharine of Racconigi*

Blessed Catherine was born at Racconigi, Italy, June 14th, 1486. When very young she became a Dominican Nun and received the Stigmas of the Five Wounds, and the Crown of Thorns on the Tuesday after Easter at twenty-four years of age, namely in 1510. This great servant of God died September 4th, 1347, sixty one years old. She was beatified by Pope Piùs VII, April 9th, 1808. (Marchese compendio delle cose mirabili della Beata Caterina da Racconigi, Turin 1858)

213

16. *Catherine of Jesus*

This admirable servant of God was a Spaniard and became a worthy companion and spiritual daughter of St. Teresa in the Carmelite reformation. She had a special devotion to the passion of our Lord. One day, whilst meditating before a picture of our Lord crowned with thorns, Catharine felt deeply penetrated at the consideration of his sufferings and earnestly entreated him to allow her to experience a share of the pain which he suffered in his adorable head. In answer to the prayer of his loving spouse, our Lord miraculously bowed down his head and allowed a real Crown of Thorns to drop down on her extended hands. Catharine profoundly venerated this precious gift, kissed it with a lively transport of devotion, and pressed it with great fervor upon her head. She continued to wear it during the twenty three remaining years of her life, though it caused her great physical pain. It was only at the command of her spiritual director, to whom she was ever most perfectly obedient in everything, that she laid it aside during her frequent severe illnesses. This great servant of Jesus died on the 24th of February, 1586 (History of the Reformed Carmelites, by Father Francis of St. Mary, and life of St. Teresa by Bouix)

17. *St. Catharine de Ricci*

This is another of the many beautiful and fragrant flowers of sanctity, given to the Church by the good city of Florence. Catharine was born from the noble family de Ricci April 15, 1522. In her earliest youth she became a Dominican Nun in the town of Prato, Tuscany. She was only twenty years of age when she received the stigmata of the five wounds on the Octave of Easter, April the 14th, 1342, from which exhaled a most agreeable preternatural odor. Moreover, the form of the cross was marked in relief by elevation of the flesh upon her shoulders. This admirable servant of God received also the impression of the Crown of Thorns. She died in the Convent of St. Vincent in Prato, February 2nd 1589 and was beatified by Pope Clement XI. Benedict XIV, in the Bull of her canonization 1746, gives an interesting account of her numerous miracles and her wonderful gifts. (See life of the Venerable Mother Catharine de Ricci by Father Philip Guidi, Florence, 1622. Also life of St. Catharine de Ricci, extracted from the authentic documents of her beatification, and canonization, Rome 1746. Consult above all the acts of canonization by Benedict XIV)

18. *Sister Raggi dé Scio*

This servant of God was born in 1552, and lived for some years in the married state. At the death of her husband she was left a widow with two sons whom she brought up so well that both became Dominican Friars, in the famous Convent of the Minerva in Rome. This virtuous widow and most pious mother, went to live near them and took the Habit of the Third Order of St. Dominic. On the feast of Pentecost 1583, whilst praying in the chapel of the Blessed Virgin, in the Church of the Minerva, she received the stigmata of the five wounds and the Crown of Thorns. She died January 7th 1600, and was buried in the same church. (Marchese 7, January) The Bollandists mention this servant of God among the saints previously omitted, and quote two lives written about her by two Dominicans. One was published in Barcelona, Spain by Father Raphael da Ribera, 1606, the other by Father Arnaud Rayseins of Douai.

19. *Benedict of Reggio*

This holy servant of God was born in the city of Reggio, Kingdom of Naples. He was a religious of the Order of St. Francis among the Capuchins. Through a special devotion to the Crown of Thorns of our dear Lord, Benedict obtained the favor that at least one of the thorns should pierce his head penetrating his skull, and causing for many years a most painful ulceration. He died in the city of Bologna in the convent of his religious Order in the year 1602. (Hueber)

CHAPTER VI

SEVENTEENTH CENTURY – JESUS CROWNED WITH THORNS IN HIS MEMBERS

This century, like the former, brought trials and trumphs to the Church. The dolorous way of Calvary ends at the rocky Sepulcher, which is rendered glorious and joyful by the resurrection. Twenty-seven canonized martyrs of Japan, carry in their hands the palm of victory over Pagan persecutions. Thousands more suffered for their faith in the north-west of Europe from the malice and cruelty of the Protestant apostasy. In Italy, France and Spain, nearly twenty'saints and eminent servants of God who illustrated this century by their virtues, have been raised to the honors of the altar. Among these shine with special brilliancy St. Francis de Sales and St. Jane Francis de Chantal, the founders of the Order of the Visitation. St. Vincent de Paul, the founder of the Congregation of the Mission or Lazarists, the Sisters of Charity, and other religious congregations and pious associations. St. Joseph Calasanctius, the founder of the Regular Clergy of Pious Schools. St. Camillus de Lellis, founder of the Regular Clergy attending the sick and dying. St. Mary Magdalene de Pazzi, in Italy, and St. Rose of Lima, in Peru, South America, flourished in this century. Both suffered the Crown of Thorns. The former miraculously from our Lord, the latter from her desire of imitating our Savior. More than forty saints and servants of God, during this remarkable century, suffered the stigmata of the five wounds, or some special supernatural dolor of the passion of our Lord. The following received the impression of the Crown of Thorns.
20. *St. Mary Magdalene de Pazzi*

The illustrious city of Florence, at this epoch a beautiful garden of sanctity, was honored by the birth and life of this great saint. She belonged to the noble family de Pazzi, and was born in 1566. When very young, she became a Carmelite Nun. Sister Mary Magdalene was only nineteen years of age, when, like St. Catharine of Sienna, she suffered the mystic and invisible Crown of Thorns, and the interior stigmata of the five wounds. This was in the year 1585, when she was made to pass through all the stages of the passion of her divine spouse. She died in 1607, being 41 years old and was canonized sixty-two years later by Pope Clement IX, April 28th 1669. Her feast is celebrated May 27th. (Bollandists 25th May)

21. *Sister Ursula Aguir*

This holy servant of God was born in Valence, Spain in the year 1554. When very young, she became a member of the Third Order of St. Dominic. Sister Ursula often participated in the dolors of the passion of our Lord. On the 21st of March 1592, she received the impression of the five wounds and her heart was pierced. She suffered likewise the Crown of Thorns, and was often ravished into ecstasies. Sister Ursula died 1st September 1608 and was buried in the chapel of the third Order of St. Dominic in her native city. (See Steill and Marchese)

22. *Sister Magdalene Caraffa*

This great servant of God was no less eminent for her sanctity, than for her nobility of blood. She was the Duchess of Andria in the Kingdom of Naples. But generously renouncing all the pomps and pleasures of the world, she embraced a life of poverty and humility, obedience, self-denial and penance in a Dominican convent. During several years, at her fervent request, she experienced every Friday, the sufferings of the Crown of Thorns. She was born in the year 1566 and died 1615 being 49 years old. (Marchese 29th December)

23. *Blessed Passidia Crogi*

This holy servant of God was a native of Sienna, another Tuscan city remarkable for her illustrious saints and persons of eminent virtue. Passidia was a member of the Order of St. Francis. She received the sacred stigmata and Crown of Thorns, which occasionally bled profusely. At the pressing instance of Queen Maria de Medicis, Mother Passidia twice traveled to France, on which occasion she plainly foretold the assassination of King Henry IV. This holy religious died in the year 1617.

See the incomparable life of blessed Passidia of Sienna in the French language, published in Paris 1627 by order of the Queen Mother, Maria de Medicis. This life was translated from the Italian by De la Brosse.

24. *Catharine Ciaulina*

She was a native of Italy and a member of the Third Order of St. Francis. The celebrated mystic writer, Gorres, cites this holy servant of God among the number of ecstatics, who suffered the pain of the Crown of Thorns in the head without any external mark. She died 1619, 27th January according to Hueber.

25. *Sister Hyppolyta of Jesus*

This holy servant of God was born January 22nd, 1553, in the city of Barcelona, Spain. She embraced the religious state in the Dominican Convent of the Holy Angels in her native city. Like St. Catharine of Sienna, Sister Hyppolyta received from our Blessed Lord, the Crown of Thorns in her hands, which she so forcibly pressed on her head, that it caused her intense pain for several years. She died in the odor of sanctity 1624, 6th of August, according to Marchese.

26. *Sister Delicia di Giovanni*

God is admirable in all his saints, but according to the purpose of his will, he is more wonderful in some than in others. The wonders of divine Wisdom and Goodness have in a remarkable manner shone in the life of Sister Delicia di Giovanni. Palermo, the capital of the island of Sicily, was the place of her birth which occurred December 15th, 1560. She became a Dominican Nun in her native city. In the year 1635, Sister Delicia experienced the sufferings of the passion in general. In the following year she received the stigma in her right hand and the next year in her left hand. In the fourth year she was stigmatized in her left foot and in the following year, in her right. In the sixth year, Delicia received the wound in her side, which produced a considerable visible enlargement of her heart. In the seventh year this admirable servant of God endured the torture of the flagellation, with effusion of blood from her virginal body. The year following, she suffered most intense pains all over her body, as if it were hanging upon the cross. Finally in the last year of her life this faithful spouse of Jesus and ardent lover of his passion was impressed with the Crown of Thorns, the emblem and sure pledge of her crown of glory. This holy religious died in the odor of sanctity on the 16th of July 1642. (See Marchese 16th July) The acts of the Dominican General Chapter held in Rome, 1656 state that Sister Delicia endured all the sufferings of our Lord's passion.

27. *Sister Louisa of Jesus*

Neuralgia headaches are painful and saddening afflictions of our humanity which are often intended by God to call to our minds the sufferings endured by his most holy Son, Jesus, our Lord, through the Crown of Thorns. Sister Louisa of Jesus should, in this respect, be our model. She was born in Paris, November 9th, 1569 and lived some years in the married state. After having edified the world, she joined the Reformed Carmelites of St. Teresa, and was the second Carmelite Nun professed in Paris in the year 1604.

Sister Louisa had an ardent devotion to the Passion of our Lord, and felt a lively compassion for his sufferings ccasioned by the Crown of Thorns. Our Blessed Lord wishing to make his loving spouse more conformable with himself, permitted her to endure the most acute pains in her head. These sufferings became so violent as to make her often fall into a swoon. It seemed to her as if some sharp instrument pierced her very skull. At other times she experienced a sensation as if an invisible hand armed with sharp points, pressed heavily upon her head. These terrible sufferings became daily more intensified, during the last six months of her life. Her religious sisters in the Convent of Dole, where she lived for some years, were of opinion that Sister Louisa suffered the impression of the Crown of Thorns. In effect the infirmarian, and other religious observed red cavities and inflamed rays, upon her forehead and round her head, similar to those caused by a real Crown of Thorns. The Nun who wrote her life describes the painful marks which she saw, but she observes that Mother Louisa never told her that they were the effects of the Crown of Thorns. This holy servant of God died in the Carmelite Convent of Dôle February 28th 1528. (Chronicles of the Carmelites in France Tom. 2 Page 526, Troyes, 1850)

28. *Maria d'Escobar*

Maria d'Escobar was born at Valladolid, in Spain February 8th 1554. She was made to suffer the Crown of Thorns, the flagellation and crucifixion. She had the stigmata of the five wounds. The stigma of the side was surrounded by five smaller wounds, from which blood and water issued. Maria died on the 9th of June 1633. (See her life published at Madrid, 1665. Also the life of Father Louis du Ponté her confessor)

29. *Sister Mary Paul of St. Thomas*

This admirable servant of God, passing through different states of life, reached an eminent degree of sanctity and received extraordinary favors from our Lord. She was born in the city of Naples, on the 16th of July 1572. She lived twenty two years in the married state, and at the death of her husband, she was left with the care of a numerous family of young children. She was a member of the Third Order of St. Dominic. During the year 1620, Sister Mary Paul received the impression of the Crown of Thorns, and about Christmas the stigmata of the five wounds, which during the night were luminous. In her profound humility, by long and fervent prayer, she entreated our Lord to conceal these favors from the eyes of men, and in conformity with her desire they became invisible. This holy woman said to her confessor, that the image of our crucified Savior was impressed on her heart. After her death August 3rd 1639, the prodigy was found realized. This miraculous heart is preserved in the Dominican Church of our Lady of Health in the city of Naples. The acts of the General Chapter of the Dominicans, held in Rome in the year 1644 mention the prophecy and the miraculous impression in the heart of this wonderful servant of God.

30. *Venerable Mother Agnes of Jesus*

Age or condition of life, instead of being an obstacle, are made subservient to the manifestation of the wonders of God's wisdom, power and goodness. This admirable servant of God was born at Puy, in France, on the 7th day of November 1502. Prevented by divine grace, little Agnes, *innocent lamb*, was only twelve years of age when she received the stigmata of the five wounds, but they remained invisible so long as she lived in the world. Having entered a Dominican Convent at 22 years of age, the stigmata became apparent. She had also the impression of the Crown of Thorns. This venerable religious often endured all the sensible sufferings of the passion. At her fervent prayer the stigmata of the five wounds disappeared again, but the Crown of Thorns remained visible during all her religious life. Mother Agnes of Jesus died October 19th 1634 in the Dominican Convent at Langeac, Haute Loire where her precious relics are preserved. The cause of her beatification has long ago been introduced in Rome. See Life of the Venerable Mother Agnes of Jesus by Lantages. A new edition of this life, considerably augmented, has been published by the Abbé Lucet, in two volumes, Paris 1862. Her life was also printed in the German language in Cologne 1671.

31. *Blessed Margaret Marie Alacoque.*

The devout worshippers of the Sacred Heart of Jesus will be pleased to see the humble, but fervent apostle of this holy devotion, enumerated among the privileged servants of our Lord, who have shared in the dolors of his Crown of Thorns.

Margaret came into the world on the feast of St. Mary Magdalene July 22nd 1647, in the village of Versovre, in the Charolais, diocese of Autun, France. When 24 years of age, she entered the convent of the Visitation Nuns at Paray-Le-Monial, and pronounced her solemn vows in the following year 1672, November 6th. The year after her divine spouse gave Sr. Margaret a new pledge of his love, by presenting her with a Crown of Thorns. Going one morning to receive Holy Communion, the Sacred Host appeared to her eyes more resplendent than the sun, so that she could not endure its brightness. In the midst of this light she saw our Lord, who holding a Crown of Thorns over her head, affectionately said to her: *"My child, receive this crown as a token of that which will soon be given thee by conformity with me."* We learn from these words, that the Crown of Thorns is a token and an emblem of a soul's conformity with Jesus Christ. This fervent spouse of Jesus strove hard to become so. She had much to suffer, and suffered all with admirable humility, sweetness and heroic patience. Two years later, namely in 1575, Sr. Margaret Marie had the vision of the Sacred Heart which has been mentioned. One day after holy Communion our Lord, she says, showed me a rude crown composed of nineteen very sharp thorns that pierced his divine head; and which caused me such great sorrow that I could speak to him only by my tears. Our blessed Lord told me that I might draw out these thorns, which had been thrust into his head by an unfaithful soul. "She pierces my head with thorns as many times as, through pride, she prefers herself to me." Not knowing how to draw them out, this sad object kept continually before my eyes, causing me much suffering. My superior, having told me to ask our Lord in what manner I should be able to remove them; he told me to do it by acts of humility, performed in honor of his humiliations. This admirable servant of God died pronouncing the sacred names of Jesus and Mary, between seven and eight o'clock in the evening October 15th 1590, being 43 years, 2 months and 3 days; of which she passed nearly eighteen in the monastery of Paray, that has of late become so famous throughout the Catholic world on her account. Blessed Margaret was beatified by Pope Pius IX, April 24th 1864. May her prayers in heaven accelerate the complete and universal triumph of the Sacred Heart of Jesus upon earth. (History of blessed Margaret Marie by Father C. Daniel S. J. published by P. O'Shea, New York, 27 Barclay street 1857 and other lives of this admirable saint, which we strongly recommend for perusal to the devout readers of this sketch.)

32. *Sister Catharine of St. Peter, Martyr*

This is another bright star in the firmament of the Dominican Order. This holy servant of Jesus was born in San Severino, a town in the Kingdom of Naples. She became a Dominican Nun in the Convent of St. Catharine of Sienna in the city of Naples, about ninety miles distant from her native place. This fervent religious had a particular devotion to her holy Patroness of Sienna, and strove hard to imitate her eminent virtues. Our Lord allowed Sister Catharine to participate very largely in the manifold sufferings of his passion. She received the impression of the Crown of Thorns, was made to feel the weight of our Savior's cross, and her heart was pierced with a sensible dart of divine love. This holy religious died May 28th 1648, according to Marchese.

33. *Sister Maria Benigna Pepé*

Mary Benigna Pepé was born in 1590, at Trapani, a town in Sicily, and became subsequently a Dominican Nun. After her death the pious Nuns, who took care of her virginal body, saw the sacred names of Jesus and Mary perfectly formed on the region of the heart and the Crown of Thorns with a cross impressed upon her shoulders. Marchese, 25th December.

34. *Sister Maria Villani*

This is another worthy daughter of the holy Patriarch St. Dominic. The city of Naples was the place of her birth, which occurred on the 18th of September 1584. Maria became a Dominican Nun in her native city, and was the foundress of a new convent under the title of Santa Maria (Holy Mary) of divine love. The city of Naples has been favored by God in the natural and supernatural order, and rendered illustrious with many saints and eminent servants of Jesus Christ.

Mother Mary Villani received the Crown of Thorns, June 26th, 1620, when she was thirty-six years old. She was often made to experience in a visible manner all the sufferings of the passion of our Lord. She received also the wound in her side and heart. This holy religious wrote a book on divine love with the title *"De Tribus Divinus Flammis,"* "The Three Divine Flames," wherein she admirably describes the nature and effects of the mystic wound of the heart. She died March 26th, 1670, when the wound of her heart was made manifest. Father Master Domenico Maria Marchese,

Neapolitan by birth, Rector of the Dominican College of St.Thomas in Naples, knew personally this great servant of God, and wrote her life. He states that after her death he saw the heart of Mother Mary, miraculously wounded, as if it had been pierced with a red-hot lance. He is the author of the celebrated Dominican Diary, so often quoted in this collection.

35. *Sister Johanna Maria of the Cross*

This servant of God was born September 8th, 1603, at Roveredo, a town of Italian Tyrol. She was a member of the Third Order of St. Francis. Sister Johanna had the impression of the Crown of Thorns, and the stigmata of the five wounds. Her death occurred March 26th, 1673. The cause of her beatification was introduced in the last century, but was interrupted on account of subsequent political revolutions. (See Hueber, 25th March. Greiderer Germania Franciscana, 1781, and above all her life written by Reneé Weber, translated in the French by Charles Saint Foi, published in Paris, 1850)

36. *Sister Frances Maria Furia*

Alexandria near Agrigente, in Sicily, was the place of her birth, which occurred March 10th, 1639. Sister Frances was a member of the Third Order of St. Dominic. She received the stigmata of the five wounds, but at her earnest prayer God rendered them invisible, like those of St. Catharine of Sienna. The year before she died on the 25th of September, Sister Frances suffered also the impression of the Crown of Thorns. She died September 25th, 1670.

37. *Sister Philippa of St. Thomas*

Sister Philippa was a Dominican nun in the Convent of Montemor, in Portugal. After her death, which took place October 6th 1670, the traces of the Crown of Thorns were visible in her head, and the stigmata of the five wounds on her virginal body were discovered by her religious sisters. (Acts of the General Dominican Chapter held in Rome, 1570)

CHAPTER VII

EIGHTEENTH CENTURY – THORNS AND THISTLES

The heretical and hypocritical writings of the Jansenists, the impious doctrines of Voltaire, Diderot, Rousseau, the Deist and Atheist illuminati, and of the enemies of all religion and civil government, kept this century in fermentation, and a dreadful explosion towards the end of it shook Europe to its foundation, and deluged France and other nations with human blood. The storm fell upon France with fearful and destructive violence. Her pious King Louis XVI, his wife, Queen Marie Antoinette, their only son Louis, heir to the throne, Princess Elizabeth, sister of the king and other members of the Royal Family, and thousands of the nobility of France, were murdered by the impious revolutionists. The Church had much to suffer in that unfortunate country by the total suppression of Christian worship. All religious houses were abolished and their property confiscated. More than ten thousand secular and regular clergy were put to death for their fidelity to their religion and vows. Fifty or sixty thousand more edified in their exile, Europe Asia and America by the holiness of their lives and their persevering zeal for the propagation of our Holy Faith. Many martyrs died also in China for their fidelity to religion. This century reckons more than sixty or seventy canonized or beatified saints, and a large number of eminent servants of God. Among the canonized saints shine with special luster, St. Alphonsus Maria Ligouri, founder of the Religious Congregation of our Most Holy Redeemer or Redemptorists, in the kingdom of Naples. St. Paul of the Cross, founder of the Religious Congregation of the most Holy Cross and Passion or Passionists, a native of the Republic of Genoa. St Leonard of Porto-Maurizio, in the same Republic, one of the greatest Missionaries of this century; St. Francis de Girolamo of the Society of Jesus; St Veronica Juliani; St Mary Francis of the five wounds. These two last saints are among the twenty privileged servants of God who are known to have received the sacred stigmata, and the Crown of Thorns, or suffered some special pain of the passion of our Lord. We pass to enumerate those who endured the Crown of Thorns.

38. *St. Veronica Juliani*

This truly admirable saint was born December 27th, 1660, at Mercatello, diocese of Urbino, in the States of the Church. When very young, she became a Capuchin nun in the Convent of St. Clara in the town of Castello. St.Veronica received the Crown of Thorns April 4th, 1693, when 33 years of age. In the night of Holy Saturday, 1697, she was stigmatized in her hands, feet and side, and frequently participated in a visible manner in the sufferings of our Lord's passion. This holy religious told her spiritual director, that all the instruments of the passion were engraven in her heart. This prodigy was verified after her death, which occurred July 9th, 1727. Veronica was beatified by Pope Pius VII and canonized by Gregory XVI, May 26th, 1839. See the life of the venerable servant of God, Sister Veronica Guiliani, by Father Francis Strozzi, a Jesuit. Also life of Blessed Veronica Guiliani, by Rev. Philip Salvatori, Rome, 1803. The late Cardinal Wiseman wrote an abridgment of her life, and that of four other saints canonized with her by Pope Gregory XVI, 26th May, 1839.

39. *Sister Marie-Anne Magdalene Remusat*

This great servant of God was born November, 30th, 1696, at Marseilles, France. Marie-Anne was only fifteen years of age, when she left the world, and retired to the Visitation Convent in her native city. This worthy daughter of St. Francis de Sales received the impression of the Crown of Thorns and the stigmata of the five wounds at 34 years of age. She died February 15th, 1730. See her life published by Girard in Lyons, 1868.

40. *Saint Mary Francis of the Five Wounds*

This ardent lover of Jesus crucified, was born on the feast of the Annunciation, 25th March, 1715 at Naples. When very young, she joined the third Order of St. Peter of Alcantara. Sister Mary Francis at 28 years of age began to experience every Friday all the sufferings of the passion, passing in a sensible and visible manner through all its dolorous stages. The different scenes of our Savior's passion were distinctly represented in her person, by the various pains which she successively endured with heroic patience. The agony in the garden of Gethsemani was visible in the extreme anguish of her soul and prostration of her body. The blows and

225

the lashes inflicted on our Savior, could be seen in the blue marks, contusions, swellings and bleeding wounds on her person. The impression of the Crown of Thorns appeared in the streams of blood, flowing from her brow and round the head. During Lent, 1743, this holy religious received the stigmata of the five wounds in her hands, feet and side. In her profound humility, she continually entreated our Lord, to conceal these extraordinary favors from the eyes of men. This prayer was granted, but only after twenty-seven years of their visible duration. This wonderful servant of God died at Naples, October 6th, 1761. She was beatified by Gregory XVI, 15th October, 1843, and canonized by Pope Pius IX, together with St. Paul of the Cross, St. Leonard of Porto Maurizio and the twenty-seven Japanese Martyrs, on the eighteenth centenary of St. Peter and Paul, June 29th, 1867. The humble room where this great saint lived and died in the city of Naples is continually visited by large numbers of devout people and many have therein obtained extraordinary graces and favors through her intercession. See life of Maria Francesca by Father Bernard Lavioza published in Naples at the beginning of the present century. This interesting life has since passed through eight editions. Another life of blessed Maria Francesca was published at Naples in 1866 by Rev. Luigi Montella.

CHAPTER VIII

NINETEENTH CENTURY – THE CROWN OF THORNS
IS THE DIADEM OF VICTORY

Century of my birth, measure of my fleeting time, gate to my eternity, I like to hear and re-echo thy praises. God in the admirable designs of his wisdom and goodness, has been generous with thee. I sincerely admire the wealth of thy gifts, thy natural talents, thy industrious skill, thy unflagging energy; the powerful activity and rapidity of thy steam engines, the ubiquity of thy voice through thy wire's electric flash, rushing with lightning speed through mountains and oceans. Knowledge under thy fostering care, has fledged and extended her wings; and science has soared to the stars, dived to the bottom of the sea, and penetrated to the bowels of the earth. All this is in thy praise, venerable mother of seventy-seven. *How good is God to Israel, to them that are of a right heart.* (Ps. 72)

But the majority of thy children, in their pride, impiety and sensuality, have abused the gifts of God, and turned them against their divine benefactor. *Pride has held them fast; they are covered with their iniquity, and their wickedness. Their iniquity has come forth as it were from fatness; they have passed into the affectation of the heart. They have thought and spoken wickedness and blasphemy; they have spoken iniquity on high. They have set their mouth against heaven and their tongues have passed through the earth. (Ps. 72.) If I have said: I will speak thus: Behold! I should condemn the generation of thy children. I studied that I might know this thing, it is a labor in my sight.*

I have learned that at thy birth, old lady, thou wert steeped in human blood by the cruel tyrant of despotism and war. Thy youth and beauty have been prostituted and dishonored by the treachery of sedition and by the impiety of revolution. Scarcely one nation can be found on the face of the earth, during the cycle of thy existence, that has not been humbled, and suffered violence from the pride and impiety of thy rebellious children. Too many of them are, like blind moles, clandestinely boring deep pits and snares of seduction, and becoming proud and arrogant at the sight of their mole-hills, which they call *progress*. Like black coal-diggers, with the dim lamps of befogged reason stuck to their soiled caps, some of thy gifted children are day and night lowering their manhood in their insane efforts to undermine the earth, with the impious and cruel design of speedily causing a universal explosion, upsetting the established order of civil society, and completely destroying the Christian religion. Venerable matron! thy noble figure will in a few years be enveloped in dismal clouds of black smoke, and lurid petroleum flames, and thy hoary head will be singed and covered with the accumulated ashes of ruins, precipitated by the perjured craft of impiety. The Church of ages, divinely built upon the impregnable rock of Peter, from whose beneficent hands thou hast received all thy worth and honor, will suffer some temporary breach in her more exposed and weaker ramparts, but these will be made available for the reception and safe refuge of repentant prodigals, returning home to their afflicted but ever merciful mother. This holy Church of the living God, in her heavenly wisdom, inexhaustible goodness and creative energy, will collect the scattered ruins of betrayed human society, and console and crown thy expiring years, by the reconstruction of a manly, noble and vigorous Christendom over the renovated surface of the earth. "The Lord our God will send forth his spirit, and holy apostles shall be created, and the face of the earth and of Christian society shall be renewed." (Ps. 103)

The ground work for this magnificent structure is being extensively prepared, and its foundations are actively dug, in spite of their intentions and calculations, by the blind agents and deluded slaves of the prince of darkness. Our Church's wisest and best architects have already met in council at the Vatican. They have designated, solemnly proclaimed and permanently installed on the pontifical throne our unerring leader, and after having paid homage to his supreme authority, they have quietly adjourned, determined to meet again at the most propitious opportunity to arrange, organize and accomplish their wisely matured plans of action. Those privileged souls, intended by God to co-operate in a special manner in this mighty work of re-edification with their prayers, penances, zeal and rich stock of merits, are under skilful training. About twenty of them have already received their diploma with the divine seal of the five stigmata, the Crown of Thorns and other tokens of our Savior's predilection. Those supernaturally wounded hands of his visible sanctity, are constantly lifted up towards heaven, like

228

those of Moses in fervent supplications to the throne of Mercy, and working hard preparing the proper materials for the erection of God's holy Temple. The humble heads of thorn-crowned virtue are day and night bowed down in prayer of self immolation before the altar of the Most High to implore the help, and obtain the protection of his omnipotent hand, for the speedy and complete success of this noble enterprise undertaken for the promotion of his honor and glory, and for the conversion and salvation of mankind.

Venerable Mother and Matron of the nineteenth century, in spite of the deep impiety and widespread wickedness of many of thy wretched children, thou wilt expire in the warm embrace of the Holy Catholic Church. With heartfelt sentiments of sincere joy and gratitude for this great mercy, thou, in the words of holy Simeon, wilt with thy dying lips bless God and say: *"Now thou dost dismiss thy servant, O Lord, according to thy words in peace; because my eyes have seen thy salvation, which thou hast prepared before the face of all people; a light to the revelation of the Gentiles, and the glory of thy people of Israel."* (Lk. 2:29) In this cheering and hopeful expectation, I consecrate, venerable Matron, to thy memory and to thy honor, the following list of some of thy holiest and noblest children, carefully trained in the school and genuine faith of Jesus crowned with thorns and crucified.

41. *Sister Maria Josepha Kumi*

This great servant of God was born February 20th, 1763, at Wollaran, Canton of Switz. She was nineteen years of age when she became a Dominican Nun in the convent of Wesan, diocese of Saint Gall. Sister Maria Josepha was stigmatized gradually. First she received the wound in her side, then the Crown of Thorns; finally, twenty years after her religious profession, namely in the year 1803, stigmatization was completed in her hands and feet. She died November 7th, 1817. A brief account of her life was published in the German language in Saint Gall, Switzerland, 1868.

42. *Venerable Maria Louisa Biagini.*

Maria Louisa was born in the city of Lucca, Tuscany, March 14th, 1770. At eighteen years of age she received the habit of the second Order of St. Francis in the Convent of San Micheletto (Little Saint Michael) in her native city. She often suffered the stigmata of the five wounds and the impression of the Crown of Thorns, especially on Good Friday. This great servant of God died March 29th, 1811, in the odor of sanctity in her Convent in Lucca where her body is preserved as a precious relic. The cause of her beatification is favorably advancing in Rome. See life of Sister Maria Louisa

Biagini, Luchese, Lay Sister of the second Order of St. Francis, by Rev. Canon Raphael Mezzelli, extracted from the memoirs of the Marquis Cesare Luchesini, and from other documents, Lucca, 1864, published by G. Giusti.

43. *Sister Ann Catherine Emmerich*

This admirable lover of Jesus crucified was born September 8, 1774, in the village of Flanike, about two miles from Coesfield, a town in the diocese of Munster, Germany. She became an Augustinian nun in the Convent of Agnetenberg at Dulmen on the 28th August 1812. Sister Ann Catharine received on her virginal body a stigma in the form of a cross. Another similar impression was made just above the first, during the Christmas feast. On the 29th December of the same year, this holy religious was stigmatized in her hands, feet and side. She received subsequently, the impression of the Crown of Thorns. Sister Ann Catharine was often made to undergo in a visible manner, all the sensible sufferings of the passion of our dear Lord. She wrote a wonderful book of her visions and revelations, with the title *"The dolorous passion of our Lord Jesus Christ."* The stigmata and all these terrible pains continued until the end of her life. She died February 9th, 1824, and was buried in the cemetery of Dulmen. See Ann Catharine Emmerich, by Dr. Krabbe, Germany. Much better however, is the life of Ann Catharine Emmerich by Father Schmoager, translated into French by M. de Lazales, published in Paris by Bray, 1808, 1872, in three volumes.

44. *Venerable Elizabeth Canori Mora*

This truly admirable servant of God, and heroic victim of self-immolation, in expiation of the sins of mankind, was born in Rome, of respectable parents, November 21st, Feast of the Presentation in the year 1774. In due time she was married to Christopher Mora, an advocate in the Roman Court, by whom she had several children. Elizabeth had much to suffer from these, but more especially from her husband. She made, however, such good use of these and other trials, that she rapidly advanced to the highest degree of Christian perfection. She ever had an ardent devotion to the passion of our Lord and was particularly penetrated with the mystery of the *Ecce Homo*, behold the man. The Stations of the Cross were the exercise of her special predilection. On Christmas day Elizabeth saw in a vision our infant Savior in the cradle, drenched in his blood. She was given to understand that he suffered all this through the negligence of Christian parents and of those who are charged with the education of children, and neglect this grave duty of Religion. On the feast of the

230

Purification February 2nd, our blessed Lady presented to her servant his divine Son wounded and bleeding profusely, and said to her: *"Behold, my daughter, how wounded he is. Oh! Hide him in thy heart."* The most holy Mother of our Lord exhorted Elizabeth to offer often the sacred blood of her divine Son, to the Eternal Father, to obtain the conversion of sinners, and the salvation of souls, to whose welfare she was so ardently devoted. Our blessed Lady added: *"Join with this offering, my daughter, that of thy sufferings and trials with the love with which thy heart is penetrated."*

These heavenly visions and exhortations enkindled in her heart, a most ardent desire of offering herself as a victim for the satisfaction of divine justice, and for the conversion of sinners and infidels. Her generous offer was accepted. She was made to suffer in a sensible manner, a real crucifixion when her side and heart were really pierced with a lance. Her sufferings were excessive. She felt that she was dying when our Lord appeared to her and detached her from the cross, praising and consoling her for her generosity. She was in an instant restored to perfect health. Elizabeth received also the Crown of Thorns. God through her prayers, and meritorious sufferings, converted many sinners, and delivered the Church and the Pontifical States from serious calamities. It was she who cured the young Count John Maria de Mastaï Ferretti, the present gloriously reigning Pontiff, Pius IX, from epilepsy, which had so far prevented his desired admission into the ecclesiastical state ... Through the spirit of prophecy Elizabeth very likely foresaw the future eminent sanctity of the noble youth. Whilst we write these lines, we learn from a high authority in Rome, that Pius IX is working great miracles. The letter is dated Rome, 8th February, 1876. On the 18th of June, 1814, she obtained from God the deliverance of the soul of Pope Plus VI, from the pains of purgatory. He had been dead about fifteen years. He had been an exemplary Pope and died in exile, and a martyr of persecution, yet it seems, he had to suffer so long in purgatory. Can we dear leader, flatter ourselves that we shall escape it? Too many Catholics are under this flattering illusion.

In the year 1820, by a special inspiration of God, Elizabeth became a member of the Third Order of the Reformed and Barefooted Trinitarians. She died in Rome, 5th of February, 1825, in great odor of sanctity. The process of her beatification is progressing favorably. (See *Voix Prophetiques*. Vol 2, Chap 13)

CHAPTER IX

THE WONDERS OF THE CROWN OF THORNS IN THE NINETEENTH CENTURY

45. *Maria Rosa Adriani*

If God is admirable in His saints, His mercy is not less wonderful in behalf of sinners. *The Lord is gracious and merciful; patient and plenteous in mercy. The Lord is sweet to all, and His tender mercies are over all His works.* (Ps. 144:9)

Sanctity is the work of God: and saints are made and intended by God for the welfare of sinners. Saints are the ripe fruits and the perfection of the Incarnation, which was principally intended for the redemption and salvation of sinful man. In the Venerable Elizabeth Canori Mora we have just admired a heroic victim voluntarily sacrificed for the welfare of poor sinners. In Maria Rosa Adriani we have another holy victim of self-immolation in behalf of a sinful world. Maria Rosa was born, lived and died at Francavilla, head city of the Province of Lecce, Kingdom of Naples. Like a bright morning star she appeared in the horizon of life, early in January, 1786. She was only five years of age, when the brightness of her precious virtue began to shine upon earth. She was violently attacked by the painful and loathsome disease, small-pox. This little and innocent sufferer, beholding her small body covered with putrid sores, prevented by divine grace, began to meditate in the best way she could, on the sufferings of our crucified Lord. On that occasion she felt a strong inspiration and an ardent desire to become like unto him, and to bear in her body the wounds of his sacred passion. The fervent prayer of this innocent child was promptly heard by her heavenly Father. From that moment she felt intense pain in her little hands, feet and side. Her heart was inflamed with a deep and tender compassion for the sorrows of our blessed Lady at the foot of the cross.

As soon as she recovered from this serious illness, little Maria Rosa manifested a strong love for retirement, solitude, prayer, mortification and penance. Some years after she wished to consecrate herself entirely and forever to God in the religious state of life, in the Franciscan Convent of St. Clare in her native city. But her urgent request was sternly refused by her parents. In obedience to them whom she ever venerated as the representatives of God, this good child remained at home keeping herself in deep recollection of spirit, secretly practicing severe penances and almost continual prayer. Her greatest delight was to remain for hours before the most Holy Sacrament in the Church.

When twenty-two years, with her parents' permission, she became a member of the Third Order of St. Francis, in the Church of the Conventual Friars at Francavilla, 19th April, 1808. This new favor increased the fervor of the youthful servant of God. Her supernatural sufferings became more intense and the stigmata began to appear exteriorly, on the principal feasts of our divine Lord, and of his most holy Mother. By degrees the impression of the wounds appeared more visibly marked and the pain was intensified. At last, during the Octave of Corpus Christi, June, 1820, the stigmata were completely formed in her hands, feet and side. This alarmed the humility of Maria, who fervently entreated her divine Spouse to keep them concealed from human sight. Her request, however, was not granted and the stigmata remained visible until her death.

When our Lord finds correspondence with His extraordinary favors, he rapidly multiplies and increases them, in his privileged servants. This he certainly did with Maria Rosa. On the 8th day of June the same month, being Friday and the Feast of the Sacred Heart, she was, late in the evening, raised to a sublime degree of contemplation, when she was favored with a vision. Our Blessed Lord appeared to his servant accompanied by his most holy Mother, took her heart from her bosom, and entrusted it to the special care and guardianship of our blessed Lady, the Virgin of Virgins. He then exhorted Maria Rosa to prepare herself to endure for his sake, and without consolation, one of the most painful martyrdoms. On the following morning, she went to see her spiritual director, and with her habitual simplicity and candor, related to him the heavenly communications with which she had been favored by our Blessed Lord and his most holy Mother. With heroic courage she added, that she was fully disposed, and firmly resolved to endure for God's sake, and with the assistance of his divine grace, any and every affliction, privation and suffering, that his divine Majesty would be pleased to send her. These noble and generous dispositions of his penitent were encouraged by the pious and enlightened Franciscan Father, the spiritual director of Maria Rosa. Fully expecting that her patience and fortitude were to be severely tested, he placed her under obedience, to give her greater confidence, and more to augment the merit of her sufferings. Her confessor then commanded her to offer herself to God, as a willing victim for the sins of men, in imitation of her crucified Spouse. She promptly and gladly complied with the order of her spiritual director. The voluntary victim was immediately placed by God on the altar of mystic sacrifice. On the following night our Lord appeared to her, nailed to the cross: and darting forth from his wounds five most resplendent rays, like beams of burning fire, he transpierced with them the hands, feet and side of his seraphic servant. The extreme pain which Maria Rosa suffered from this divine operation, made her swoon and fall on the floor of her room as if dead. On the following morning, being unable to move, she sent to her spiritual director, who examined her hands and feet, and found them transpierced from side to side and bleeding profusely. The heroic sufferer told him that the wound in her side caused her intense pain, extending to her shoulder. This generous victim of charity and patience, could truly say with St. Paul: *"I bear the marks of the Lord Jesus in my body."* (Galat. 6:17)

Beside these five visible and permanent wounds, people could see blood flowing from the interior angle of her eyes, but more abundantly from the right side. This was a consequence and effect of the Crown of Thorns, which Maria Rosa continually suffered internally, and the punctures of which were often visible on her head and brow. She explained this mysterious phenomenon to her director, by stating that the blood flowing from her eyes, was caused by a long thorn which seemed to her to pierce through her whole head its points penetrating to the eye. She added that this long thorn was pressed into her head, when forced to lean against the wood of the cross invisibly placed by our Lord upon her shoulders, by which she was almost crushed down to the earth with an immense weight. After enduring for some days this terrible martyrdom, with heroic courage and fortitude, our Lord enriched the soul of his noble servant, with the abundance of his heavenly gifts and graces. These in return inflamed her heart with an insatiable thirst for more sufferings.

To this end, this truly admirable heroine made use of numerous instruments of penance, which have been preserved at Oria as precious relics, the mere sight and even mention of which, cause a pious horror. She often scourged her innocent body to blood with a dicipline made of strong wire, the numerous thongs at the extremity of which were armed with sharp steel points that cut and tore her flesh. A tin cross nearly a foot long, with arms in proportion, is also shown, the whole length and breadth of which is armed with small tacks about half an inch long. Maria Rosa, as a lover of the cross and victim of charity, when still very young, so closely tied upon her chest this terrible instrument of penance, that it sunk in her flesh, and became in the course of years incarnated with it. She bravely wore it almost all the time of her life. More frightful even were five large needles, a foot long, with which she occasionally transfixed her body through from side to side. All these terrible instruments of penance are religiously preserved in the Monastery of the Franciscan Fathers in the city of Oria.

This admirable servant of God had a profound veneration for, and sincere devotion to the seraphic Mother of Carmel, St. Teresa, whose virtues she earnestly strove to imitate. The saint in return obtained for her many favors from God. On the 15th of October, Feast of St. Teresa, 1824, Maria Rosa was ravished in a deep ecstasy. A seraph appeared to her, holding a burning dart of divine love, with which he pierced her heart. This divine operation was renewed every year on the same day, during the last twenty-three years of her life.

On the 10th of September, 1848, being the Sunday within the Octave of the Nativity, and the feast of the Holy Name of Mary, our holy heroine felt, in fact knew by special revelation that her mortal course was drawing to an end. All her life had been a fervent and faithful preparation for death. She received with extraordinary devotion and joy, all the sacraments and spiritual helps, that our holy Mother the Church lavishes upon her dying children. Maria Rosa, having been during her whole life, upon the cross, she wished in imitation of her crucified spouse, to die a victim of obedience. She had previously agreed with her confessor that, in her last agony, she was to give him a sign to obtain his command, in virtue of holy obedience for her soul, to depart from this earth and proceed immediately to the eternal embrace of Jesus, her heavenly Spouse. He promised to do so on condition that, if admitted without delay to the beatific vision, she would, if permitted by God, cause the bells of the Monastery Church to ring miraculously a joyful chime. The long wished-for moment arrived. The dying servant of God raised her last supplicating look to her confessor praying at her side. He immediately imparted to her his last blessing, and gave to her the desired command of holy obedience. Maria Rosa about noon September 10th, 1848, with an angelic smile upon her virginal lips, calmly closed the eyes of her body to the earth, to open those of her innocent and pure soul in the light of the beatific vision of God in heaven. A most joyful chime was heard over all the city of Francavilla from all the bells of the city churches. At her death Maria Rosa Adriani was 72 years, 7 months, and 20 days old.

This brief but edifying sketch has been written by the spiritual director of this holy servant of God, who assisted at her death, and who is actually engaged in writing more fully her life. The following is his declaration.

Declaration
Oria, Apirl 17th, 1872.

I declare that the Church has not yet given any decision on the subject of the deceased. God will in due time make her worth known by means of stupendous prodigies. I do hereby protest that all I have said about Maria Rosa Adriani has no other authority than that of a purely human historical record, and completely submit it to the decrees of Pope UrbanVII and of all the other Supreme Pontiffs.
Father Master Francis Della Pace,
Minor Conventual Director
(See *Les Stigmatisées*, Louise Lateau, 1. Vol. Appendice)

46. *Venerable Anna Maria Taigi*
Though we are not aware that this venerable servant of God suffered in a visible manner the impression of the Crown of Thorns, yet we believe that she deserves to be enumerated in this catalogue. Our object is to promote devotion to the Crown of Thorns of Our dear Savior. Now, as we have mentioned before, this holy woman had continually for forty-seven years this holy crown before her eyes. We humbly believe that, one at least of the objects of this wonderful manifestation was to promote a special devotion towards the crown of our Lord. The vision of the mysterious sun, fit emblem of the Eternal Sun of justice, who assumed human flesh, and came upon earth to enlighten those who sit in darkness, deserves some notice in this place. As we said above, Anna Maria was favored by God during forty-

seven years with a clear and uninterrupted view of a most brilliant sun. *Around it shot forth rays from the center and a very closely set crown of thorns intertwined, encircling the superior disk of the sun, stood upon the points of the upper rays. Two of the thorns, lengthened on either side beyond the others, descended below the disk where, crossing one another, they formed with their points a figure like a cross.* This we deem sufficient for this place. We may observe that this description admirably tallies with what we have just read about the long thorns in the head of Maria Rosa Adriani. A few details about Anna Maria Taigi will be agreeable.

She was born May 29th, 1769, at Sienna, in Tuscany. At six years of age she with her parents went to reside in Rome. In due time she was married to Dominico Taigi, or rather Taegi, a virtuous young man, but of uncouth and abrupt manners, which contributed much to her sanctification. She was the mother of seven children. Some died very young. The rest she brought up with the greatest care and diligence in the practice of their religious duties. One of her daughters is still living. Anna Maria was a perfect model of a pious Christian wife and mother. She was never idle, yet always praying. She led a life of continual self-denial, mortification and penance, yet she never neglected any domestic duty. She was full of active charity for the poor and indigent; and inflamed with an ardent zeal for the conversion of sinners, and salvation of souls. For the suffering souls in purgatory, she had the most lively compassion; and her devotion to the passion of our Lord, and the dolors of his most holy Mother, was boundless.

Through the supernatural light of his mysterious sun, this wonderful servant of God was enabled to see everything past, present and future. Nothing was hidden from her knowledge, which had relation to the Church, or the Pope. She knew in an instant, by a simple glance at the sun, the secret designs of governments, all the plots of secret societies, the intentions of individuals, their state of conscience, the doom of souls after their death. She possessed in a very eminent degree the spirit of prophecy, and foretold many important events to take place to the end of time, which, according to her knowledge, is fast approaching. Through her spiritual director she often warned the Pope and his ministers of the dangerous machinations of earthly princes, secret societies, treacherous officials, and malevolent individuals of any kind. She prayed and practiced severe penance for the conversion of the enemies of the Church, of sinners and of infidels, and succeeded in converting many. The conversion to Catholicity of the Emperor of Russia, Alexander I, his death on the 1st December, 1825, and the salvation of his soul, were revealed to her on the same day; and she announced these events to the Russian ambassador in Rome at that time. Anna Maria Taigi died in Rome in great odor of sanctity, June 9th, 1837. The process of her beatification is progressing rapidly. She has been declared venerable by Pope Pins IX. (See her very interesting life by Edward H. Thompson, published London, 1873)

47. Sister Bertine Bouguillon

Bertine was born at St. Omer, France, 1800. When very young she became a religious in St. Louis' Hospital in her native city. At 22 years of age Sister Bertine was stigmatized in her hands, feet and side, and received the Crown of Thorns. These suffering and miraculous representations were manifested every Friday, and on the principal feasts during the year so long as she lived.

By order of the Bishop of Arras, Mgr. De la Tour d'Auvergne, theologians and medical men were commissioned to examine into the extraordinary phenomena manifested in the person of Sister Bertine, and after a most searching and minute inquiry they came to the unanimous conclusion that they had a supernatural origin; in short, that they were from God. The Bishop confirmed their decision by an official and definite sentence. Sister Bertine died January 25th, 1850. (Voix Prophetiques by L'Abbé Curicque. 1. Vol. Paris, 1872.)

48. Maria Domenica Lazzari

This suffering child of the cross, was born March 16th 1815, at Capriani, Italian Tyrol. Maria Domenica was stigmatized in her hands, feet and side, January 1st, 1834, and three weeks later she received the impression of the Crown of Thorns. Every Friday, until the year 1847, this victim of the passion suffered intensely; all her wounds and the Crown of Thorns bleeding profusely. She died on Easter Sunday, 1848. See Les Stigmatizisées du Tyrol, by Leon Bori, Paris 1840. Also, Louise Lateau. The Ecstatic of Bois du Haine, Belgium, by Shepard, London, 1872.

49. Crescenzia Nierklutsch

Crescenzia was born June 15th, 1816, at Cana, a Tyrolese village. She lived for some time at Tschermes, and more lately at Méran, where she received the stigmata of the five wounds, and the impression of the Crown of Thorns. In the year 1844 she was living in Méran, and is supposed

238

to be still alive at the present time. Rev. Antonio Riccardi mentions her in his book with the other two Tyrolese stigmatized. Domenica Lazzari, and Maria de Moerl, the famous ecstatic. See likewise, the bleeding wounds of Christ reproduced on the persons of three Christian virgins actually living in Tyrol, by Veyland, Metz. 1844.

50. *Dorothea Visser.*

Dorothea was born at Gendringen, Holland, in the year 1820. When she was a very young child, a little boy miraculously appeared to her, informing the pious girl that some extraordinary things should happen to her. About the 23rd year of her life, Dorothea received the impression of the Crown of Thorns, and soon after she was stigmatized in her hands, feet and side, but in a new and singular manner. The five wounds of her stigmata were cruciform. The medical doctor Te Welscher published in 1844, at Borken a work about this servant of God with the title: *"The Stigmatized of Gendrigen."* Mr. Riko of Haye, who communicated this information to Dr. A. Imbert Gourbeyere, thinks that Dorothea Visser is still living in Holland.

CHAPTER X

THE MIRACULOUS IMAGE OF OUR INFANT SAVIOR AT BARI, KINGDOM OF NAPLES, ITALY

"May the glory of Christ, who is the image of God shine unto all men." (2 Cor. 4:4)

This nineteenth century, being destined by God to form an epoch in the Catholic Church, is pre-eminently the age of prodigies. In the foregoing pages we have already noticed many of them and more will be found in what follows. Were we not circumscribed within the hallowed circle of the Crown of Thorns, we could fill an entire volume with prodigious events of different kinds, that have illustrated the Christian chronicles of the present century. The learned, judicious and devout author of the Voix Prophetiques (Prophetical Voices) Rev. I. M Curicque, in two large volumes of above 1,500 pages 12mo. has collected, especially in the first volume, a great number of them, which we trust will soon appear in an English dress. For our present object, in connection with the Crown of Thorns, we compile the following facts from the 1st volume, chapter V.

1. Many weak Christians are not only surprised, but also somewhat scandalized, in beholding the present degraded condition of Italy, from a civil and religious point of view. Might seems to have prevailed against right. Cunning, duplicity, and hypocrisy persecute and oppress truth, candor, and honesty. Impiety, vice, corruption and sacrilege boldly stalk in the usurped states of the Church, domineer in the capital of the Christian world, and like the monstrous beast prefigured in the thirteenth chapter of the Apocalypse, partaking of the nature of the leopard, of the bear, lion and dragon, blaspheming against Jesus Christ, and holding his Vicar a prisoner in the Vatican. But to the eyes of enlightened faith these are some of the scandals that the impiety and malice of wicked men have rendered inevitable

in these evil days. Woe, however, to them by whom such scandals come. Christian faith should enable us to see and to feel that the revolution, or, apostasy as it is better termed in the Apocalypse is dominant all over the face of the earth. Hence, why should we be surprised, and much less, why should anyone be scandalized in seeing it rear its impious and defiant head in Italy, the only country that after receiving the light and life of Faith from the apostles of our Lord, all the might of Pagan persecution, heretical perfidy and human impiety, could never succeed in extinguishing it from the mind and heart of that Catholic people? If old paganism warred against Palestine, the land of promise, and the chosen country for God's true worshippers; what wonder is it that revived paganism, in these latter days, aims its most deadly blows against Italy, the Palestine of Christianity, and especially against Papal Rome, the center and fountain-head of Catholicity, the divinely chosen seat of the infallible head of Christ's Holy Church? The Papacy is the only irremoveable rock and insurmountable barrier, that checks the ever surging billows of Satan's fury and of human impiety. Rendered proud and bold, by their success in almost every part of the world, these emissaries of Satan are becoming mad at the resistance offered to their impious designs and desperate efforts, by the venerable octogenerian sitting calmly and hopefully in St. Peter's chair in the Vatican, who by his powerful words and inspired messages of wisdom and warning, makes the revolution tremble, like Attila in its apparently victorious career against the seat of his universal government. The Pope fully and firmly relies upon the infallible promise of Him whom he represents upon earth. For he said: *"Thou art Peter, and upon this rock I will build my Church, and the gates of hell shall not prevail against it."* (Mt. 16:18) Let us be calm and hopeful, in fervent prayer, and we shall soon see the present Crown of Thorns transformed into a brilliant crown of universal glory and triumph for the whole Catholic Church. We have a guarantee for our hope, in the manifold, frequent and extraordinary prodigies, manifested in different parts of the world, but especially in Christian France and Papal Italy.

The general ignorance of the Italian language, and the comparatively few Americans who travel in Italy, and who feel any interest in visiting the more secluded portions of that classical land, the affected ignorance and studied silence of the secular and Protestant press in relation to Catholic events, and last, but not least, the habitual caution, and almost extreme reserve of Italian writers, in giving publicity to the prodigies so frequently

241

occurring in that country of faith, deprive the Christian reader of many most interesting and edifying facts, and cause some weak-minded Catholics to suppose that God has almost forsaken that privileged people. We are desirous of supplying this omission, as far as circumstances will permit, and correcting, if possible, the mistake. Let us then proceed to examine another extraordinary event connected with a chain of prodigies intertwined with the mystic Crown of Thorns.

From time immemorial, but more especially since the twelfth century, stimulated by the devotion and zeal of the seraphic Patriarch, St. Francis of Assisi, and by his fervent religious of both sexes, veneration for our Infant Savior has ever been a peculiar feature in the devotions of Italian Catholics. It is now nearly a century since a most beautiful figure of the Divine Infant, made of the purest virgin wax, has been religiously preserved in some pious families in the archi-episcopal city of Bari as an object of domestic devotion. It is intended to represent our Infant Savior in the cradle. About twenty years ago, this beautiful figure fell by inheritance into the Providential possession of two very pious middle-aged sisters, surnamed *Parlavecchia*. They are now far advanced in years, the elder being nearly seventy years old, the other only a few years less. The Christian name of this latter is *Maria Gaetana*. During many years, both have been most exemplary members of the Third Order of St. Francis, which is very numerous in Italy, and especially in the kingdom of Naples. These pious maidens lead a secluded life at home. They have been remarkable for their strict exactness in the observance of their simple and holy rule of life, and are justly regarded as models of general edification in their native city, on account of their exemplary conduct, their fervor, persevering prudent zeal and active charity. They are respected by all as faithful living copies of the two privileged sisters, Mary and Martha, mentioned in the Gospel. The elder sister represents the activity of Martha, whilst the younger, *Maria Gaetana*, has chosen with Mary the better part, of sweet contemplation. Being satisfied with the bare necessaries of life, they live upon a small income derived from a moderate house rent. They scarcely ever consent to receive any visitor, except a saintly and venerable old priest, a near relative, the Rev. Laurence Lapedota, and some other ecclesiastic and devout lay person, when no other conversation is permitted, except upon pious and edifying subjects. In short, their conversation, as St. Paul says, is in heaven. This will be better understood when we state that *Maria Gaetana* is so favored by our Lord as to have been for many years impressed with the miraculous stigmata of the five wounds, in her hands, feet and side. These facts are well known in the city of Bari.

The devotion of these saintly sisters towards our Infant Savior is universally admired. By ecclesiastical authority, they have been allowed to transform a large room in the upper story of their house, contiguous to their humble cell, into a chapel, with a beautiful altar, on which the cherished object of their devotion is preserved. In fervent acts of devotion, prayer and meditation they spend some hours of the day, and many more during the night, imploring the mercy of God, for the conversion of sinners, the perseverance of the just, and for the speedy triumph of our holy religion. Pious Catholics have free access to this domestic chapel for motives of devotion. But they find it very difficult to enter into conversation with the two sisters, or to be admitted into their private rooms. God has rewarded their faith and devotion with a number of extraordinary prodigies, through the sacred image of their cherished *Santo Bambino*. These may be classified in the following five categories:

1. Since the 19th day of March, feast of St. Joseph, 1866, being Monday in Passion Week, and a short time after the exile of the learned Archbishop of Bari, Monsignor Pedicini, by the so-called Italian, but in reality Freemason and anti-Christian Government, the sacred wax image of our Infant Savior, reclining in a beautiful cradle, was observed to exude a miraculous sweat in such abundance that being carefully collected in clean linen cloths and pressed into a vessel, several small glass bottles have been filled with it, and are religiously preserved. This prodigious sweat has been the means of many other miracles, one of which is its frequent multiplication.

2. The sacred figure oftentimes *sweats blood*. This miraculous blood— fresh, lively and rosy—exudes in such abundance, sometimes from one side, then from another, varying with the different feasts in the year, that being carefully collected in clean linen placed under and over the sacred image, several vials have been filled with it, and are devoutly treasured up as precious relics, by means of which numerous prodigies have been and are wrought at the present time.

3. A sweet and most agreeable odor exhales from the little cradle wherein the sacred image is kept, that can be perceived at some considerable distance from it, and is observed, not only through the sense of smell, but it wonderfully affects the souls of the faithful, inspiring heavenly sentiments

of piety and devotion in all those who visit this privileged chapel with true Christian dispositions of mind and heart.

4. Though the sacred wax figure is, by order of ecclesiastical authority, kept under a glass shade, fixed with seals, so that it cannot be reached by human hands, or by any other instrumentality, yet it has been occasionally observed moving from one position to another, from right to left, from left to right, sitting up or standing upon its feet, exactly like a living child, two or three years old.

5. Lastly, what is still more wonderful, and more deserving our consideration, are the bloody impressions produced over or communicated in an instant, to the linen, to engravings, or pictures and other objects placed, with due permission, over or in contact with the sacred image of the Divine Infant, *il Santo Bambino*, of Bari. As a general rule, these miraculous impressions exhibit symbols expressive of mysterious and prophetic signification, as we shall have soon to remark. We proceed now to explain more fully, and in greater detail, these five prodigious events. The following facts are faithfully translated from the official account given of these prodigies by the very Rev. Father Bruni, a member of the congregation of the mission of St. Vincent de Paul, more generally known as the Lazzarist Fathers, from the original title of their mother house in Paris where their general superior resides. Very Rev. Father Bruni, when commissioned by the Archbishop of Bari, Mgr. Pedicini, to investigate and report these facts, was superior or president of the ecclesiastical seminary in that city. But since, like other religious in Italy, he has been banished from the seminary and from his religious establishment by the impious and persecuting government of Victor Emmanuel.

These facts were first published in France in *Le Rosier de Marie*, "the Rosary of Mary," an excellent weekly periodical, very ably edited by the French Dominican Fathers. The account may be read in the number of Saturday, 19th of August, 1871, page 647.

FIRST SECTION

BLOODY SWEAT OF THE SACRED IMAGE

According to the statement of Very Rev. Father Bruni, this prodigious sweat of blood began about two o'clock in the afternoon of the 19th of March, 1866, Monday in Passion Week, and continued without interruption in the daytime, until Palm Sunday, ceasing, however, in the night. Since that time, this miracle has been repeated thousands of times, lasting more or less, several hours, according to the circumstance of the feasts which were being celebrated in the Catholic Church. During the principal feasts of our Divine Lord, and of his most holy Mother, this miraculous bloody sweat was more abundant and remarkable. It lasted several hours, and was observed flowing in the day, and also in the night-time.

After having been observed and carefully examined, on their first appearance, by the Rev. Laurence Lapedota, a venerable priest with an exquisite delicacy of concience, he considered himself conscientiously bound to make these prodigious events known to the Very Rev. Archdeacon Petruzzelli, administrator of the archdiocese of Bari, during the exile of his Grace, Mgr. Pedicini. The Archdeacon, prudently wishing to verify the reality of these reports, visited the miraculous image, in company with the learned capitular theologian, Canon d'Aloja, Canon Maggi, of the Metropolitan Church, Rev. Joseph Gatta, Rev. Peter Cassano, and several other respectable and intelligent gentlemen of the city. Very Rev. Father Bruni was also present, and, as an eye-witness, affirms that all saw the prodigious sweat of blood exuding from the sacred waxen image of our Infant Savior, and testifies that the same prodigy has since the 19th of March, 1866, been observed by large numbers of persons of every class and condition. He justly remarks that this is an event of public notoriety, and can be witnessed by every person desirous of verifying the reality of this prodigy.

In the year 1867, during Holy Week, "I and many other persons," says Father Bruni, "observed a large drop of white sweat on the body of the sacred image, and a similar one on the head; whilst at the same time drops of blood of a heavy color flowed from the forehead, *indicating the punctures of the Crown of Thorns,* and also from the right hand, manifesting the wound of the crucifixion. These drops of blood flowing from those two parts of the sacred figure were gradually increasing. These two extraordinary prodigies were taking place, from the same waxen figure, precisely at the

245

same moment. This circumstance should not be overlooked. On the 13th of April of the same year, a person of high dignity (Mgr. Pedicini), having consented to visit the miraculous image, observed a drop of fresh red blood exuding from it. He ordered the glass shade to be removed, took the image of the *Bambino* (Infant Savior) in his left hand, and with the index of his right hand he carefully wiped off this bloody sweat. But another drop immediately appeared, which, having been similarly removed, the second, third and fourth time, the same prodigy was instantly renewed. Having diligently examined the wax figure in every direction, and, being fully satisfied that no foul means or deceitful contrivance could naturally have been used by any human ingenuity, firmly convinced of the reality of the miracle, and deeply impressed by the supernatural phenomenon, in a calm, dignified and reverential manner, he replaced the sacred image in the venerated cradle.

SECOND SECTION

ORDINARY SWEAT OF THE MIRACULOUS IMAGE

As soon as this prodigious sweat became frequent, and copious in quantity, pieces of clean linen were carefully placed over the sacred image of our Lord, and with the necessary permission of ecclesiastical authority were removed when observed to have become saturated with this prodigious liquor. This having been wrung into a small vessel, it was put aside into a closet, and almost forgotten. But after some time the Rev. Laurence Lapedota, having had occasion to look for it, remarked that it had somewhat increased in quantity. This prodigious multiplication becoming daily more evident, the pious priest, through his private devotion, poured out a portion of this liquor into another vial; it continued, however, to increase. On several occasions the first vessel was entirely emptied, but in a short time was found replenished to the brim, occasionally overflowing into a saucer or salver, placed under it for this purpose. Still more surprising is the fact that some empty vials, having been left for future use near this vessel, were found filled with the same miraculous liquor. This experiment was purposely repeated several times, and always with the same result.

The ordinary color of this prodigious liquor is similar to that of dry straw, but occasionally it becomes light and clear, and at other times more heavy and sub-obscure. Ordinarily, in tasting it, the liquor has no particular savor, but sometimes it tastes like cinnamon. At the bottom of this glass bottle a sediment can be perceived, exhibiting the appearance of bloody traces deeply marked.

The following remarkable circumstances are connected with this miraculous sweat.

1. It is incorruptible. Vials full or partially filled with this sweat, since the year 1866 have been preserved, but not the least deterioration can be detected.

2. This prodigious liquor changes color when given to different persons. With some it is limpid and clear, like crystal; with others it becomes turbid, and even blackish. This last gloomy color generally forebodes imminent misfortunes and serious evils.

3. A peculiar odor usually remains in the vial or vessel wherein this miraculous liquor is collected. With some persons, however, the fragrance is more persistent, whilst with others it is more intermittent. Sometimes this odor becomes disagreeable to some persons, and at the same time it is very pleasant to others. Without pretending to penetrate the hidden secrets of the human health, we may suppose that the state of conscience of individuals contributes much to these different sensations.

4. The miraculous liquor having been given in small doses to drink to sick persons, has often produced more or less instantaneous cures, or it has certainly been the beginning of physical amelioration. There is no doubt that all those persons who have used this liquor with sentiments of a lively faith, and in good moral dispositions, have always been benefited thereby in body and soul.

5. This miraculous perfume, the nature of which cannot be described by human experience, not only exudes from the sacred waxen image of our Infant Savior, but also, from its little cradle, from the linen, and other objects placed in contact with it. On the following occasion this heavenly perfume was particularly remarkable:

6. In the month of November, 1866, Father Bruni, in company with several other persons, having had occasion to remove the glass shade covering the sacred image, all were suddenly refreshed with a most agreeable perfume of roses, as if they had been in a flower garden, surrounded with roseplants in full bloom.

7 In April, 1867, one of the Sisters of Charity at Bari, having by permission placed an artificial lily on the sacred image for a short time,

in taking it back she perceived that it had received miraculous impressions, and exhaled an extraordinary fragrance. Without mentioning these facts, the good sister forwarded this lily, enclosed in a letter, to a pious friend in France, who, in acknowledging its safe receipt, expressed great admiration at its indescribable perfume.

THIRD SECTION

MIRACULOUS MOVEMENTS OF THE HOLY IMAGE

The image of our Infant Savior at Bari has evidently been chosen by God as an instrument of the most wonderful prodigies on record. It may be considered a concentration of supernatural phenomena intended by Divine Providence to confound the impiety of the wicked men, and to enlighten the faith and strengthen the hope of the faithful. Let us, for our edification, consider its prodigious movements.

The Rev. Father Bruni, in his official report to the Archbishop, Mgr. Pedicini, mentions the following miraculous motions:

1. The eyes of the waxen image have often been observed by many persons to move in different directions, and with various expressions in the looks, quite in the same way as if it were a living and·intelligent child.

2. The face of the figure, artistically fine, often assumes various physiognomic expressions. Sometimes it appears full of life, and beaming with an heavenly smile; at other times it becomes painfully sad and suffused with a deadly pallor. These miraculous physiognomic motions have been very frequent.

3. In the year 1866, July 25th, towards evening, this wonder-working figure was by several devout persons found holding in its right hand a mysterious oriflamme, or small golden flag, and a cross in its left hand. Neither of them had or could have been placcd there, as they were found in the waxen hand of the little image. To effect this, it would have been necessary to open the small wax fingers to receive, then to close them again in such way as to make them grasp and hold in a natural manner, both the small golden flag and the cross. But this could not have been done without breaking both hands. Moreover, all persons allowed to have access to the sacred figure were by their known characters above the shadow of suspicion, and nobody could have attributed to them the horrible crime of such deceitful and sacrilegious profanation. The reality of this prodigy has never been

doubted by well-informed persons in the metropolitan city of Bari.

4. On the 20th day of March, 1866, the Rev. Canon Maggi and the Very Rev. F. Bruni, and several other trusty persons, had left the holy waxen figure in its usual position in the cradle, under its ordinary glass shade. Two days after, it was found in a transversed position, which could only have been effected through a miracle, because the glass shade, by order of ecclesiastical authority, had been sealed or otherwise closed in such a way that no person could touch or move the prodigious image. Rev. Michael Farchi was the first in remarking this new prodigy, which he pointed out to other persons present. Upon the same occasion a profuse sweat was seen flowing from the same miraculous image.

5. On the 25th of July, of the same year, the Holy Infant was found standing at the end of the cradle, and was seen by many devout visitors often changing its position. It was upon this remarkable occasion that the oriflamme and cross were found in its hands. This wonderful prodigy continued, from the 25th of July to the 6th day of December, 1866, nearly four months and a half, during which time it was witnessed by a multitude of persons of every class and condition.

In order to certify the reality of the prodigy, the wax figure of the Holy Infant, then reclining in the cradle, was carefully examined by a committee of competent ecclesiastic and other proper persons, designated by the learned and pious Archbishop, Mgr. Pedicini. This examination was made on the 12th day of April, 1867. It was then observed that the wax figure of our Infant Savior, at its original moulding or formation by the artist, had its left foot more drawn up than the right one, and the artistic position of this latter was such that when the commissioners attempted to place the wax figure in an upright and standing position it was observed that the forepart only of the right foot could touch the table or the bottom of the cradle, whilst the left foot could not reach it at all. It was therefore demonstrated and concluded that, according to the natural laws of gravitation, it was physically impossible for the waxen image to remain standing without any support whatever, as it had done during the long space of four months and twelve days, in the latter part of the previous year. The reality of the miracle was unanimously admitted. If modern skeptics refuse to believe, and censure our Christian credulity, we say to them, with St. Paul, *"Carnal man cannot understand spiritual things,"* and, much less, the nature of supernatural events.

FOURTH SECTION

PIOUS IMPRESSIONS AND SYMBOLIC FIGURES FROM THE MIRACULOUS IMAGE

These extraordinary impressions and mysterious figures bear upon them the seal of a supernatural power, whether we consider the manner in which this was done, or the symbols which they express.

As soon as the Rev. Laurence Lapedota perceived the prodigious sweat exuding in considerable quantity from the sacred image, he had the pious thought, or the inspiration, of covering it with clean linen, which would naturally absorb it, and thus preserve, this heavenly liquor. It will be remembered that the miraculous sweat occurred first on Monday in Passion Week, 1866, 19th of March, feast of St. Joseph, the adopted father of the Incarnate Word. On the following Good Friday, the same pious priest observed that the linen was marked with stains of blood, which was flowing from the sacred figure of the *Bambino*, and a cross had been formed in the center of the cloth as if it were erected on a little mound.

About the end of August of the same year, in changing the pieces of linen saturated with the prodigious sweat, the same reverend gentleman felt a strong desire to see impressed on the new, fresh linen the likeness of our Infant Savior. On the first of the following month of September, 1866, in removing the cloth from the sacred figure, the truly pious priest found, to his great delight, that his devout wishes had been fully gratified. From that memorable day to the present time literally innumerable have been the miraculous impressions made upon a variety of things of a pious nature, placed in the venerated cradle of the sacred image. All the emblems of our Lord's Passion have been produced many a time in various ways. The monogram of the sacred name of Jesus, the figure of his most holy heart, the monogram of Mary, the figure of her immaculate heart, the figure of the dove, emblematic of the Holy Ghost, the image of St. Joseph, and of other holy objects, have since that day been miraculously produced in such abundance, says Very Rev. Father Bruni, that it would fill a large volume, were any attempt to be made to describe them. These miraculous impressions have frequently been found conformable to the secret desires of devout visitors.

The Archdeacon Petruzzi has, however, been even more favored by the *Santo Bambino* (Holy Babe). This eminent ecclesiastic sent a small figure of the Divine Infant, reclining in a small cradle, adorned with artificial flowers, and covered with a glass shade, to protect it from dust. In conformity with his request, it was placed within the larger cradle of the miraculous image, covered likewise with a proportionate shade glass. Now, it is an undeniable fact, known to the whole metropolitan city of Bari, that this smaller image of our Infant Savior did receive on that occasion the impressions of the five wounds in the hands, feet and side. Moreover, it has, like the larger and more famous image, been occasionally seen to exude a miraculous sweat. These facts are taken from the report of the ecclesiastical commission presided over by Very Rev. Father Bruni. His Grace Mgr. Pedicini, Archbishop of Bari, naturally very cautious and prudent in everything, but more especially in these extraordinary events, being determined to ascertain in person the truth of these prodigious reports, on the 23d of March, 1867, hence more than one year after they began, sent a piece of linen, enclosed in a double envelope, and secured with several wax seals, bearing the Archiepiscopal arms. In obedience to Mgr. Pedicini's orders, this double envelope was placed in the cradle close to the miraculous image of our Infant Savior. It was soon after observed that this wax figure had miraculously moved over, and reclined upon the Archbishop's envelope. On the following day, a priest, charged with this duty, took the double envelope from the cradle, and found it moistened outside with a bloody sweat. In presenting it to the Archbishop, this illustrious prelate perceived immediately a very agreeable perfume exuding from it. Having carefully examined the seals on the outward envelope, and having found them intact, he opened it. He did the same with the smaller inward envelope. This also being carefully opened, an incomprehensible phenomenon presented itself to the Archbishop and to other ecclesiastics present. His Grace observed that this envelope, being moistened in some parts, was perfectly dry in others. Moreover, where the envelope was wet outside, it was dry in the corresponding portion inside; and where outside it was perfectly dry, it was moistened inside.

In extracting the small piece of linen from the interior envelope, Mgr. Pedicini found it soaked with a miraculous sweat; and, although this wet cloth touched inside the whole paper envelope, yet this, as we have already said, was moistened only in some parts, and perfectly dry in others. Behold, here, already a chain of prodigies! ...

Miraculously impressed on this white linen was found a mysterious pine-tree, round which were entwined two ugly serpents, irritated against each other, one of which had the head of a horrid dragon. Both were transpierced with a sword. We will now give the very plausible and probable explanation of these symbols:

1. This mysterious pine-tree is evidently the figure of ecclesiastical authority. The essential authority, established, protected and defended by the power and wisdom of God, and perpetually guaranteed to His Church by the infallible promises of Jesus Christ, her founder and Divine Head, cannot be upset, and much less destroyed by the power of darkness, *for the gates of hell shall never prevail against it.* This magnificent tree, deeply rooted in the mind and heart of the most enlightened and most noble portion of mankind, strong in divine power, erect in justice, elevated in truth, and ever green with unflagging vigor of life, is the Church of Jesus Christ. Even in her greatest and most severe trials, this glorious Church is always as strong, firm, sound, green and full of energy, as the stoutest pine or cedar on Mount Lebanon during the fiercest storm. Nay, more, the Church is purified and strengthened by the persecutions of her enemies.

2. The serpents graphically represent the pride and hatred of Lucifer, and spirit of impiety and insubordination of the modern, anti-Christian revolution, coiled round the tree of the Church, eager to pull her down to the ground, or to squeeze out her very life. But, finding their united Satanic efforts and impious stratagems absolutely impotent and vain, in their bitter disappointment, they turn their maddening rage and fury against each other.

We should, moreover, reflect that modern revolution or apostasy, like all other rebellions, being the offspring of proud minds and of corrupted hearts, bears necessarily within its bosom the germs of discord and dis-solution. This fact is daily becoming more and more apparent in the divisions and subdivisions of political parties, and still more so in the endless splits of heretical and Masonic sects, which, like envenomed broods of scorpions, tear each other to pieces, and must consequently soon disappear from the face of the earth. The sooner they return to the pit whence they issued forth, the better for the general happiness of mankind ...

So far, however, we are obliged to acknowledge the existence in Europe of two leading parties, namely, Moderates and the Radicals, the Monarchists and the Republicans; in short, the Girondists and Jacobins of the French bloody revolution and impious apostasy of 1790. This is more particularly the fact in the present civil condition of unhappy Italy. The Ministerial and the Opposition parties in the Italian Parliament are in reality nothing else but the slow resuscitation of the defunct Girondist and Jacobin

252

parties of horrible memory ... Now, how could this wretched state of society have been more graphically and more prophetically expressed than by the terrible figures of the two horrid serpents entwined around the large, strong, and ever green tree of the Catholic Church? ...

A mysterious sword transfixes both serpents, and holds them together in writhing pain of agonizing fury. This deadly weapon represents the ever-effective and victorious two-edged sword of St. Peter. In this striking emblem we behold the marvelous effect of the definition of the dogma of the Papal Infallibility by the Ecumenical Council of the Vatican. The masterly blow has been well directed; it has been truly unerring in its aim, and shall prove decisively crushing in its inevitable consequences against the proud head of the infernal dragon, and against the impious spirit of modern revolution. The two wounded serpents, unable to injure the huge, sound tree of the Church, shall, in their rage of despair, bite and tear each other to pieces. During their fierce and bloody combat, and their violent contortions, they will cause sad havoc among the nations of the earth. But enough of this; we will return to our main subject of the miraculous and symbolic impressions.

The Reverend President of the seminary, Father Bruni, relates that on a certain occasion a pious ecclesiastic was allowed to place near the miraculous image a corporal, which is a square piece of white linen, used by Catholic priests at the altar. Upon this cloth a cross was found engraven with blood, and over this cross was a *crown of bloody thorns*. At the foot of the cross, our Lady of Dolors is represented standing in an attitude of profound sorrow. At each side of the cross there are two hearts, one of which is surmounted by a small cross, the other is pierced with a sword. Above these appear the sun and moon. In different directions stains of fresh and vermilion blood can be seen. All this is very wonderful and significant. We should not forget to remark that the mystic Crown of Thorns is ever united to the cross of our redemption and salvation. Blessed Crown of Thorns, through which we obtain the diadem of eternal glory! ...Our hope of salvation is strengthened when we behold at the foot of our Savior's cross his most holy Mother, shedding tears of love for him, and of maternal compassion for us; and with a heroic spirit of self-immolation offering to the Eternal Father her Divine Son's sufferings, and her agonizing sorrow, to obtain mercy and pardon for a sinful world ... The union, however, of the two most holy and most loving hearts that have ever animated, and warmed two human breasts is the surest and sweetest guarantee of our final victory. In this miraculous picture the adorable heart of Jesus and the immaculate heart of his Virgin Mother are united together in the same object of merciful charity. They are near the cross, and painted with miraculous blood. This blood seems clearly intended to announce the necessity of future victims of faith and love before the Church enjoys the full triumph of the Cross. The martyrdom of many of her children will be the *Red Sea* of her deliverance from her persecutors. These two hearts are the furnaces of Divine love, the source of merciful compassion for sinners, the centers of the sweetest and most exalted devotion. They are an expressive invitation to all the faithful to retire within them as the most secure and safest harbors during the fearful storm of the present anti-Christian revolution.

The sun and moon are miraculously painted in the picture in characters of blood. We could interpret this prodigy as a mystic realization of our Savior's prophecy, *that the sun will be changed into blood.* But we prefer to interpret the symbol as indicating that the Sun of Eternal Justice is there to warm the heart and illumine the mind of the faithful; and the moon, the mild figure of Mary, is there shining for the guide and help of poor sinners encompassed by the dismal darkness and gloom of error and vice. The mysterious and significant stains of fresh, living and vermilion blood, so miraculously sprinkled in different parts of that white linen cloth, seem to foretell and announce that the blood of many innocent victims will soon be required by Divine justice to atone for the crimes of mankind, and to adorn the white tunic for the glorious day of her universal triumph. Let us, then, in union with the august Virgin, Mother of our crucified Savior, at the foot of this cross, send forth our fervent supplications to the throne of grace and mercy in the firm hope that brighter days and more happy years will speedily shine over the face of the earth.

We close this long, but, we trust, interesting chapter with another remarkable prodigy, related by the Rev. J. M. Curicque, mentioned more than once in the foregoing pages. "An engraving," he says, "has been shown to us by a pious gentleman with whom we are well acquainted. It was sent to him from Bari by a Sister of Charity, after having been placed in contact with the miraculous image of our Infant Savior. This pretty large steel engraving represents our Lord upon the cross, with St. Mary Magdalene weeping, in a kneeling position at the foot of the cross. Through its contact with the miraculous waxen image of our Infant Savior the following prodigious effects were produced on the engraving:

First.	The head of our crucified Lord has been marked with traces of blood diverging into four rays.
Second.	Blood is likewise seen on the hands, feet and side of our Lord.
Third.	The cross from top to bottom is literally covered with blood.
Fourth.	But, what is more wonderful, is the fact that the prodigious blood stopped flowing immediately above the arm of the kneeling Magdalene, wherewith she embraces the cross, and over which her head sorrowfully reclines. Not a drop of blood is seen upon the loving penitent, but it appears again under her arm, running down to the ground, all the way over the cross.
Fifth.	The alabaster vessel engraved near the cross is entirely covered with this prodigious blood.
Sixth.	The side of our crucified Lord is deeply marked with a large bloody semicircle, one side of which branches out in three mysterious red points or rays.
Seventh.	The sun, the moon, and more than a hundred starry points round about the crucifixion are formed with this miraculous blood.
Eighth.	The inscription of the picture engraved at its bottom has the monogram of Jesus marked with blood.
Ninth.	And lastly, the central letter is surmounted by a cross of blood.

The pious writer concludes by saying: "We have been deeply struck and moved to contemplate this engraving, which receives from these miraculous bloody impressions a supernatural mark of originality. This prodigious event is evidently intended to recall to our ungrateful minds the sacred blood of our Divine Savior, who cries out to us from the cross: 'Ah! why do you abandon me, ye wretched sinners! Why will you remain obstinate in your determination of asking from impious and crafty impostors that water of life which can come to you only from me, your Lord and God, bleeding for your sake upon this cross.' *Be astonished, O ye heavens, at this: and ye gates thereof, be very desolate ....For my people have done two evils. For they have forsaken me, the fountain of living water, and have dug to themselves cisterns; broken cisterns, that can hold no water.* (Jerem 2:12) In your utter disappointment, learn, my people, a salutary lesson; and return at last to my open arms, and to my wounded and bleeding heart, *All ye that labor, and are heavy laden, and I will refresh you; and you under the shadow of my cross shall find rest to your souls."* (Mt. 11:29)

CHAPTER XI

THE THREE LIVING WONDERS OF EUROPE AND AMERICA

Palma Maria, Louise Lateau, Sister Esperance of Jeus

God, in His infinite wisdom and goodness, keeps bright beacons of brilliant sanctity in different parts of the earth for the edification of mankind. They are raised on the light-house of the Church to indicate the true harbor of safe refuge to minds in the darkness of error, agitated in the stormy sea of doubt. All these favorites of Heaven, all without a single exception, are sincere, devout, and eminently virtuous members of the Holy Roman Catholic Church. During the nineteen centuries of Christianity, Catholic history records by thousands, we might say by millions, eminent saints and servants of God who have been endowed with supernatural gifts, and with the power of working miracles; whilst not a single one can be satisfactorily indicated outside the pale of the Catholic Church. The fact is that Protestantism and infidelity, despairing of seeing a miracle which is not a direct condemnation of their apostasy and impiety, boldly deny the existence, and even the possibility of miraculous events. They charge Catholics as guilty of imposture or credulity, when they speak of existing miracles. For our justification we are satisfied to appeal to God and to facts.

The growing materialism, wickedness and impiety of the present century have an extreme need of bright examples of living virtue, to rebuke vice, to correct error, and practically to demonstrate the reality of Catholic dogmas and doctrines to a perverse and infidel generation. Our calumniators exert all their skill and strength, their lungs and pen, to represent our Church as corrupt and corrupting, and this divine Spouse of Christ, conscious of her truth and holiness, with calm dignity, practically confutes their malicious or insane charges by multiplying before the eyes of mankind living models

256

of Christian virtues and heroes of sanctity. The presence of such brilliant examples of holiness, illustrated by miracles, is a triumphant confutation and divine condemnation of schism, heresy, infidelity and vice. It is a solemn rebuke and warning to crowned tyrants and to earthly governments that harass and persecute the holy Spouse of Jesus Christ, the only mother of saints upon earth and in heaven. These living saints, with the eloquent voice of miracles, never cease exhorting sinners to speedy repentance, and animate and strengthen the attachment of true Catholics to their holy faith. So many eminent servants of God, decorated with the stigmata of the Passion, and crowned with the thorns of our Savior, distributed by him like heavenly sentinels at the most important points of his Church, are a sure presage of speedy victory and triumph for Catholicity, and a certain warning of inevitable and fast-approaching defeat to the enemies of our holy religion. In this firm hope and confident expectation, we proceed to give a brief notice, of the three living wonders announced at the head of this chapter. The first is Palma Maria Addolorata Matarrelli, of Oria, Kingdom of Naples. The second is Louise Lateau, of Bois-d'Haine, Belgium. The third is Sister Esperance of Jesus, of Ottawa, Canada. We begin with the first and most wonderful:

51. *Palma Maria, of Oria, Italy*

Palma Maria Addolorata Matarrelli was born on Thursday in Holy Week, March 31st, 1825, in the episcopal city of Oria, province of Lecce, Apulia, Kingdom of Naples. The name of Palma is rather singular among Catholics, who at baptism should receive the name of a saint recognized by the Church. Her second name, however, fully satisfies the requirements of religion. Moreover, the name of Palma, meaning *Palm*, was evidently given to this privileged child in a Providential manner; for it signifies victory and triumph after a fierce combat. It seems that God has chosen Palma Maria as an effective living instrument for obtaining great victories over Satan and his infernal legions in human shape, fighting against his holy Church. By her extraordinary mode of life, by her severe penances, continual prayers, by her heavenly lights, prophecies and miracles, this wonderful woman has already contributed much to the edification of the faithful, and will, we hope, accelerate the fast-approaching universal and lasting triumph of our most holy religion.

Palma Maria seems to possess the marks described by the Apostle for her grand mission. St. Paul says: *"See your vocation, brethren, that*

*not many are wise according to the flesh, not many mighty, not many noble.
But the foolish things of the world hath God chosen, that he might confound
the wise; and the weak things of the world hath God chosen, that He might
confound the strong; and the mean things of the world, and the things that
are contemptible, hath God chosen, and things that are not, that He might
destroy the things that are; that no flesh should glory in His sight."* (1 Cor.
1:26) This is a masterly portrait of our Palma. Daughter of a poor shepherd,
she was married to an humble shepherd. Totally illiterate, she knows not
how to write or read a single letter of the alphabet. This fact should not
be overlooked by those who attach more importance than necessary to the
material education of children, especially girls of the poorer class. Knowledge of our holy religion is by far more essential and useful. At twenty-
eight years of age Palma Maria was left an orphan and a widow. Her father
and husband died, and her three infant daughters were taken home by their
Heavenly Father. Extremely poor, weak and suffering, absolutely unable
to work, she, with her aged mother, entirely depends on the charity of a
Christian family. A pious gentleman, Federico Mazzella, by urgent request
induced Palma, with her mother, to make their residence in his hospitable
house, where his virtuous daughter, Antonietta, is day and night entirely
devoted to her father's guests. That house will be very likely changed into
a future sanctuary, and the name of this charitable family will be forever
associated with that of one of the most remarkable servants of God in this
century.

Palma Maria is apparently a living miracle. During the last twelve
years she has never swallowed a morsel of food. Her only nourishment
is the Bread of Life. By the Bishop's permission, a large room contiguous
to her humble apartment has been transformed into a private chapel, whither
every morning Palma is carried, seated upon a chair of suffering, to assist
at Mass, and to receive from the hands of the priest the Holy Communion
in company with the pious Antonietta, her visible guardian angel. After
Holy Communion Palma Maria is ravished into an ecstasy of grateful love
for about fifteen minutes. Brought again to her room, she is ordinarily visited
three or four times everyday, and also during the night, by our Lord, by
some angel or saint, from whom she visibly receives again the Eucharistic
Sacrament. Thus, by a singular privilege, as far as we know, never granted
before, this extraordinary woman receives Holy Communion several times
daily. Her prudent and saintly spiritual director, Father Francis della Pace,

and other ecclesiastical superiors, at first objected to these unusually frequent Communions. But our Lord manifested to Palma Maria that he had two objects in these frequent and visible Communions to her. The first was to rebuke the growing infidelity and the skepticism of the age, the coldness and indifference of Christians, and to stimulate a more lively devotion towards the Holy Eucharist among well-disposed Catholics. His second object was to communicate the needed strength and courage to herself, who had to endure a continual martyrdom of the most intense sufferings for his honor and glory, for the welfare of the Church, for the conversion of sinners and infidels, and for the salvation of souls. Palma has since been permitted to communicate as often as her Divine Spouse judges best for her spiritual welfare. In reality, she has need of these extraordinary helps. Her sufferings are beyond description, and above human comprehension. To deliver souls from purgatory she often endures in their behalf, the pains to which they are condemned by the justice of God. She occasionally suffers the sensible torments of hell to obtain the conversion of some great sinners in imminent danger of being eternally lost. She has the stigmata of the five wounds, which, however, at her earnest request, our Lord has made to disappear, being visible and bleeding only during the Fridays in Lent. But from the Crown of Thorns blood flows frequently in great quantities. This blood, falling in drops upon, or being wiped off with any cloth, leaves upon it the impression of crosses, of various instruments of our Lord's Passion, or other sacred emblems. The same and more wonderful impressions are occasionally produced upon her ordinary clothes, or upon other articles, as white handkerchiefs, which have been applied to her body and chest. In writing this sketch we have before our eyes these wonderful impressions, which have been photographed. They represent more than fifty different figures or signs. The principal and more striking of these are Calvaries, crosses, nails, hammers, pincers, crowns of thorns, scourges, monstrances with Hosts, hearts in large numbers and of different dimensions, some figures of our Lady of Seven Dolors, frequently the number seven in Arabic figures, often figures of roses, long rods with branches ending with thirteen stars, rods branching out with seven lines, the same with two lines, a cross of thin green branches; the cross of La Salette, with hammer and pincers; a longer branch, with twelve stars on each side, ending with another on the top of it. The letter "L" is seen very frequently, and some other emblems, the meanings of which are fully understood by Palma Maria. She explains them to her directors only, who write her words down for future reference. We venture to give the following explanation:

Naturally speaking, there is a mutual relation between the mind and sense, the soul and body. The mind draws its ideas from the senses, and the strong affections of the soul react upon the body. When these mental affections or emotions are very intense they seem to pervade the entire frame of our being, and to infuse a mysterious fluid in our very blood, from which, on some peculiar conditions, emblems will be produced, indicating the state or disposition of the soul.

We can understand even better this explanation on supernatural grounds. Divine grace, principally intended for the soul, acts also on the body. This is particularly the fact with some of the seven Sacraments. Moreover, for our final glorification and admission into heaven, not only the soul, but also the body, must undergo some process of preparation, and sanctification. This is one of the motives why self-denial, mortification and penance are so often and so strongly recommended to us in the Bible and in Christianity. Lastly, as our Lord in his glorified body retains the bright stigmata of the five wounds, and the glorious impression of the Crown of Thorns, so the bodies of the elect will be adorned, with glorious emblems, representing the virtuous labors they have performed, the privations, sufferings, pains and tortures they have endured for God's sake, and in God's service. Now, a Christian soul raised to a very high degree of perfection is very near her final state of glorification, and consequently very conformable to the image of her glorified Head, our risen Savior. But if our Blessed Lord left the marks of his sufferings upon his glorified body, and the bodies of the elect will be adorned with heavenly emblems in reward of their physical labors and sufferings, we have no great difficulty in believing the fact of the miraculous emblems produced on different articles of dress that come in contact with the body or blood of Palma Maria d'Oria. If these emblems are miraculous, they are consequently the effects of Divine interposition.

We do not hereby pretend to forestall the supreme judgment of the Holy See; we merely express our humble opinion. We are inclined to believe and to hope that the emblems we have enumerated are intended by God for our instruction and edification. He may wish to make us understand what is the habitual state of the soul of Palma Maria. Her mind and heart seem thoroughly penetrated with the grand and affecting mystery of our Lord's sacred Passion. Like St. Paul, Palma Maria glories in nothing but

260

in the Cross of Christ. Her whole being, like a sponge, appears penetrated and saturated, as it were, with the Passion of her Divine Spouse. Oh! what wonder that this living sponge of Christ, when slightly pressed, gives impressions of the emblems of the Passion. Being continually on Calvary, steadily at the foot of the cross, her looks fixed on Jesus crucified, and her heart and body crucified with him, what wonder if Palma Maria leaves on what she touches the impressions of Calvaries, crosses, scourges, hammers, nails and crowns of thorns? She has been for years steeped in them, she is impregnated with them in mind and heart, in soul and body. With St. Paul, she can truly say: *"I bear the marks of the Lord Jesus in my body."* We say the same in relation to the Sacrament of the Holy Eucharist. Palma has passed not only hours daily and nightly before our sacramental Lord; but this wonderful mystery of love is, we may say, the subject of her continual meditation, and the object of her most ardent aspirations and seraphic love. How ardently must she love our Lord in the Blessed Sacrament, to deserve from him, as we are informed, the singular privilege, never known to have been granted before to any living saint, of receiving him several times daily? Again, how must these frequent Communions, if really from God, make her seraphic ardor of devotion blaze forth into immense flames of love. This heavenly fire in fact becomes so intense, not only in her soul, but also in her body, that the cold water she is forced to drink to cool her, and which, burning interiorly, she cannot retain more than a few minutes in her stomach, comes out of her mouth literally boiling and steaming; and her inside dress is singed and burned as if her body were a red-hot iron. When we consider, these facts, we may be surprised, but we should not be incredulous about the figures of Hosts, remonstrances and other emblems impressed on her clothes. In explanation of these figures, we are of opinion that the number seven is intended to express her ardent devotion to the seven dolors of our Blessed Lady. The thirteen stars may signify her great veneration for the Apostles. The letter "L" means labor, suffering. The roses may be taken as the emblems of her burning charity, and of the odor of her sanctity. The cross of La Salette is a miraculous confirmation of the reality of that apparition. Moreover, a certain mysterious liquid, like honey, occasionally issues from her mouth, which, by order of her spiritual director, being collected and enclosed in bottles of clear glass, is gradually transformed into large Hosts, like those used by the celebrant at Mass. These prodigies can be witnessed at Oria, and Dr. A. Imbert Gourbeyere solemnly testifies having seen these as well as other astonishing wonders. Twice he saw her miraculous Communions and the wonderful Host on her extended tongue. He witnessed her ecstasies, the bleeding of the Crown of Thorns; he perceived the smell of her burning clothes, he saw them burned and covered with emblems. He had them photographed, and brought with him to France some handkerchiefs miraculously emblematized. Palma Maria is supernaturally bi-located, or transported to distant and different nations, to assist some privileged souls either in their severe sufferings or at the point of death. She often assists at the ecstasies and sufferings of Louise Lateau in Belguim. She is acquainted with living servants of God and other eminent Catholics living in different parts of the world. She speaks of a little girl living at present in Paris, near the great Convent of the Sisters of Charity, who is destined to become a famous saint, whom she calls Rita. She is stated to be in frequent spiritual communication with the celebrated seer, Melanie de La Salette, now called Sister Mary of the Cross, who lives at Castellamare, not far from Naples. She mentions a holy person living in Jerusalem, called Pasqualina, who has been stigmatized. Palma Maria seems to have the spirit of prophecy, by having foretold events before their realization, and this on several different occasions. She speaks of trials in store for the Pope, for Rome, and for the Church in general. She has announced impending massacres of priests and religious persons, especially in the kingdom of Naples, as also the three days' darkness, and other terrible calamities, which will be speedily followed by brilliant victories and the universal triumph of the Catholic Church. These biographical details we have compiled from the French work of Dr. A. Imbert Gourbeyere, mentioned several times in the preceding chapters. Since our compilation. We have heard that Palma Maria, on account of these truly extraordinary phenomena, is kept under a cloud. But we are personally inclined to believe that this is only a temporary, though very severe trial, permitted by God for the final purification of her soul, and for a great increase of merit for eternity.

CHAPTER XII

52. *Louise Lateau, Belgium*

Behold another admirable servant of Jesus crucified, living at the present time in Belgium. Louise is the youngest of three daughters of very poor and humble, but pious Catholic parents. She was born January 30th, 1850, in the small village of Bois d'Haine, diocese of Tournay, in Belgium. Her father died soon after her birth, and her mother a few months ago. She lives with her two sisters, Rosina and Adeline. Louise is a child of Providence. In her earliest infancy she was three or four times miraculously preserved from imminent danger of death. In the year 1866, when sixteen years of age, she already showed herself a heroine of charity, in attending her afflicted neighbors, stricken down with the terrible plague of cholera, and abandoned by their nearest relations, giving burial with her own hands to those who succumbed to the disease, carrying the corpses upon her weak shoulders to the public cemetery. In the same year she became a member of the Third Order of St. Francis. During the month of April, 1868, Louise had a very severe attack of illness, when her death was every moment expected, but, according to her prediction, she recovered suddenly early in the morning, and was able to go to the parish church to receive Holy Communion. She was incipiently stigmatized on the 24th of the same month, after an apparition from our Infant Savior. The stigmata became complete in a few months. On the 20th of September of the same year, being the third Sunday of the month and Feast of the Seven Dolors of our Blessed Lady, Louise received the Crown of Thorns. From the beginning of her stigmatization, and of the impression of the Crown of Thorns, Louise suffers a repetition of these stigmatic pains every Friday during the year, the wounds bleeding profusely. After the long agony mentioned below, our Lord appeared to his brave servant, impressed upon her shoulders the wound caused to him by the weight of the cross, enriched her soul with new lights and gifts, among which is the gift of prophecy. Hence Palma Maria's predictions begin to be verified. During her ecstasies on Friday she accompanies in spirit our Lord through the different stages of his Passion. In the ecstatic state Louise is perfectly insensible to any sound, and does not feel in the least any wound inflicted upon her body. When placed by visitors in her hands she can immediately distinguish any devotional article, as, for instance, relics of saints, crosses, medals, rosaries, which have been duly blessed and indulgenced, from those that have not. She also recognizes instantly the hands of priests, whilst she takes no notice of those of any lay person. The loudest noise does not affect her, but she can hear the least whisper of any pious prayer. Her confessors or ecclesiastical superiors can recall her instantly from her most profound ecstasy, but she does not hear the loudest call of any other person, not even her mother or sisters. Louise is often visited in spirit during her ecstatic sufferings by Palma Maria d'Oria, who prophesies that she will work great miracles, when Belgium shall be in serious political convulsions and dangers. Hence we may hope that her precious life will be preserved by God for some years to come. Different accounts having appeared in the English and American Catholic periodicals, we refer our readers to them, and to *Les Stigmatizées*, first volume, for further information upon this subject. The following extract will be found interesting:

THE AGONY OF LOUISE LATEAU

"We are enabled," says the *Journai de Bruxelles*, to publish some correct information concerning the stigmatized girl of Bois d'Haine. We have it from an eye-witness who within the last few days visited the humble abode of Louise, and who has given us the result of his observations as follows:

"On the afternoon of the 3rd of February, 1876, I knocked at the door of the cabin which now, more than ever, appeared to me like the sanctuary of some reparatory suffering.

Everything within was peaceful. A look of pain overspread the faces of Rosina and of her sister Adeline, who, for the last month, have been the victims of poignant sorrow, caused by their sympathy for the excessive sufferings of Louise. The subject of our conversation was suggested by these very sufferings. We spoke, but in a low tone, of all that had taken place in this abode for the last month; "Louise is so gentle and so resigned in her sufferings," Rosina said to me.

"I now went into the room where this holy girl has been agonizing for more than a month. Louise was stretched upon a bed that was remarkably clean; her face, a little pale at this moment, stood out from the white pillow like a virginal apparition. Though bearing traces of pain, it still retained its wonted sweetness and resignation. Her eyes, which were almost closed, opened only at intervals, when answering such questions as were put to her. There was no atmosphere of sickness in the little room; the air was as pure as in other parts of the House. Louise does not, as far as I could see, even during her most violent crises, have the slightest perspiration, nor that clamminess of the skin incident to prolonged sickness. Although confined to her bed for a month, in the same position, she does not feel any pain nor stiffness in that portion of her body stretched upon her poor straw mattress.

"The Doctor, who at this moment came in to see her, confirmed my observations; he found her pulse weak, quick, but regular. "There is no symptom of sickness in Louise," said he, "medicine fails to find a remedy applicable under circumstances like these."

"Louise constantly displays all the dolors of the Passion of the Savior of the world, from the agony in the Garden of Olives, to the crucifixion on the summit of Mt. Calvary. Her sufferings are only interrupted every morning during the presence of the Blessed Eucharist.

"On the following day, at 6:15 A.M., I accompanied the priest who had been authorized to give Communion to Louise.

"On our arrival in the room the stigmatized one appeared to be the victim of the most intense sufferings; these gradually subsided. Although the presence of the Blessed Sacrament had diminished the intensity of her pain, her difficult breathing could be distinctly noticed.

"Louise received her Communion with pious eagerness, and without opening her eyes, she consumed the Sacred Host.

"Immediately, and without a shadow of transition, it worked in her a complete transformation. Her suffering disappeared in the twinkling of an eye. The pale countenance of Louise brightened up with celestial rays and seemed overspread by a divine beauty. Everything was calm and motionless in that virginal body, which had become the tabernacle of the living God in the Eucharist. Not a wrinkle on her transfigured countenance, nor upon her lips closed in ecstasy. Even her chest was motionless; it seemed as if her heart had ceased to beat and that life was suspending its laws, through respect for the real presence of Jesus Christ.

265

"The eye could see in Louise at this moment only the mysterious quiet of death, but under this deceptive exterior one felt that a fullness of supernatural life was coursing, and that from the heart, as from a spring, it flowed into every part of this sainted girl's body. "How beautiful!" repeatedly exclaimed Rev. Father C., who, with tears in his eyes, was contemplating with me this magnificent spectacle. And indeed, I do not think it possible, on earth, to witness a more wonderful scene.

"We fell upon our knees to adore Jesus Christ, whose presence was so visibly made manifest to us, and we recited the prayer, "O good and most sweet Jesus." During the recitation of this prayer Louise opened her lips as if joining in with us; this was the only motion we could detect in her for more than ten minutes during which we were at her side."

ANOTHER ACCOUNT, DATED MAY

There I was, when meeting a dear bosom friend of my sacerdotal youth, resolved at once to go to Bois d'Haine and see Louise. We started from Paris on the eve of Ascension Day, and arrived at Manage the same day, towards 3 o'clock P. M. There we inquired for the road leading to Bois d'Haine, which is about one mile and a half from Manage. After a walk of about three-quarters of a mile, on a good pleasant road, planted all along with fine trees, and undulating through fine harvests, we arrived at a small cottage, lying close to the main road, and we were told by a passer-by that it was Louise I.ateau's dwelling. Who can imagine our emotions and joy at the mere sight of that dear little house in which we were to witness such great wonders! Not daring then to call in before being introduced, we contented ourselves with happily looking at the form and appearance of that fortunate dwelling. It is a brick house, having about twenty-four feet front, and eighteen feet depth, and ten of height. Its walls are very slightly painted a yellowish stone color, and the roof is covered with red shining tiles. There are in front, two windows, protected by an iron railing, and also by green shutters, which were then open. At an equal interval between is the door, also painted green. Exactly above the door is an enclosed opening, to go to the garret. This little cottage is divided into five little rooms; and it is only a few years since, that the two back rooms were added to the building for, previously, the house was scarcely ten feet deep. After we had gazed with some love on that humble, but neat cottage the scene of so many wonders from Almighty God, we pursued our course towards the church of the village, not without emotion, and as if we had already been struck by something supernatural. Soon we arrived at Bois d'Haine, and after a visit to Our Lord to ask success for the object which had brought us there, we called at the parsonage, and introduced ourselves to the Reverend Pastor of the place. *Monsieur le Curé* is a fine looking gentleman, of about fifty years of age, and bears on his face much sympathy and kindness, though he is very sober in words. Father Niels is his name. We could not resist his pressing invitation, and thus made ourselves at home at the parsonage. As I stayed four days at Bois d'Haine, I had fully the time of witnessing and investigating many things concerning Louise. O! happy moments, which I shall never forget!

LOUISE LATEAU IN THE MORNING AT THE TIME OF COMMUNION

Up to last January, Louise could attend to her daily work, and thus could go to church every morning, to receive Holy Communion. The only day of the week she was unable to do so was Friday. But on the three first days of January she was excruciated with such sufferings that it was thought that her last moments had arrived. In fact she was anointed on the 2nd of January, and her saintly soul was thought to have fled away from her virginal crucified body. Many times during those three days did her weeping sisters call her, but it was in vain; she had all the symptoms of death. But as soon as Father Niels called her: "Louise!" immediately, as by enchantment, she seemed to awaken from an ecstasy. She would soon fall again into the same forlorn position, and would be called back again by the priest's voice and, command. It was a kind of ecstasy different from her other ecstasies. Nobody can imagine what she suffered during those three days, either in her body or in her soul. Besides the excruciating sufferings of the stigmata, she felt then all the dolors of the agony of our Savior in the Garden of Olives, and had also what Father Seraphine, who is one of the examiners appointed by the Bishop of Tournay, calls "the deadly sufferings," that is to say, she felt all the sufferings which are previous to death, and had all the symptoms of a last agony. This explains why, at that time, several papers published Louise's death. Nevertheless, those intense sufferings abated afterwards, though on Good Friday it was also thought that she would die. But if Louise's sufferings abated, she has been unable to do any work ever since; and she is almost always confined to her bed, except a few hours of the day, during which her sisters help her to sit on a poor old family chair. Being thus unable to go to church, she receives every morning Holy Communion in her room. I have twice had the inestimable privilege of personally bringing to her our Lord, and once of being present at that great moment. The spectacle is always exactly the same, every morning, either before or after Communion. The only detail which is special to Friday is the bleeding of the stigmata. So, to have it complete, I will describe the scene of Friday. It is generally at six o'clock that the Holy Communion is carried to Louise. It is a walk of three-quarters of a mile. Oftentimes high personages, in order to have a chance of penetrating into Louise's room, are happy to carry the bell or the flambeau, or to escort the Blessed Sacrament: and there would be large crowds following the priest, if they could be admitted, which is not possible, as the room is exceedingly small. As soon as the priest arrives at the house, it is assured that the sufferings of the angelic maiden begin to abate in order to cease entirely when the Host is put on her tongue. Louise's room is quite small, and is perhaps not more than nine feet square. She lies on a small iron bedstead, and rests on her back. Her eyes are shut, and remain so during the whole ceremony. Her face at that hour is generally pale, but her cheeks are full. She seems to be the victim of very acute sufferings, causing on her face continual oscillations or vibrations. Her lips are half open, and she seems to be out of breath. Is that suffering caused by her mystical sufferings, or by her unspeakable eagerness to receive her Divine Spouse? It may be caused by both. As usual the Confiteor is recited; then the priest recites the *Misereatur* and *Indulgentiam*, she extends her tongue, which she advances far down on her lips, and as soon as the Host is laid on it, she quickly draws it back. I have been struck with the rapidity every time. Then her lips close up; you do not perceive any longer any oscillation or vibration on her face. She becomes as motionless as a marble figure. The colors of lily, which before were visible on her face, are united to rosy hues. Her eyes remain always perfectly shut. You cannot perceive any breathing, and you have to look very closely to notice a slight, slow heaving of her chest. A few seconds after Communion, I noticed once on her closed lips the last vibration of a murmured prayer. Her whole countenance seems to breathe her soul, and seems to be transfigured. I have never seen so beautiful a face. All of us were so struck with respect and wonder, that we remained many minutes on our knees uniting our weak adorations to the burning adorations of that loving, enraptured maiden. Her ecstasy is so perfect that her body is completely insensible to any piercing, however painful it might be.

Physicians, appointed to verify this fact, have repeatedly pierced her with sharp instruments in the most sensitive parts; but there was not the

268

least contraction or oscillation in her body. During her daily morning ecstasy, Louise does not see any vision; but her soul is united to our Lord by the most intimate fusion; and she is enraptured with so many delights, that it is a beginning of the heavenly bliss, and she is rather in heaven than on earth. On her forehead there was only one large drop of blood, ready to flow. I must notice, that since last January her forehead has bled perfectly only three or four times. But previously, every Friday there was around her head, a crown of blood, two fingers wide. The blood begins generally to ooze from her stigmata at midnight, and sometimes at the time of Communion it was very difficult to lay the Host on her tongue, as the blood was trickling from all directions of the head, and there was danger that the Host might be sullied with blood before being received. The blood ran down in such abundance, that it flowed around her neck like a crimson collar. After a few minutes of silent prayer, we all rose up to leave that fortunate room. Towards the direction of her hands, the napkin which was put around her neck as a communion-cloth, was stained with fresh blood. Having previously asked from *Monsieur Le Curé* the permission of examining Louise's hands, I drew close to her and took off the napkin; I found some folded linen lying on her hands in order that the blood should not go over her dress and her little couch. These linens were entirely sullied and damp with blood. I also took them off, and, O my God! what a spectacle! It seemed that Louise was bathing in her blood: so great was the abundance of blood, either fresh or coagulated on her hands. Her fingers were connected together, and the palms of her hands rested flat on her chest. A beautiful crimson blood was oozing from her stigmata or piercings of both hands. These piercings are exactly in the middle of the hands, between the third and fourth fingers. After we had all contemplated with an unspeakable emotion that touching scene, I replaced the napkin, in order that Louise's sisters should not be aware of our curiosity; and, not without some regret we went out, after having addressed a few words of encouragement to Rosine and Adeline, sisters of Louise. This ecstasy of the morning lasts about half an hour. Then, suddenly Louise comes back to herself, and for several minutes does not feel the least pains of her previous sufferings. She recites then the prayer, *"En ego, O bone Jesu, etc."* Then her pains come back by degrees. During the forenoon, except on Friday, her sisters help her to rise, and to sit on a chair at the foot of her bedstead, and close to the wall. Thus she remains also a part of the afternoon, and sometimes the whole night.

THEODORE

A gentleman of the *Germania*, describing a visit he paid, on Good Friday, to Bois d'Haine, writes the following, concerning Louise Lateau:

"I have often seen the stigmatized lose a great deal of blood, but never as I did to-day. The blood, which literally gushed out of her hands, was absorbed by a quantity of large white pieces of cloth that were lying on her bed. The blood-stains showing themselves on her cap and the garment thrown over her shoulders, indicated that the head also and the right shoulder were bleeding much. Her eyes were not quite closed, and seemed to be fixed on the wall. From her continual sighs, the violent shaking of her hands, and the exclamation, *'Mon Dieu,'* which escaped her from time to time, it was evident that the sufferer had to bear immense pain. In the afternoon, towards two o'clock, I went in again, soon after the ecstatic state had set in. I found myself in the company of the Belgian Minister of Justice, a doctor of Brussels, the director of the Seminary for Foreign Missions in Paris, a professor of Tourcoing, in France, and several French and Belgian noblemen. A German who was dressed in every respect like a layman brought his hand close to Louise. Immediately a bright smile became visible on her face. "What's that?" whispered several. 'Monsieur est prêtre,' said the curé. 'Ah, voila!' The same priest gave the doctor a picture which was not blessed. It was held up to her, but she did not smile. Then the priest took it back, blessed it, and returned it to the doctor, who held it near Louise. Her face was at once lighted up with a strikingly bright smile, which lasted as long as the picture remained near her. With regard to visitors, the writer says that very few laymen are admitted, and that ladies are not allowed to enter the house at all. Only last week the Grand Duchess of Toscana and the Duchess of Aremberg, who begged hard to see Louise Lateau, had to return home, without having their wish gratified. On the other hand, Count Perponcher, German Ambassador in Bruxelles, got permission to visit her. It is now thought that she is really approaching her death."

270

CHAPTER XIII

53. *Sister Esperance of Jesus, Canada*

This youthful servant of God was born in 1853, near Quebec, Lower Canada. Her parents are poor, but humble and pious Catholics. Her name in the world was Vitaline Gagnon. From her earliest infancy this privileged child of God gave signs of precocious piety and devotion. Her sweetest delight was to go to the Catholic cemetery, and, kneeling down near some grave, recite with angelic recollection, and with her innocent little hands joined on her breast, *Hail Marys* for the souls in purgatory. When thirteen years of age Vitaline was admitted as a postulant among the Sisters Hospitaliers of Quebec, but with deep regret she had to return home to her parents, because the physicians declared that a life of religious enclosure would not agree with her delicate constitution.

Physicians, however, are very often mistaken in these supernatural matters. Such was the case in regard to Vitaline Gagnon. Some time after her return home she applied for admission among the Gray Sisters at Ottawa, and was received after being in an extraordinary manner cured of a serious cold. Her malady, however, returned accompanied by a distressing cough, which caused grave uneasiness. The religious threatened to send her home again if she were not soon cured. Vitaline, with childlike confidence, had recourse to her dear mother, our Blessed Lady, and she was again immediately cured. Being admitted to the novitiate, she took the religious name of Sister Esperance of Jesus. Two years later she made her religious profession, and on the same happy day she received the stigmata of the five wounds. Her wounds bleed every Friday, and every time this innocent victim of charity offers her prayers and sufferings to obtain some special grace for those who have recourse to her intercession. She is continually on the cross of suffering. For some years she has been living without any other food than that of the Eucharistic Bread of immortal life. Apparently she seems to enjoy perfect health, and looks remarkably well. The water that issues from her wounds emits a very agreeable perfume; it is sufficient to remain in her poor cell a few minutes to become impregnated with this celestial fragrance. It is now eleven years since Sister Esperance made her religious profession and received the stigmata of the Passion. She is often made to pass through the different stages of the Passion of our Lord. When scourged at the pillar her body is raised by an invisible hand, and the blows inflicted upon her can be heard. These are so terrible that her whole body is covered with wounds and bruises. After this she is placed on the cross, and suffers all the torments of a real crucifixion. She offers frequently her sufferings for the souls in purgatory. This good religious is often raised up into ecstatic raptures, during which the spiritual condition of persons recommended to her prayers is made known to her. The souls in purgatory often appear to her, asking her prayers and suffrages for their speedy deliverance. To give her a sensible proof of the intensity of their sufferings, they touch her body with a mysterious hand, leaving upon it a distinct and visible impression, as if it had been made with a hand of red-hot iron. In eight months she suffered six or seven of these painful marks. Sister Esperance has made several prophecies which have been literally verified. Contrary to the opinion of physicians, she told her confessor that one of his sick penitents would die soon. The person died within a week, and the departed soul appeared to her, asking her prayers and suffrages, because she was in purgatory; then, placing her burning hand upon the foot of Sister Esperance, she left upon it a visible impression, which the humble religious showed to her confessor. Her religious sisters venerate her as the visible guardian angel of the community. Her advice and exhortations are full of heavenly wisdom and prudence. When consulted by any person about spiritual or temporal affairs, she seems to know by intuition all their wants, and the most secret dispositions of their souls. Sister Esperance possesses the gift of discernment of spirits. Before being admitted to her presence she knows the internal dispositions and motives of visitors who ask to see her. She humbly but firmly refused to see some ladies who traveled a long distance for this purpose, but through motives of feminine curiosity. On the contray, she sent an invitation to a virtuous religious, well known to the writer of this notice, who, having to go to the convent to see his own sister, abstained through humility from asking for Sister Esperance. This good religious has much to suffer, but he has been highly encouraged and consoled by her kind words, prayers and letters. We have read one of these messages of charity. These details have been given by two eye-witnesses. May God make Sister Esperance of Jesus a great saint, the *hope* and advocate of Canada and of America, according to the meaning of her religious name. North America needs some powerful native saint and advocate with God in her impending trials. (See *"Les Stigmatizées,"* 2 Vol, note about the end. Also, *"Voix Prophetiques,"* tome 1, livre 4, chap. 4)

CHAPTER XIV

CONCLUDING REMARKS

We close this catalogue with the following names of servants of God who might have been added to the list of those who have been stigmatized.

1. *Blessed Mary of the Angels*, born at Turin, Piedmont, Italy, January 7th, 1661. She was a Carmelite nun, and suffered the sensible dolors of the Passion of our Lord. She died December 16th, 1717, and was beatified by Pope Pius IX, 1865.

2. *Mary de Aiofrin, or Aiostrin*. She lived at Toledo, in Spain, and was stigmatized in the side. She is mentioned by Rayssius, Raynaud and Alva, who refer to Vallega, *Florilegium Sanctorum*, tom. 3.

3. The virgin *Eustochia*. She was a Franciscan nun. After her death the holy names of Jesus and Mary were found impressed on the region of her heart. She is mentioned by Raynaud, who refers to Alano Copo. She may be the servant of God whose life has been written by Michael Pio. A similar name is mentioned by Bagatta and by Scardeone.

4. Sister Nympha, a nun of the Order of St. Francis de Paola, mentioned by Rayssius and Alva, who refer to the general history of the same order, published in Paris by Dony de Attichy, 1624.

The five following living servants of God have also been stigmatized or crowned with thorns:

1. Madame Moillis, living at Dragiugnan, France.

2. Sister Francis Xavier de Requisita, Aveyron, France.

3. Pasqualina, mentioned by Palma Maria d'Oria, living in Jerusalem, Palestine.

4. Sister Mary of the Cross, better known as Melanie de la Salette, is reported to have been stigmatized and to have received the Crown of Thorns.

5.	From two sources of high and reliable authority, both eye-witnesses, the compiler of this has learned that a religious of the Precious Blood in Canada has been stigmatized, and impressed with the Crown of Thorns. This is Mother Catharine, and the founder of this new religious institute in Upper Canada.

We venture to say that this list, notwithstanding its imperfections, is the most complete that has ever appeared in any book. It may be considered an abridgment of the history of those saints and servants of God that have received the miraculous impression of the Crown of Thorns. A real history of these extraordinary facts is rather difficult, and would require the combined talents and efforts of an able physician and a learned and pious mystic theologian. A more perfect study of the chronicles of sanctity would certainly enlarge the catalogue of holy persons who have supernaturally shared in the sufferings of our Lord's Passion. Moreover, we are not always permitted to penetrate, within the sacred retreats of Christian humility, wherein those favorite servants of God like to remain concealed in obscurity. Many of them have succeeded in concealing themselves from human observation.

In the Theological Dictionary of Gosschler, one of the editors justly observes that the miracle of the stigmatization is perhaps more frequently produced during our present time than it appears to have been in past centuries. There are few epochs, he says, wherein there have been in different parts of Germany so many cases of stigmata as there are at the present moment. The more commonly known are Catharine Emmerich, Maria de Moerl, etc. But, to the knowledge of the writer of this article, there are many others who have succeeded better than these in concealing their supernatural gifts from public notice, and remain unknown in holy and salutary obscurity. The same remark is true in relation to other servants of God in Italy, France, Spain, and in other countries. Sanctity is inseparable from humility, which lives and thrives in voluntary obscurity and quiet seclusion.

From St. Francis of Assisi, in the beginning of the thirteenth century, to the present day, there has been an uninterrupted living chain of saints and servants of God, stigmatized or crowned with thorns. This consoling and edifying fact can be mathematically demonstrated. Since that memorble epoch there has not been a day wherein the glorious family of living persons mystically crucified have ceased to represent in the Catholic Church the sublime mystery of Calvary.

275

From the general catalogue of the stigmatized we learn that twenty were men and one hundred and thirty-six women. The vast majority of these privileged persons were members of different religious orders or congregations.

1. The illustrious Order of St. Dominic marches at the head of this glorious procession, with the standard of the Cross. No less than sixty children of this great Patriarch have been decorated with the sacred stigmata of our crucified Lord, sixteen of whom endured only the internal sufferings of the Passion.

2. The seraphic Order of St. Francis comes next, with the holy founder at its head. Including St. Francis of Assisi, forty-three members of the various Franciscan families have been stigmatized, fourteen of whom suffered only the internal dolors of the Passion.

3. Carmelites have seven.

4. The same number is found among the Augustinians.

5. The Cistercians have five stigmatized.

6. Nuns of the Visitation have three.

7. The Theatines, or Nuns of St. Cajetan, two.

8. The Hospitaliers Sisters have two.

9. The Benedictines, one.

10. The Servites, one.

11. The Premonstratense, one.

12. The Beguine Sister in Belgium, one.

13. The Canadian Gray Sisters, one.

14. Sisters of the Precious Blood, one.

The rest, in a very small proportion, were secular persons, living in the world.

Twelve of these stigmatized servants of God had lived in the married state, one only, of whom was a man, namely, Blessed Roberto Malatesta. Two of these received the stigmata while living with their husbands. They were Blessed Mary of the Incarnation (Madame Alcario) and Johanna of Jesus and Mary, the latter in Spain, the former in France. As far as we know, all these privileged saints and servants of God belong to the following nationalities:

1. Italy, the center of Christianity, is at the head of the list. This country has been wonderfully blessed by God. She is justly recognized as the land of miracles. Out of one hundred and fifty-six stigmatized

or otherwise supernaturally impressed with the marks of our Savior's Passion, Italy alone numbers at least seventy, nearly the half of the whole list. She is still more favored with the Crown of Thorns. Among the fifty-three, known to have received the miraculous impression of the mystic crown, thirty-three are Italian saints or eminent servants of God. We should, moreover, observe that they are, as Dr. A. Imbert Gourbeyere says, the most illustrious in the entire catalogue of stigmatization.

2.   Catholic Spain comes next to Italy, with fifteen stigmatized and four crowned with thorns.

3.   France has eleven stigmatized and four crowned with thorns.

4.   Different parts of Germany have eleven stigmatized and three crowned with thorns.

5.   Belgium counts five stigmatized and two crowned with thorns.

6.   Portugal has five stigmatized and one crowned with thorns.

7.   Tyrol, three stigmatized and one crowned with thorns.

8.   Holland, two stigmatized.

9.   Switzerland, two stigmatized and one crowned with thorns.

10.   Hungary, two stigmatized.

11.   Canada, two stigmatized and crowned with thorns.

12.   Scotland, one stigmatized.

This was Father John Gray, a Franciscan Friar, who suffered martyrdom for his faith, at Bruxelles, from the hands of the Calvinists, January 5th, 1579. He is mentioned by Father Thomas Burchier, an English Franciscan, in his *"Ecclesiastical History of the Martyrdom of the Franciscan Friars who suffered in England, Ireland, and Belgium, from the year 1536 to 1582."*

Among the cities more particularly illustrated by these privileged saints and servants of God are: Naples, which counts eight of them; Florence, four; Foligno, Mantua and Sienna, in Italy, three each; Valencia, in Spain, four; Paris, in France, two.

More than forty of these have been raised by the Holy See to the honors of the altar, which means that they have been canonized, or at least beatified. They have all died in the odor of sanctity, and the cause of the beatification of many of them has been introduced in Rome.

Three members of this glorious family of saints, all three Italians, who have been decorated with the true cross of honor of our Divine King, crowned with thorns and crucified, have been canonized or beatified in the

277

present century. They are St. Veronica Juliani, 1839, by Pope Gregory XVI; St. Mary Francis of the Five Wounds, 1867; and Blessed Charles of Sezia, 1873, by Pope Pius IX.

As the Passion of our Lord began with the fall of man from original justice, so the Crown of Thorns commenced to be plaited for him from the moment that the offended Majesty of God said to Adam: *Cursed is the earth in thy work ... Thorns and thistles it shall bring forth to thee.* In the company of Moses we have contemplated this Crown on Mount Horeb at the light of the burning bush, and we venerated it with him in the Tabernacle round the Ark of the Covenant. In the figure of the Azazel we saw our Savior meekly receiving upon his adorable head the curse due to our sins, and beheld him sacrificed on Mount Moriah, to save all the elect, in the person of Isaac, the obedient son of Abraham. Following the path indicated by these and other figures of the Old Testament, we arrived at Bethlehem, and, with St. Bernard we meditated on the crown of poverty and misery placed by his Virgin Mother on the head of our Infant Savior. We have accompanied him to the hall of Pilate, and witnessed in the cruelty of his stepmother, the Synagogue, the full realization of all the prophetic figures of the Crown of Thorns. We contemplated the sufferings and humiliations of the King of Sorrows, and accompanied him to his final victory and triumph. We admired the devotion of the holy Empress Helena, and with profound gratitude received from her hands the precious relic of the Crown of Thorns.

During the last seven centuries, including our own, we have seen this sacred Crown miraculously bleeding in the Church of the living God, and adorning the heads of more than fifty successive privileged servants of Jesus Christ. Several of these heroic persons are suffering and are adorned with it whilst we write and read these wonderful facts.

PRAYER

Crown of our Savior, we venerate thee. Oh! why shall we not adore thee, after having been sanctified by the sufferings and by the sacred blood of the Divine Victim of our redemption? Crown of Jesus, thou art very dear to his sacred heart. We see thee entwined round it, the cherished object of his divine predilection. Thou and the Cross are most dear to him. Intimately convinced of this truth, spurred on by thy gentle pricks, encour-

278

aged by thy fervent lover, St. Bernard, I have gathered this small bunch of flowers in thy praise and in thy honor. I humbly lay it in the bosom of the afflicted and sorrowful Mother of my crucified Savior, at the foot of the Cross. She knows my wants, my wishes, my object. I sincerely desire to see her Divine Son, the King of Sorrows, glorified in thee, with thee, and through thee. Crown of Thorns, obtain for me and for all the pious readers of this little work, the grace to bear the trials and humiliations of this life in imitation of our Divine Savior crowned with thorns; that we may deserve to receive from his glorified hands the crown of eternal bliss and glory. Amen.

"Spinea Corona Capitis Jesu,
Diadema regni adepti sumus." Fiat.

THIRD PART

PRACTICAL DEVOTIONS IN HONOR OF THE CROWN OF THORNS

CHAPTER I

GENERAL EXHORTATION

1. *Go forth, Ye daughters of Sion, and see King Solomon in the diadem wherewith his mother crowned him.* (Cantic. 3:2)

With these words our holy Mother the Church exhorts all Christian souls to contemplate the King of Kings, Jesus Christ, her Spouse, crowned with thorns. There are strong and pressing motives for this invitation. Jesus crowned with thorns is a singular spectacle in the history of human sorrow and suffering. The malice of the human heart has invented, and the cruelty of the human hand has inflicted all manner of tortures on guilty or persecuted victims. But the horrible martyrdom of the Crown of Thorns was exclusively reserved for the Divine Victim of Calvary. If the novelty of an event is sufficient to excite the curiosity of mankind, surely the unexampled torture inflicted upon our dear Lord, should draw the attention of Christians to this new development of human malice and cruelty. From the two great doctors of the Church, St. Athanasius and St. John Chrysostom, we have learned that the horrible invention of the Crown of Thorns, must be attributed to the infernal malice of the devil, who wished to torment and to humble our Divine Lord beyond the experience of any other human sufferer. *"It was the devil that had taken an entire possession of all those impious executioners,"* St. John Chrysostom says. *"The devil,"* St. Athanasius adds, *"the devil excited and impelled those cruel soldiers to torment and deride our blessed Lord."* (Serm. de Pass. Domini.)

We are confirmed in this well-founded opinion when we reflect that those Pagan soldiers, in violation of military discipline, trampling under foot every law of order, justice and humanity, acted this bloody tragedy without the knowledge, and contrary to the intention of Pilate, the Roman Governor and their superior officer. *"Milites, pecunia corrupti, hoc ad gratiam Judaeorum faciebant,"* John Chrysostom says. Two conclusions follow from this fact. We learn, first, that the torment of the Crown of Thorns must have been extremely painful and humiliating to our Divine Lord, having been inflicted upon him by those barbarous men, possessed and instigated by the malice of the devil. All tortures inflicted through malicious hatred and against law, order and justice, are always more cruel, more painful and more humiliating for an innocent victim, than chastisements deserved by crime and decreed by legitimate authority. But in this great and profound mystery of the crowning with thorns of our Lord Jesus Christ, all on the side of men, all is disorder, all is malice and extreme cruelty. The second conclusion to which we would come is that devout Christians should practice some special devotion adapted and intended to make the best reparation in our limited power to our Divine Lord for this new and horrible outrage. He will surely be pleased with our humble efforts and pious intention.

2. This is our earnest desire in proposing the beads and badge of the Crown of Thorns to the attention of devout Catholics. We venture to make the proposal, after having asked the advice of competent persons, who have approved it and have encouraged us in our understanding. Convinced of ultimate success, because we know in whom we believe, and for whom we work; yet we are not without some apprehension that our humble efforts may evoke some opposition. We expect that one of the principal objections will be directed against the novelty of this devotion. This objection may proceed from two very different kinds of persons. The first will be found intelligent and conservative. The second may be denominated timid and selfish. This latter class of easy-going persons does not like to be annoyed with many, much less with new practices of devotion, which require a little time to learn them and cost some slight inconvenience

in actual execution. They are fully satisfied with those few prayers which they learned in their childhood without much labor, and which they ocasionally recite without any effort, and, for this reason, very likely without much advantage to their souls. They imagine that, like themselves, the Church of Christ is getting old now, and does not like to be bothered with new practices of devotion. Persons in this state of mind will scarcely have patience to await calmly, and listen to arguments: hence, we will not attempt to disturb their equanimity, but we will, with hope of better success, address our humble remarks to the first class of more intelligent and generous souls.

Every intelligent Catholic is habitually disposed to use prudence and reflection when any new practice of devotion is proposed for his acceptance. Before approving, sanctioning and practising it, he will carefully examine its origin and nature, its object and authority. Being satisfied that the origin of a new form of practical devotion is derived from a sacred source, that it is good and useful in its nature, that its object is holy and desirable, and, finally, that it is recommended by the sanction of legitimate ecclesiastical authority, surely he will not oppose it, but he will rather uphold and encourage its practical development. It will not require, dear reader, any deep or extensive study to find out that devotion to the Crown of Thorns possesses all these qualifications.

3. Its origin is derived from a well-known fact of sacred history, related in the Gospel, by the three holy Evangelists, St. Matthew, St. Mark and St. John, whose testimony is true. The form of a devotion intended and adapted to recall to the mind of Christians, the physical sufferings and moral ignominies and humiliations endured by the Incarnate Son of God, with the pious intention of compassionating him in the horrible torture suffered for our sake, on account of our sins, should certainly be considered both good and desirable. Good! ... Oh, is it not good, dear reader, to contemplate Jesus, our Lord, crowned with thorns, seated upon a cold stone, made to hold in his hand, quivering with pain, the reed of derision as his royal scepter, covered with the scarlet cloak of ignominy, whilst Pagan soldiers, encouraged by the approving shouts of an insolent rabble, strike with heavy sticks his thorn-crowned head, spit upon his sacred face, and impiously bend their knee to salute him in mockery, *King of the Jews?* ... Is it not good and desirable for Christian souls to consider often the patience, the meekness, the humility and charity of the King of Sorrows in his keenest anguish and deepest public humiliations? ... St. Bernard, by happy expe-

rience, found this meditation very good and profitable. He tells us that from his first entrance into the cloister, which he considers the beginning of his conversion, he formed for his daily meditation a crown of all the sufferings and sorrows of his crucified Lord and Savior, and pressed it closely to his loving heart.

"During my life," he says, "I shall never cease proclaiming the torrent of delights which this salutary devotion brought to my soul. During all eternity I will hold in grateful remembrance the abundance of Divine mercies wherewith my spirit has been refreshed. This holy crown is very dear to my heart. No one can ever take it from me. I press it closely to my bosom. To meditate upon it often is the secret of my wisdom, the fullness of my knowledge, the perfection of my sanctification, the guarantee of my salvation, the treasure of all my merits. This meditation supports me in my trials and sufferings, keeps me humble in prosperity, and like two thorny hedges at the right and left side of the road, it makes me walk safely midway, where prudence leads and true wisdom follows, keeping away from me the snares of presumption and the pit-falls of despair. Do you likewise, dearly beloved, plait for your devotion this precious Crown of Thorns. Clasp it to your breast, press it deeply to the very core of your heart, meditate frequently upon it. It will become your surest protection in life, your consolation in death, and the crown of glory in a blissful eternity." (St. Bernard, Serm. 24 in Cantic.)

This devotion of the Crown of Thorns should, therefore, be considered good and desirable in its nature, as it is holy and profitable in its object. The principal object of the devotion of the Crown of Thorns is the promotion of the honor and glory of our Divine Lord by means of the frequent remembrance of and pious meditation on the sufferings and humiliations endured by him at his crowning of thorns. Every Christian will readily acknowledge that this is a holy exercise. St. Bernard believed it to be both holy and sanctifying, he considered it desirable, because he warmly exhorts us to practice it continually with fervor and fidelity. By happy experience, this eminent saint found this pious exercise highly conducive to his spiritual progress in the way of Christian and religious perfection. He assures us that God rewarded his devotion with an abundance of heavenly lights and graces. From this fact, we are given to understand that God was pleased with the devout practice of this holy doctor of the Church, and that in his Divine goodness he sanctioned it with his heavenly gifts.

Fully persuaded of these advantages, St. Bernard blames the careless apathy and want of devotion of some effeminate Christians, who neglect this holy exercise. *"Egredimini, filiae Sion.* Come forth, daughters of Sion," he says. "We call you daughters of Sion, ye worldly Christians, because in your conduct, you show yourselves weak and delicate. You are daughters, and not sons, because you do not manifest any strength of devotion, any manly courage, in your Christian life. Rise from your carnal indolence to the intelligence of spiritual truths, from the slavery of sensual concupiscence to the liberty of the children of God. Come out bravely from your earthly notions, from your worldly maxims, and from the selfish and vain pretexts of old customs. Come and see your Heavenly King crowned by his step-mother, the Synagogue, with a crown of thorns. (St. Bernard, Serm. 2 in Epiph. Domini.)

"Let sinners," this holy doctor says in another sermon, "Let sinners look at their Savior crowned with thorns on account of their sins, and be moved to compunction and sorrow. If they obstinately refuse during life, to see him crowned with thorns in pain and ignominy, they will be obliged to behold him as their Judge in a crown of justice, when he will condemn them as reprobates to everlasting punishment. But all pious souls that have often meditated on his painful and ignominious Crown of Thorns, will behold him in his crown of glory, and receiving from his divine hand the diadem of the heavenly kingdom, they will be made eternally happy in his blessed company. (Serm. 50, de Diversis.) Surely, all this makes the devotion of the Crown of Thorns very desirable.

4. The celebrated stigmatization of the seraphic patriarch, St. Francis of Assissi, may be adduced as a satisfactory proof that a special devotion in memory of the Crown of Thorns will be agreeable to our Lord and profitable to our soul. The Church has instituted a special feast on the 17th of September, with its proper Office and Mass, in order that every year the remembrance of this extraordinary prodigy of the Passion, may be renewed among the faithful, and the mystery expressed by the stigmatization may be more profitably meditated upon, to inflame our hearts with love for our suffering Savior. In the prayer of the Office and Mass of that day the following words are used, which express the principal object of the Feast: *"Lord Jesus Christ, when this world is become cold in thy love, thou hast renewed the sacred stigmata of thy Passion in the body of blessed Francis, in order to inflame our hearts with the fire of thy charity."*

To keep this sacred fire of Divine love ever burning in the hearts of Christians, the striking prodigy of stigmatization has been continued without interruption in the persons of some privileged members of the Church, from the time of St. Francis to the present day. We have seen that more than one hundred and fifty saints or servants of God have since received the complete or partial stigmatization of the Passion. Not merely with words of mouth, but with gaping wounds and flowing blood, the great mystery of Calvary is proclaimed by a chain of prodigies to a cold, thoughtless and selfish world, and is perpetuated in the Church of the living God, to inflame the hearts of Christians with the fire of Jesus' love.

It is a fact deserving our most serious attention that the prodigies of stigmatization have been almost invariably connected with the miraculous impression of the Crown of Thorns. This remarkable event is contemporaneous with the stigmatization of St. Francis. Blessed Emilia or Emily Bicchieri, of the Third Order of St. Dominic, born in Vercelli, Piedmont, Italy, May 3rd, 1238, is the first person known to have suffered the supernatural impression of the Crown of Thorns. She died in her native city on the Feast of the Invention of the Holy Cross, May 3rd, 1278. St. Francis of Assisi died October 4th, 1226. From that period the miracle of the Crown of Thorns has been visibly perpetuated in the Catholic Church without interruption to the present day. Palma Maria of Oria, in the kingdom of Naples, and Louise Lateau in Belgium are the most celebrated instances of our time.

We humbly believe that God has some special object in keeping the Crown of Thorns, miraculously bleeding in the Church during more than six hundred years. We believe that He desires to excite in the faithful a special devotion to this profound, moving and instructive mystery of His Son's Passion. As the stigmatization of St. Francis, continued ever since in so many saints and servants of God, was, according to the infallible judgment of the Church, intended to promote devotion to the Passion of our Lord in a general way; so we venture to say that a similar chain of prodigies relative to the Crown of Thorns, seems to indicate that our Lord desires to excite in the minds and hearts of the faithful a special devotion towards this sacred and sublime mystery of the Passion.

5. We sincerely and heartily rejoice at the rapidly increasing devotion among the faithful towards the Sacred Heart of Jesus. We believe that this Divine Heart is the invincible bulwark of the Church against the desperate

assaults of her numerous and powerful enemies conspiring together to effect her utter destruction. The Sacred Heart will soon be our salvation.

From what we read, however, in the edifying life of Blessed Margaret Mary Alacoque, a nun of the Visitation, who received from the blessed hands of our Lord the Crown of Thorns, we venture to say that the beads and badge of the Crown of Thorns will form the complement of this sublime and practical devotion. The following are the words of this great and glorious saint. "The Divine Heart was represented to me on a throne of fire and flames, radiant on all sides, and more brilliant than the sun, and transparent as crystal ... The wound which our Lord received upon the Cross was visible. *There was a Crown of Thorns around the Divine Heart, and a cross above it.*" (Life of Blessed Margaret Mary) The emblem of the Sacred Heart of our Lord, by the command of the Church, is always represented in paintings and devout pictures, with his Crown of Thorns. These thorns must then be very dear to our Blessed Savior; for he wishes to have them entwined round his sacred and glorified heart. May we not, then, reasonably and devoutly hope that the beads and badge of the Crown of Thorns are some of the many precious fruits of this holy devotion, very agreeable to our Blessed Lord? If the devout lovers of the Sacred Heart think so, we feel sure that they will pray and interest themselves for its adoption and propagation among the faithful.

We see another hopeful sign in favor of this devotion of the beads and badge of the Crown of Thorns in the famous prodigy of Anna Maria Taigi's mystical sun surrounded and crowned with thorns, which she continually contemplated during forty-seven years, and which was mentioned in the first part of this book. As the devotion to the Sacred Heart of our Divine Lord is evidently intended to cure the corruption of the human heart in these degenerate times; so we humbly hope that the devotion to the Crown of Thorns will help to correct the perverse thoughts, erroneous judgments and extravagant opinions of this proud world. The Sacred Heart of Jesus will purify and sanctify our hearts, and devotion to the Crown of Thorns will rectify our reason, sanctify our minds, and thus thoroughly perfect human nature.

6. In the history of mankind we find no epoch where these two vital remedies were more needed than at the present time. Our limits forbid a long discussion upon this important subject. A little knowledge and experience of human society is sufficient to demonstrate that the human heart

in the generality of men, is deeply corrupted by its attachment to material objects and by sensual indulgence. The more material and self-indulgent man becomes, the less he loves God. Moreover, because the law of God is diametrically opposed to the self-indulgence and materialism of man, who has been created for higher and nobler ends, hence arises the modern rebellion against the Divine law, and an actual hatred in the hearts of the most vicious men against the Divine Legislator. Such is the present terrible condition of human society. The Sacred Heart of Jesus only can apply an effective remedy for this frightful disorder.

But another evil is prevalent in human society. This is what St. John calls *"the pride of life."* It is the pride of the mind, the pride of intellect in a superlative degree. It is the preference given by self-conceited men to human reason, to secular knowledge and to natural science, above divine revelation, against the essential dogmas of religion and in a spiteful opposition to the infallible judgment of the Church, and of the Vicar of Jesus Christ, the Pope of Rome. This is the present disorder of modern human intelligence, which strives to restore the Pagan worship of Minerva and of the more modern goddess of reason of Voltairean fashion. Among the common classes of the people, this spirit of pride is evident in the self-conceit, in the aspiration for independence from all authority, human or divine, in the contempt for superiors, in the disregard of law and duty boldly manifested by many in their socialistic, or, rather, anti-social tendency. Outside of the Catholic Church the people, or at least their secular leaders, have impiously constituted themselves the makers and unmakers of their ministers of religion, the supreme judges of the doctrines and of the mode of worship of their peculiar sect. This baneful and destructive maxim of human pride, called private judgment, a crime in religious matters, worse in many respects than original sin, was proclaimed by the first leaders of the so-called Protestant Reformation; it has now reached its full development to the lowest degree of practical infidelity. The spirit of pride and rebellion of the fallen angels has, to a great extent, usurped the dominion of the world. It is only the Sacred Heart of Jesus, crowned with thorns, that can succeed in healing this deep and wide wound of the human heart, and in curing the towering pride of the human intellect through his meekness and humility. *Learn from me*, Jesus crowned with thorns says, *learn from me to be meek and humble of heart*. Oh! what lessons of humility, what examples of meekness and obedience, what respect for authority, shall we learn from the Incarnate Son of God, if we meditate often on the profound mystery of the Crown of Thorns. The Sacred Heart and the Crown of Thorns are destined to cure and save humanity in this last age of the world.

7. Finally, we feel fully convinced that a sincere and practical devotion to the Crown of Thorns among the faithful is conformable to the spirit and intention of our holy Mother the Church, the loving Spouse of the Lamb. This holy Church, under the guidance of the Holy Ghost, and prompted by her own devotion, has instituted a special Office and Mass in commemoration and honor of the Crown of Thorns of her Divine Spouse. The Catholic clergy, and all ecclesiastical and religious persons bound to the choir, are strictly commanded to recite this office, and the priests, to say this Mass, every year, on the first Friday in Lent. The same Mass may, through a special devotion, be repeated on different suitable occasions. Through the good example and zeal of the clergy, the Church surely desires to propagate this salutary devotion among the faithful. The special honor and veneration paid by the Church to the genuine Crown Of Thorns of our Savior or to any portion of it as a sacred relic, manifests to us, what is her spirit and intention in relation to this sacred and memorable instrument of our Lord's Passion. Here we may justly call to our mind the decree of Pope Innocent VI about the lance and nails of our Lord, which, we have mentioned in the introduction of this work. The spirit and mind of the Church can likewise be understood by the fact of her canonization or beatification of those privileged persons who have been miraculously impressed with the Crown of Thorns. All these considerations leave no doubt in our mind that it is the desire of our holy Mother the Church to promote among the faithful, by every legitimate means, a salutary devotion to all the instruments of our Lord's Passion, and especially to his Crown of Thorns, which caused him such long and intense sufferings, and so many deep humiliations.

We should, moreover, observe that the miraculous impression of the Crown of Thorns upon the head of God's holy servants has in no previous century of Christianity been perhaps so frequent, certainly never so extraordinary and so remarkable, as in this present nineteenth century. As far as we know, no less than fifteen privileged persons have received already this miraculous impression. We cannot foretell how many more will be decorated with this glorious badge of the Passion during the twenty-three years that still remain of this memorable age. For the present time it will be sufficient to mention the illustrious names of Palma Maria of Oria, in the kingdom of Naples, and of Louise Lateau in Belgium, to show that the circumstances attending their miraculous coronation have never been so remarkable and so glorious for Jesus Christ and for his holy Church.

Therefore, when overwhelmed with bodily afflictions and mental anxieties, on account of our temporal affairs or spiritual concerns; when, like holy King David, our soul refuses the consolations of creatures, let us then at least look up to the Divine King of Sorrows, crowned with thorns, and saturated with opprobriums. When our poor head is tortured with pain, which our irritated brain, the source and center of the nervous system, diffuses through every limb and part of our prostrated body, some pious reflections upon, or at least a devout look at our Divine Head and Master, crowned with sharp thorns, will be found very good, very comfortable, and highly profitable to our souls. Members of a Divine Head crowned with thorns, we will learn from his example to bear our physical sufferings and humiliations with patience, meekness, and humility.

For this end we have written this work. We are not aware of the existence of any similar book, or of any formal devotion in memory and honor of the Crown of Thorns of our dear Savior. With entire and absolute dependence on the judgment of the Church, we humbly offer to the public this small volume, and venture to propose to the acceptance of our fellow-Catholics, in these days of trial, the beads and badge of the Crown of Thorns.

Competent ecclesiastical authority will, in its wisdom and prudence, have to decide whether the book and the proposed devotion are suitable and proper for the end for which they are intended. If they are approved, as we trust, we will rejoice for the honor and glory that will be given by many devout souls to our Blessed Lord, and for the spiritual and temporal blessings which this salutary devotion will bring upon mankind. But, if our incapacity and unworthiness render useless our humble efforts, we will remain satisfied with our good intention and expect for it our reward from our Lord, for whose honor and glory we have attempted this work. We will also pray and hope that some more worthy and more able person may be induced to accomplish in a more sarisfactory manner what we have attempted to indicate, and have ventured to begin. We close this chapter with a pious hymn by the Rev. Father Caswall, translated from the Office of the Crown of Thorns, "*Exite, Sion Filiae.*" Then, in the following chapters we will venture to propose our idea of the devotion of the beads and badge of the Crown of Thorns in memory and honor of our Lord Jesus Christ:

1. Daughters of Sion! royal maids!,
      Come forth to see the Crown
   Which Sion's self, with cruel hands,
      Hath woven for her Son.

2. See! how amid his gory locks,
      The jagged thorns appear.
   See ! how his pallid countenance,
      Foretells that death is near.

3. Oh! savage was the earth that bore
      Those thorns so sharp and long,
   Savage the hand that gathered them
      To work this deadly wrong.

4. But now that Christ's redeeming blood
      Hath tinged them with its dye,
   Fairer than roses they appear,
      Or palms of Victory.

5. Jesus, the thorns which pierce thy brow
      Sprang from the seed of sin.
   Pluck ours, we pray thee, from our hearts
      And plant thine own therein.

6. Praise, honor to the Father be
      And sole-begotten Son;
   Praise to the Spirit Paraclete
      Whilst endless ages run. AMEN.

CHAPTER II

THE BEADS OF THE CROWN OF THORNS

"The Crown of Thorns is a Diadem of Love."

No form of popular devotion is known to exist in the Church specially intended to honor our Divine Lord, the King of kings, for wearing during the most painful portion of his Passion, the Crown of Thorns, for our sake and instruction. The beads and badge of the Crown of Thorns, described in these pages, are humbly and respectfully intended, with all due regard to ecclesiastical authority, to supply this want.

Though we are nbt with exact accuracy informed of the real number of thorns that pierced the adorable head of our suffering Lord, yet a pious tradition mentions that they were seventy-two. The truly learned and pious Suarez states that such is the opinion of several Christian writers. From the information that we receive from devout and learned Catholic authors, the Crown of Thorns may have contained more, but not less of these thorns. St. Bernard and St. Anselm, quoted by Taulerus, affirm that thousands of these sharp thorns pierced our Savior's adorable head.(A Lapide, in St. Matt. 27:29, Suarez, 3 pars, a. 46, art 3. Disp. 35)

The beads of the Crown of Thorns are prepared on the supposition that they were seventy-two. Hence they are composed of seven decades. The seven usual mysteries for consideration during the recital of the beads are entirely taken from the Gospel, and give the history of the crowning of our dear Lord with thorns. The recitation of these beads is begun in the usual manner, with the addition of two short versicles specifying its object. After announcing the so-called mystery, or subject for pious reflection, during the respective decade, the *Pater Noster* and *Ave Maria* are recited once, then the doxology or *Gloria Patri* is repeated ten times. Thus these

292

beads are composed of seven *Our Fathers* and as many *Hail Marys* intended to commemorate and honor the seven dolors of the most holy Mother of our Lord, who had a very large share of internal sufferings in the Passion and death of her Divine Son. The *seventy Glorias* contained in the seven decades, with one at the beginning and another at the end of the Rosary, after the *Pater Noster* and *Ave Maria* for the Pope, give seventy-two *Glorias* in memory of the supposed wounds in the adorable head of our dear Lord and Savior Jesus Christ.

We wish explicitly to state that by this form of prayer it is not intended to fix the number of wounds in the head of our Lord, crowned with thorns, but only to honor and thank him for his sufferings in the best practical way that we know. The beads of the Crown of Thorns will close with a suitable prayer translated from the Office of the Crown of Thorns approved by the Church. The beads of the ordinary Rosary of the Blessed Virgin Mary may be used instead of those of the Crown of Thorns, until a pair of these can be procured. The only difference will be the addition of two extra decades, and reciting the *Gloria Patri* in place of the *Ave Maria.* We give now the detailed form and mysteries of the beads of the Crown of Thorns.

Manner of Reciting the Beads of the Crown of Thorns.

V. Come let us adore Jesus Christ, our King.

R. Crowned with our thorns, wounded by their sting.

O God, come to my assistance.

Lord, make haste to help me.

Glory be to the Father, and to the Son, and to the Holy Ghost.

As it was in the beginning, is now, and ever shall be. Amen.

First Decade

Let us consider that Pilate, to satisfy the people, released unto them Barabbas, and after having scourged Jesus, our Lord, delivered him up to be crucified. (Mk. 15:15)

Recite one Our Father, one Hail Mary, followed by ten Glory be to the Father. Then say.

V We venerate, O Lord, thy Crown of Thorns.

R We meditate, O Jesus, on thy glorious Passion.

Second Decade

Let us consider how the Pagan soldiers led Jesus into the court of the Governor's palace, and called together the whole band. (Mk. 15:16)

293

The rest as in the first decade.

Third Decade.

Let us consider how the soldiers, having stripped Jesus, put a scarlet cloak about him. (Mt. 27:28)

The rest as above.

Fourth Decade.

Let us consider how those cruel executioners, platting a crown of thorns, put it on the head of Jesus, and a reed in his right hand. (Mt. 27:39)

The rest as above.

Fifth Decade.

Let us consider how those malicious men, spitting upon the face of our Lord, took the reed from his hand, and with it struck his adorable head. (Mt. 27:30)

The rest as above.

Sixth Decade.

Let us consider how those impious men, bending the knee before Jesus, our Lord, mocked him, saying: Hail, King of the Jews. (Mt. 27:29)

The rest as above.

Seventh Decade.

Let us consider, in this last decade, how our Lord, Jesus Christ, bearing the Crown of Thorns and the purple garment, was led before the people, and Pilate said to the Jews: *Behold the man.* (Jn. 19:5)

The rest as above.

Then say:

Our sins, O Lord, have sown the thorns
　　The points of which thy head transfix.
Convert our souls, remove our guilt,
　　And in our hearts thy thorns infix.
Oh! may all men, thee, King of Kings,
　　In faith adore, in worship love;
And in our infallible Pope
　　Behold thy pledge of truth and hope.

Recite one *Pater, Ave* and *Gloria* for the Pope.

Then say:

V Having platted a crown of thorns,

R They placed it upon his head.

294

Let us pray.

Grant we beseech thee, Almighty God, that we, who in rememberance of the Passion of our Lord Jesus Christ, venerate here upon earth his Crown of Thorns, may deserve to be crowned by him with glory and honor in heaven, who liveth and reigneth with thee and the Holy Ghost. World without end. Amen.

In reciting these beads we may have the following intentions: First decade, to promote this devotion; Second decade for our parents or immediate superiors: Third decade, for our temporal rulers; Fourth decade, for the conversion of all sinners and infidels; Fifth decade, for our pastor or confessor; Sixth decade, for our bishop; Seventh decade, for the Pope.

CHAPTER III

THE BADGE OF THE CROWN OF THORNS

Be thou faithful unto death, and I will give thee the crown of life.
(Apoc.2:10)

The Crown of Thorns having been for our dear Lord the most painful, the most humiliating, and the most protracted torture of his bitter Passion, it seems very just and proper for us Christians to use some devout emblem, calculated to remind us and others of these dreadful sufferings and profound humiliations, endured for our sake by our Divine Savior. The beads of the Crown of Thorns are not a badge, but a form of prayer. They bear, indeed, a more immediate and a clearer relation to the Crown of Thorns than other similar forms of prayer, as the common Rosary of the Blessed Virgin Mary, the Bridgitine beads, the beads of the five wounds, or those of the seven dolors of our Blessed Lady. But these beads will at most be recited once a day, and then they are laid aside during the remainder of the time, without, perhaps, bestowing upon them or their special object, another thought. It seems, therefore, very desirable that some other emblem of devotion more adapted in its form and use for recalling more frequently to our mind the sufferings and humiliations undergone by our Divine Lord and Sovereign King at his crowning with thorns, might be adopted by Catholics. Now, the badge of the Crown of Thorns appears, in our humble opinion, to answer in a peculiar manner this desirable end. Moreover, as our head is the ever active forge of so many vain, proud and sinful thoughts, which so largely contributed to the plaiting of the Crown of Thorns for our dear Lord; it seems but just and proper that it should co-operate in the promotion of his honor and glory. Again, because many worldly persons manifest such extravagant and ridiculous vanity in adorning their heads: so we confidently trust that many pious Catholic ladies will be induced to use this badge of the Crown of Thorns as a protestation against this vicious extravagance, and as an expiation for the offenses offered to our Savior crowned, not with flowers, but with thorns, not with gold and precious stones, but with wounds and blood. Their piety and devotion will surely please our blessed Lord, who will reward them with the unfading crown of everlasting glory. To them we address in a special manner the words of the Canticle: *Go forth, ye daughters of Sion; and see King Solomon in the diadem wherewith his mother crowned him.* (Cantic. 3:2)

1. This badge is intended to be worn in memory and honor of the painful Crown of Thorns of our Divine Lord and Savior, the King of Sorrows.

2. It will be white in color, as an emblem of the purity of our intention in this devotion and in all our moral actions, and of the purity of our heart in all our affections.

3. This badge will be marked with seventy-two red spots to express the seventy-two wounds very probably inflicted upon the adorable head of our Divine Lord, crowned with thorns. It may be pierced in seventy-two places, and underlined with red tape or ribbon. The red tape or ribbon, appearing through the holes of the white badge, will represent the punctures caused by the thorns in the head of our Savior.

4. On the front of the badge a small cross will be either stamped, or formed by two small pieces of red ribbon. Polished brass, silver or gold in the form of a cross may be used.

5. This crown is intended to be worn on the head either by itself, or it may be attached inside or outside any head-dress, convenient and proper for any class or sex of Catholic persons, according to the duly approved and legitimate customs of society in any country.

6. Like the beads, we Catholics intend to use this crown badge as a perpetual pledge of our sincere and hearty homage, love, devotion and obedience to Jesus Christ, the King of Kings, crowned with thorns for our sake and instruction. As the ancient monarchs wore a small white bandage round their head, as a symbol of their dignity, authority and power; so we intend with this crown badge to acknowledge and proclaim that Jesus our Lord is the Sovereign King of the Universe, the sole Redeemer of mankind, and the only Savior and Master of our soul.

7. Next to Jesus Christ, we profess our first and supreme spiritual allegiance to the Pope, his Vicar upon earth, the visible head of the Church, the first and highest ecclesiastical authority, and the infallible teacher of mankind.

8. We intend using the beads and wearing the badge of the Crown of Thorns as a sacred pledge of our sincere respect for all legitimate authority, spiritual or temporal, ecclesiastical or civil. On our side both the beads and the crown badge will be a practical protestation, and a pious defensive weapon against the modern spirit of libertinism, insubordination and revolt, aiming at the utter subversion of all natural and positive, human and divine law, authority and order. May our devotion to the Crown of Thorns of our Divine King prove an effective remedy for these serious evils, threatening the very existence of human society.

CHAPTER IV

ADVANTAGES TO BE DERIVED
FROM THIS DEVOTION

Through the thorny crown of Jesus' head
To glory's didem we are led.

—St. Jerome

There is a considerable number of Catholics who refuse to practice devotional exercises, unless they are enticed by a list of indulgences. Indulgences are without doubt desirable spiritual advantages, which we should all be eager to obtain whenever we can. But we should not mistake the means for the end of a Christian devotion. Many Catholics speak and act in relation to indulgences as if these were the principal end of their practices of devotion. But we should in our pious exercises consider the honor and glory of God of higher importance than our own personal advantage. We should not behave like hired servants, who refuse to work for a master except wages are bargained for beforehand. We should not act as selfish little children, who neglect a task imposed on them by their parents or teachers, except some sweetmeats or a premium is promised them. Obedience to paternal authority, and the gratification which good and docile children will give to their parents and teachers by their virtuous conduct, should be their sweetest and most precious inducement in the accomplishment of their duties and the manifestation of their filial affection. Those children who study to please their parents through disinterested motives of filial love, surely deserve greater praise and a richer reward than those who act only through selfish interest and personal gratification.

The same principle is sound in relation to our devotional practices towards God. Let us by all means try to gain as many indulgences as we can. But we should not make them the inseparable condition and much less, the principal object of all our devotional exercises. Let us be more generous and noble in the service of God. Love should be our noblest motive, and His divine honor and glory our highest ambition. With St. Ignatius Loyola, let us often say, and always act, *For the greater glory of God.* "If when you perform any good work agreeable to God," St. John Chrysostom says, you expect any other reward, you show that you do not understand how good it is to please him. Did you comprehend the sublimity and excellence of this privilege, you could never reckon any other reward equal in value to that of pleasing the infinite Majesty of God. (De comp. Cordis ad Stellam, lib. 2.) The sweetest happiness and highest reward of the angels and saints in heaven is their perfect knowledge that they are pleasing, praising and glorifying God. These maxims are not less true because they are sublime and little appreciated in practice. Let us remember that true devotion must have God, and not man, for its principal object and final end. For true devotion, according to the angelic doctor, St. Thomas of Aquin, is an habitual disposition of the will that makes us prompt and cheerful in everything that tends to the service, honor and glory of God. We should never suspect that God will ever allow Himself to be outdone in loving generosity. The less we seek ourselves in the service of God, the more abundant reward we shall receive from Him, *"who is our reward exceeding great."*

1. This should in a more special manner be our rule in all our devotional exercises relative to the sacred Passion of our Lord Jesus Christ. This Divine Victim of charity did not seek himself in the sufferings and humiliations of his bitter Passion, but, on the contrary, he completely sacrificed everything to the honor and glory of his heavenly Father, and for the redemption, salvation and glorification of our soul. *"Because with the Lord, there is mercy, and with him plentiful redemption."* (Ps. 129:7) The promotion, then, of the honor and glory of God will be the first and best fruit of our devotion to the Crown of Thorns.

2. The second and next to it will be an increase of loving compassion for our dear Savior crowned with thorns and saturated with opprobrium for our sake.

3. The third will be an increase of true Christian respect and genuine obedience to all our legitimate superiors but more especially to the Supreme Pontiff, the infallible, Vicar of Jesus Christ, the visible head of the Church upon earth, the first and highest ecclesiastical authority, the unerring teacher of mankind, so impiously misrepresented, so maliciously persecuted and oppressed in these evil days of arrogant infidelity. We may be confident

that our devotion will shorten the time of trial, and rapidly accelerate the epoch of universal triumph for the Holy See and for the whole Catholic Church.

4. When harassed with internal anguish of spirit, occasioned by scruples of conscience, by temptations, and especially when oppressed by calumny, when embittered by reproaches, by insults, by treachery, by injustice, by persecutions, we will find comfort and courage to bear these trials with Christian resignation and merit, by devoutly reflecting on the example of our Divine Lord and Sovereign King crowned with sharp thorns, and subjected by cruel and impious men to the most painful sufferings, and to the most degrading humiliations. He was our Master, we are his servants. The beads and badge of the Crown of Thorns will by happy experience be found highly conducive to the attainment of this important object in a time of trial.

5. Persons afflicted with headaches, so numerous in these days, will through this salutary devotion, obtain physical relief, or at least moral and spiritual comfort in their painful sufferings, through a special compassion and help of our Lord, who knows how to compassionate our infirmities. Strengthened by his Divine grace, encouraged by his example, they will bravely endure these painful trials with greater merit, and thus obtain an increase of joy and glory for all eternity in heaven. We trust that it will not be considered out of place to state, as a fact connected with this subject, that some experience of these sufferings and trials have contributed much to the idea and execution of this humble work in memory of the Crown of Thorns.

6. Because, as we learn from the Gospel, Pagan soldiers were, under the instigation of the evil spirit, the barbarous authors and the cruel instruments of those atrocious sufferings and profound humiliations of our Divine Lord, the Sovereign King of the Universe; so it is to be hoped that all true Christian soldiers, more especially those who may and *will be* in the glorious service of the Pope and of the Church, will be induced to adopt this holy devotion with the pious intention and noble resolve of offering to our Blessed Lord some atonement for the outrages heaped upon him by Pagan military men at his painful and humiliating crowning with thorns.

7. Finally, let us hope with St. Jerome that through our fidelity in practising and promoting the devotion of the beads and badge of the Crown of Thorns, we may deserve to obtain the glorious crown of eternal life.

By reciting the beads and wearing the badge of the Crown of Thorns we will, in these dangerous times of fierce conflict of Pagan might against Christian right, and of infidel error against Catholic truths, be daily reminded, that *"Through many tribulations we must enter the Kingdom of God."* (Acts 14:21)

But by our fidelity and fervor in this holy devotion we hope to obtain the gift of final perseverance in the faith, love and service of our Sovereign King, fighting manfully even unto death for his honor and glory, and thus deserve the promised crown of eternal bliss in the Kingdom of Heaven. *"Be thou faithful unto death, and I will give thee the crown of life."* (Apoc. 2:10) *"Studeamus nunc ut membrorum vita capitis sit corona."* (St. Augustin),

FINIS CORONAT OPUS